BELFAST
'69

BELFAST

'69 BOMBS, BURNINGS AND BIGOTRY

ANDREW WALSH

FONTHILL

Fonthill Media Language Policy

Fonthill Media publishes in the international English language market. One language edition is published worldwide. As there are minor differences in spelling and presentation, especially with regard to American English and British English, a policy is necessary to define which form of English to use. The Fonthill Policy is to use the form of English native to the author. Andrew Walsh was born and educated in the Republic of Ireland and now lives in Britain, therefore British English has been adopted in this publication.

Fonthill Media Limited
Fonthill Media LLC
www.fonthill.media
books@fonthill.media

First published in hardback 2015
This paperback edition published 2022

British Library Cataloguing in Publication Data:
A catalogue record for this book is available from the British Library

ISBN 978-1-78155-395-4 (hardback)
ISBN 978-1-78155-876-8 (paperback)

Typeset in 10pt on 13pt Sabon
Printed and bound in England

Contents

Acknowledgements

This is my second book on the violent and chaotic outbreak of conflict in Northern Ireland in 1969. There are many authors and historians who write about Northern Ireland; all of them most probably do it for the pursuance of 'truth', or to use other historical methodologies in understanding how the conflict developed. I write about Northern Ireland (and Belfast in particular) because I love the place, its people, and its history, and to find out, from the people themselves, how they coped with thirty years of near anarchy and chaos.

Therefore, I would like to thank Robert McClenaghan for his unequitable help to me while I was in Belfast. His patience knows no bounds. I would like to thank Tom Holland in the Sinn Fein offices, Danny Morrison for his help and support, Mrs Eileen McAuley for her time and courage in dragging back up such bad memories, Jean Canavan and her family in Bombay Street for their hospitality, and Seamus McCabe for his time in talking to me honestly about his brother.

I would also like to thank Patrick Dorrian, who toured Belfast with me, giving me an insider's view of the city, and who has since become a good friend. I thank Alban Maginness for his time, Mike Nesbitt MP, Gregory Campbell MP, Jim Shannon MP, and Baroness May Blood for her support.

I interviewed many people in Belfast, and I would like to thank some of them here: Joe Doyle, Marian Walsh, Marian O'Neill Donaghy, Paddy Mooney, Wallace Thompson, and Doreen Gilchrist. I would also like to thank the staff of the Linenhall Library and the Public Records Office of Northern Ireland (PRONI) for their great help.

Many others omitted their names, and just wanted to tell me how they felt at the time. This included Catholics, Protestants, members of the British Army, and ex-members of the RUC. To them I thank you—your contribution has made a huge difference to the story. The last words are to my family, who once again have put up with me over the months of research and writing; thank you again.

This book is dedicated to the memories of the following:

Herbert Roy
Patrick Rooney
Hugh McCabe
Michael Lynch
Sam McLarnon
Gerald McAuley
David Linton.

They were victims of events not of their making, nor of their control.

Chronology of Events in Irish History

1601: The Battle of Kinsale. This was the last major battle which ensured English domination over the Irish. Spanish troops landed in depleted numbers to aid the rebels but were defeated by the English, under Lord Mountjoy. O'Neill's lands, in Ulster, are carved up amongst the English and Scottish Protestant settlers—the beginnings of the plantations.

1620: Plantations begin in the counties of central Ireland, most notably in Kings County and Queens County (Offaly and Laois).

1641: Rebellion in Ireland. Sectarian conflict erupts between Irish Catholics and English Protestants.

1649: Cromwell lands in Ireland to clear up the remnants of the Royalist forces. Massacres at Drogheda and Wexford by soldiers of Cromwell's 'New Model Army'.

1655: By this point, since Oliver Cromwell landed in Ireland, at least 50,000 Irish Catholics have been sent to the English colonies in the Caribbean as slaves.

1690: Battle of the Boyne in County Meath.

1791: The foundation of the United Irishmen by Rowan Hamilton, Napper Tandy, Wolfe Tone, and others. It aimed to bring Protestants and Catholics together.

1795: The foundation of the 'Orange Order' after a localised battle involving Protestant and Catholic groups in County Armagh. They took their name from William of Orange, and celebrated his Battle of the Boyne victory over the Catholic King James.

1798: The United Irishmen rebellion, led by Wolfe Tone.

1801: The Act of Union between the parliaments of England and Ireland, as a direct response to the 1798 Rebellion. The new country was to be called the United Kingdom of Great Britain and Ireland.

1814: The foundation of the Apprentice Boys of Derry—celebrating the Siege of Derry, in which the armies of King James attempted to storm the city. It was ended by the forces of King William.

1829: The Catholic Relief Act is passed, allowing Catholics to sit in parliament. It is commonly referred to as Catholic Emancipation.

1841: The population of Ireland stands at just over 8 million.

1845: The beginning of the Irish Famine (an Gorta Mór) with the failure of the potato crop.

1846: A Poor Law is enacted by parliament, with the creation of a Poor Law Board. The famine enters its second year.

1848: Rebellion against British rule by the 'Young Ireland' movement ends in failure.

1851: The Population of Ireland was now just over 6 million, down 2 million on the 1841 Census.

1861: The Census of this year shows that the population of Ireland decreased to just over 5.5 million.

1871: The Population of Ireland was now under 5.5 million.

1879: The beginning of the 'Irish Land Wars'.

1881: The population now stood at 5 million.

1891: In the 1891 Census, the population of Ireland is shown at just over 4.5 million.

1893: The Gaelic League is formed.

1896: The formation of the Irish Socialist Republican Party by James Connelly, who aspired to create an Irish workers' republic.

1901: Census shows a decrease in population of 400,000 on the previous one. The population was now 4,400,000.

1905: The creation of Sinn Féin ('we ourselves') by Arthur Griffiths. Dedicated to the creation of an independent Irish Republic, free from British interference.

1912: The formation of the Ulster Volunteer Force (UVF) by Edward Carson, a Dublin lawyer who was opposed to Home Rule. It was formed to defend Ulster from Home Rule and a Catholic-dominated Irish Parliament.

1913: The formation of the Irish Volunteers in an attempt to thwart the rise of a Protestant-dominated militia force in the north of Ireland.

1914: The beginning of the First World War. The Home Rule Act was suspended for the duration.

1916: The Easter Rising. Working on the old adage that 'England's difficulty is Ireland's opportunity', the rebels staged an insurrection in Dublin, hoping for support from around the country. The insurrection failed, and the main leaders were executed. The Battle of the Somme begins in France. The Ulster 36th Division, with many UVF men, suffers heavy casualties.

1918: In the post-war general election Sinn Féin wins the majority of seats allocated to Ireland. The Unionists win seats in the north-east of the country and in Trinity College, Dublin. Sinn Féin refused to sit in the Houses of Parliament, setting up their own parliament in Dublin. This was the start of the Anglo-Irish war (War of Independence). The Black and Tans are sent to Ireland to aid the police force. They embark on an orgy of destruction, burning the town of Balbriggan and razing Cork city centre in reprisal acts.

1920: The Black and Tans kill twelve people and injure scores more at a football match in Dublin, in reprisal for the killing of fourteen undercover agents by the IRA earlier that day.

1921: A truce is called between the British government and the IRA. Subsequent negotiations create the Irish Free State and Northern Ireland. The IRA splits into pro and anti-Treaty wings. Sectarian violence continues in Belfast, with the expulsion of Catholics from their houses in mixed areas. Around 400 Catholics are killed in this period. The Northern Irish Parliament is opened, and Lord Craigavon is appointed as Northern Ireland's first prime minister.

1922: The expulsion of Catholics from their homes in Belfast continues. The introduction of the Special Powers Act by the Northern Irish government, which is to be reviewed annually. Formation of the Garda Siochana (civic guard), the Free State police force, which replaces the old Royal Irish Constabulary. The new force is disarmed, and remains so.

1923: The end of civil war in the south, with the anti-Treaty forces defeated. There is stabilisation of the new state. The expulsion of Catholics from their homes in Belfast continues; Protestants are evicted as well.

1925: The Boundary Commission ends after an alleged leak to the press. The border between the Irish Free State and Northern Ireland is to remain the same, leaving a substantial number of Catholics on the northern side.

1926: The Census in Northern Ireland shows that Catholics make up fewer than 35 per cent of the population of the state of Northern Ireland.

1932: There are riots in Belfast, involving Protestants and Catholics working together against lack of monetary relief for the unemployed.

1936: The census in the Irish Free State shows the population to be just under 3 million. A Census the following year in Northern Ireland shows the population as 1,200,000.

1937: The Irish Free State declares itself a republic in all but name by enacting a new constitution, replacing the King as the head of state with the president, and changing its name to the Gaelic 'Eire'. The constitution, however, comes under scrutiny for its territorial claim to Northern Ireland.

1938: The three 'Treaty Ports' of Cobh, Berehaven, and Lough Swilly—held by the British as part of the Treaty settlement in 1921—are returned to the Free State against the wishes of Winston Churchill, who continued to criticise the decision throughout the ensuing war.

1939: The declaration of war on Germany by Great Britain and France. Northern Ireland immediately offers her support; the south declares herself neutral. This period became known as the 'Emergency' in the Free State. There is severe criticism of her policy of neutrality from Britain and Northern Ireland.

1940: The IRA launches a renewed campaign with a raid on a British Army camp. Lord Craigavon dies.

1941: Belfast is heavily bombed as the Germans attempt to impede British shipbuilding at Harland and Wolff. However, many residential areas of the city are also bombed. Catholics and Protestants share the basement cellar in Clonard monastery, in west Belfast, to escape the bombing. Fire engines from the south are sent north to help the Belfast fire service cope with the fires. Winston Churchill allegedly tells DeValera he will end partition if he enters the war on the Allied side. DeValera does not take the offer seriously.

1942: American troops land in Northern Ireland as a prelude to the Allied invasion of North Africa. A renewed IRA campaign begins.

1943: Americans land substantially more troops in Northern Ireland in preparation for D Day.

1945: The death of Adolf Hitler and ending of the Second World War in Europe. DeValera heavily criticised for offering his condolences on the death of Hitler to the German ambassador in Dublin. Labour government wins election in Britain. Advent of the Welfare State. Formation of the Anti-Partition League.

1948: Declaration of the 'Republic of Ireland'. Britain responds with the Ireland Act, guaranteeing Northern Ireland's status within the United Kingdom as long as her parliament so wishes.

1954: The Flags and Emblems Act becomes law. The RUC could now take down any flags they considered to be a breach of the peace (in other words, the Irish Tricolour).

1956: The beginning of Operation Harvest—the IRA's border campaign—with attacks on RUC stations along the border with Northern Ireland. The Northern Irish government interns hundreds of known republicans.

1957: Internment without trial is introduced in the south by DeValera against the IRA, despite an order from their leadership banning any military action against the Republic's security forces.

1962: The IRA's campaign ends in failure.

1963: Captain Terence O'Neill assumes the role of Prime Minister of Northern Ireland. He begins a policy of attempting to bring Catholics and Protestants closer together.

1965: O'Neill invites the Taoiseach of the Republic, Sean Lemass, to talks in Belfast. This was the first time that two Prime Ministers of Northern Ireland and the Republic met on a formal basis; it is widely criticised in Unionist circles. Ian Paisley denounces the summit.

1966: Easter Rising 50th anniversary marches by republicans and nationalists take place in Belfast; this creates tension in Catholic and Protestant working-class areas. The UVF reforms, issuing a warning that all known IRA men will be shot without mercy. The first sectarian killing of the present Troubles occurs. A Catholic man, Peter Ward, is shot dead outside a pub on the Shankill. Gusty Spence, of the UVF, is accused of his murder.

1967: The formation of the Northern Ireland Civil Rights Association (NICRA). It demands an end to inequalities in housing, local election voting, and employment on religious grounds.

1968: The formation of People's Democracy (PD) by students at Queens University, Belfast. Its aims are similar to NICRA. Civil rights marches dominate the political agenda of Northern Ireland. In October, a march is attacked by the RUC. Television cameras make sure that the aggression is widely broadcast, attracting widespread criticism of the Northern Irish government. O'Neill is now under extreme pressure for the speedy conclusion of reforms; he makes the 'Ulster at the Crossroads' speech. He resigns after the election shows deep cracks in party and Protestant support for his reform policies. Chichester-Clark becomes prime minister of Northern Ireland and continues the policy of reform.

1969: A four-day PD march from Belfast to Derry in January is attacked at Burntollet by off-duty 'B' Specials and Loyalists. The tension mounts in Derry and Belfast. The summer season round of marches creates sporadic rioting, and there is rioting in Belfast at the beginning of August. An Apprentice Boys march in Derry on 12 August creates intense tension. The rioting begins, initially between Catholics and Protestant marchers—the RUC begins to fight Catholics. The Battle of the Bogside begins. Jack Lynch, Prime Minister of the Republic, gives an inflammatory speech on television. Irish Army 'hospitals' are moved to border areas. There is serious rioting in Belfast along interfaces. Catholics are burned out of Bombay Street, Conway Street, and various other parts of west Belfast. British soldiers are 'temporarily' called in to relieve pressure on the RUC. The Army begins to erect the 'peace line'.

Brief Explanation of Terms

Act of Union: After the failure of the 1798 rebellion, the parliament in London decided to disband the Irish parliament in Dublin. This was mainly because of the threat of Catholics, if given the right to partake in parliament, becoming a majority, breaking the link with England and allying themselves with France. The Act came into force on 1 January 1801 and united Britain with Ireland, thus creating the United Kingdom of Great Britain and Ireland.

Apprentice Boys: An organisation founded in 1814 to commemorate the lifting of the 'Siege of Derry' in 1689 by forces loyal to the Protestant King William. The siege was put in place by James II. Apprentice Boys march annually to commemorate this event. In 1969 the Apprentice Boys' march in Derry was the catalyst for nationalist rioting, culminating in the 'Battle of the Bogside', which lasted three days and instigated the intervention of British troops into Northern Ireland.

Battle of the Bogside: An Apprentice Boys' march in Derry on 12 August 1969 was the catalyst for three days of intensive rioting which culminated in British troops being deployed on the streets of Northern Ireland. Tension in the city had been on a razor's edge because of civil rights agitation for the past year. It finally exploded when Catholic youths began to stone the marchers. The RUC became involved, standing with their backs to the Protestants. Things degenerated with the RUC throwing stones back at the Catholics, then using CS gas. Barricades were erected at strategic points of entry into the Bogside. The area literally seceded from the state of Northern Ireland. This event was also the catalyst for serious sectarian rioting in other parts of Northern Ireland, Belfast being the place worst affected with eight deaths over a period of two days.

Battle of the Boyne: King William's most famous battle. On the river Boyne, about 3 miles west of the town of Drogheda in the Republic, was the site where the

Protestant King William's armies defeated James, the Catholic King of England, who had been deposed by William and Mary, his Protestant daughter. This was not merely a Catholic versus Protestant battle, however. It was part of a wider European conflict, and there were many Protestants on the side of James and Catholics on the side of William. The 'Orange Order' was founded in William's memory, and every July Protestant areas of Northern Ireland celebrate his victory and the ascendency of the Protestant tradition in Ireland. A monument dedicated to the Protestant victory marked the site until it was blown up by the IRA in 1922.

CCDC: Central Citizens Defence Committee. Established in 1969, after the August riots in Belfast, this brought together the numerous defence and community groups that had formed in Belfast. Jim Sullivan and Billy McMillan were involved in its creation. The CCDC was involved in regular talks with the Army about the dismantling of the barricades in Catholic areas after August 1969.

Dáil: The Irish parliament (Dáil Éireann), which was formed in 1919 after a British general election in which Sinn Féin won 75 per cent of the available seats in Ireland. Sinn Féin members would not take their seats in Westminster, but instead set up their own parliament in Dublin. Declared illegal by the British, it was restored as the parliament of the Irish Free State after 1921.

GOC: General Officer Commanding, in charge of the British Army in Northern Ireland. Responsible to the Ministry of Defence in London.

Home Rule: The principle of a limited form of self-determination within a dependency of another country. In the case of Ireland, it was seen as a practical solution to Ireland's desire to run her own affairs. Home Rule became part of British political life in the late nineteenth century. It finally became law in 1914, but was shelved at the outbreak of the First World War and abandoned in the face of Unionist criticism and rebellion in Ireland after 1920.

IRA: Irish Republican Army. Formed from the Irish Republican Brotherhood and various other groups, the IRA came to prominence during the Irish War of Independence, 1919–21. It split over the provisions of the treaty with the British that brought about Partition. The IRA lost much, if not all, of its military prowess after the failure of 'Operation Harvest' in 1962. It embarked on a socialist path up to 1969, and was heavily criticised for its 'failure' to defend Catholic areas of Belfast in August 1969. In 1970 it split again into 'Provisional' and 'Official' wings.

JSC: Joint Security Committee. This was a committee of Northern Ireland's Stormont government, containing Army and RUC representatives. Set up after the

British Army became involved in August 1969, it met on a regular basis, sometimes three or four times a week, as the situation in Northern Ireland grew worse.

Loyalist: Term used for those who support the present union of Northern Ireland with the United Kingdom and who are prepared to use violence in order to achieve their aims. They are almost exclusively Protestant. Paramilitary groupings associated with Loyalism are the Ulster Volunteer Force (UVF), the Ulster Freedom Fighters (UFF), the Loyalist Volunteer Force (LVF), the Ulster Defence Association (UDA) and the Red Hand Commandos (RHC). Many more subsidiary groups were active during the Troubles and have not been mentioned here.

Nationalist: The majority of the Catholic population of the north of Ireland are classed as the 'nationalist community'. They hold a belief in 'Irishness' within their culture but do not resort to violence in their agitation for a united Ireland. Notable nationalist MPs have included John Hume and Austin Currie, later to found the Socialist and Democratic Labour Party (SDLP) with Paddy Devlin and Gerry Fitt, the party's first leader.

PD: People's Democracy. This organisation was formed by a group of students at Queens University, Belfast, in October 1968 in reaction to the political turmoil engulfing Northern Ireland and particularly the civil rights march on 5 October in Derry. Its principles were similar to the civil rights movement: fair allocation of housing, an end to Gerrymandering and 'one man one vote'. The PD was most famous for the Belfast to Derry march in January 1969, which was repeatedly attacked by Loyalists. The organisation followed a socialist path for much of the 1970s.

Republican: Irish Republicans are more prone than nationalists to use violence to reach their goals. They are associated with the aim of ending the partition of the island of Ireland and establishing a Socialist Republic of Ireland. Mostly Catholic, they are mainly drawn from the working-class areas of Northern Ireland, of which The Falls district and the Bogside are but a couple of examples. Groups associated with Republicanism's violent strain are the Provisional IRA (PIRA), the Official IRA (OIRA) (under permanent ceasefire since 1972), the Irish National Liberation Army (INLA), the Real IRA (RIRA) and the Continuity IRA (CIRA). Splinter groups are a feature of the violent strain of Republicanism; thus there are many more not mentioned here.

RUC: Royal Ulster Constabulary, formed on 1 June 1922 out of the remnants of the Royal Irish Constabulary (RIC). Classed as acutely sectarian by the Catholic community in Northern Ireland, the RUC was replaced by the Police Service of Northern Ireland (PSNI) after the Good Friday Agreement of 1998.

Taigs: Originally a nickname for an Irishman along the lines of 'Paddy' and 'Mick'. In modern times, it has been used as a derogatory term for Catholics in Northern Ireland.

Taoiseach: (Leader) Prime Minister of the Republic of Ireland (literally pronounced 'tee-shock'). The term came into use after the enactment of the 1937 Constitution.

Unionist: Describes those who hold a desire to maintain the constitutional link with the United Kingdom. Most are Protestants, although there are Catholics who are also Unionist. They wish to achieve their aims through mainly democratic means.

UVF: Ulster Volunteer Force. Formed in 1912 to oppose with arms the formation of a Home Rule parliament, it saw action at the Battle of the Somme in the First World War. The UVF was revived in 1966 as a paramilitary organisation led by 'Gusty' Spence. It was responsible for the death of a Catholic barman on the Shankill Road in 1966, and began to increase its paramilitary activities after 1970, in direct response to the increase in IRA activity.

Foreword

Ciarán MacAirt, author of *The McGurks Bar Bombing: Collusion, Cover Up and A Campaign for Truth*

If Irish history in the last half a millennium has taught us anything, it is that history here has a creeping tendency to repeat itself. Nevertheless, we have learned little except that each community has suffered and caused much suffering. That alone is a constant.

Violence begat violence, but which pogrom came first, or why force was for many the only option, is the subtext to our politics this very day. Many within the pro-state Unionist community will argue that this most recent conflagration was the result of yet another militant Republican insurrection, which had threatened the Northern Irish state since its inception in the 1920s. The summer of 1969 realised their worst fears for lawlessness and rebellion.

However, this negates the Republican belief that the north was a rogue Orange state sustained by sectarianism and suppression of the Irish people. As for this latest conflict, many of those caught up in the violence of the summer of 1969 will argue that they had no other option but to take up arms.

Not only did they consider that the constitutional battle for civil rights and equality failed when it was batoned to the ground by the Royal Ulster Constabulary, but on a local level—street-by-street—a new generation of Irish youth felt that it had to re-arm and defend itself.

The rattle of Browning machine-gun fire from the forces of law and order underscored this need. The 'B' Specials and pro-state Loyalists pouring into their streets and setting fire to house after house burned it into the collective psyche. A failure by the state to defend the basic human rights of all citizens, never mind reform itself, legitimized their actions—in their own minds at least.

However, many, many more persevered with peaceful means, and much of what the civil rights protestors demanded was realized over the next two years.

It was too late by then. History had yet again overtaken us, and both communities played out the same bloody patterns that had underpinned the birth of the state: repression, fear, riot, pogrom, paramilitarism, armed militia, internment, and propaganda. This horrific cycle was whipped to a hurricane in the summer of '69, and this was when we slipped back into the abyss.

History itself is now the great battlefield for who was right or just in the actions they took since then. Minor battles will be fought between the pages of books like this; however, readers should be warned that if we do not attend to the great lessons of our shared history, this conflagration could happen again. Indeed, the events of the past few years have shown just how uneasy our peace can be.

Ken Wharton

On 14–15 August 1969, British troops were deployed onto the streets of a part of the United Kingdom for the first time—other than during the exigencies of wartime—since the 'General Strike' of 1926. This part was Northern Ireland, where law and order had finally broken down. The excellent *Lost Lives* states that prior to that fateful day eight people had been killed, including several some three years before the 'accepted' start of the troubles. It is not the brief of this history to cover this period, and, for the sake of a beginning, it must start the day before, with the first deaths, in what the Ulster folk call the 'wee hours' of that August day.

With the day barely minutes old, Herbert Roy (aged twenty-six), from the Loyalist Shankill Road area, became the first of five people to lose their lives before the stroke of midnight. He was involved in rioting in the Divis Street area of Belfast; he was shot, and died of his wounds around thirty minutes after the start of the new day. Within minutes, little Patrick Rooney (aged nine) had been tragically shot and killed by a stray round, dying in his own bed in the Divis Tower. The author, a young and naive soldier, watched the TV interviews conducted with his distraught parents with horror and disbelief. One remembers the black-and-white pictures of a devastated and yet calm-looking working man describing the way that he had to scrape part of his little boy's head off the bedroom wall with a spoon. That interview, those words, and the horrific images which accompany it will follow this author to his grave. Little did he or any of the watching world realize that many more grieving parents and other loved ones would suffer in the same way, before the Troubles breathed their last and finally claimed their last victims.

Private Hugh McCabe—a British soldier home on leave and merely observing the rioting—was shot and killed in Whitehall Row, also in the Divis area. He was buried, with full military honours, by his comrades from the Queen's Irish Hussars; by the end of that fateful year, 139 days later, a further five British soldiers would also be dead. Almost seventeen months after the troops had gone in, Gunner Robert Curtis was shot and killed in Lepper Street, Belfast, on 6 February 1971, along with his comrade, Gunner John Laurie, who died six days later from his wounds. Popular convention has accorded Curtis, whose pregnant widow gave birth some months later, the epithet of being the first soldier to be killed in Northern Ireland during the Troubles. I believe that there is evidence to the contrary, and that Gunner Curtis was the 22nd soldier to die during this time.

In August 1969, having sat on their collective hands, the weak and prevaricating British government led by Harold Wilson sent troops onto the streets of Northern Ireland for the first time. Its role was to keep the warring sectarian factions apart, to restore law and order to the streets, where anarchy ruled, and to protect the downtrodden Catholic population. When greeted by the news that troops were going in, one Welsh soldier told his wife that it would never happen, but if it did, then it would be all over by Christmas. Where did we hear those words before? 1914? 1939? 1950 perhaps, as Britain's National Servicemen sailed off to Korea? Major Hardy, when you said those words to me in a museum in Brecon, several lifetimes ago, you were almost 40 years out—but sir, you were there, and you did your part, and I am honoured to have met you.

The troops were initially greeted by a relieved Catholic community, which was held down by years of Protestant and Unionist domination. They were second-best in housing, in education, in jobs, and even in the voting arena. Rioting, lawlessness, and the brutality of the infamous 'B' Specials had left a violent vacuum of power; law and order had ceased to function. Once order was restored—thanks to the professional impartiality of the squaddies—the Catholics relaxed, and out came the tea cups, sandwiches, and plates of biscuits. The Protestants watched in sullen silence; trouble was brewing. Within months, those same Catholic women had swapped cups of tea for buckets of urine, they used sanitary towels thrown from upstairs windows, and the sandwiches were replaced with rocks and petrol bombs, and, before too long, by the .303, the Armalite, and, soon enough, the .50 calibre bullet.

Introduction

We are not going to build houses in the South Ward and cut a rod to beat ourselves later on. We are going to see that the right people are put into these houses and we are not making any apology for it.

Alderman George Elliott (Unionist Councillor, Enniskillen).[1]

In fact, Catholics had a disproportionately large share of local authority housing.
(1971 Census)

It was during my time in Belfast writing *From Hope to Hatred: Voices of the Falls Curfew* that I decided to write a book on the tumultuous events in the city during August 1969. Many of the numerous people that I spoke to at the time always referred back to then—in interviews, in general conversation, and in their many memories. Why were those days so ingrained in people's minds, in a city that had seen numerous bouts of sectarian violence in its past? Why did August 1969 stand alone as a benchmark for all that was wrong in Northern Irish society since the country's inception in 1921, considering that hundreds died in that outbreak of conflict? Why did it stand apart from 1935, when thousands of Catholics were forced from their homes during severe sectarian trouble? Was it because the events were so recent? Was it the real prospect that—as events around the world were showing—real change could be brought to bear on the Stormont government?

These and many other questions went unanswered in my mind. Today, Belfast still shows the scars from those few days. Walls that separate communities, dead-end roads, and symbols of loyalties on both sides still adorn working class areas. Streets that generations of families grew up in are long gone, demolished to make way for more modern homes, but their names live on in the memories of people and on the new gable ends. Likewise, the names of revered and long-dead comrades-in-arms stand out on murals on those same gable ends and walls, there to show the generation of today the sacrifices of yesterday.

Ultimately, there are many reasons that these events still hold a grip on society. Many people in Northern Ireland were heavily influenced by the revolutionary protests spreading across the globe, and television played a crucial part in this. The Civil Rights protests in the United States (the civil rights movement in Northern Ireland, for example, was heavily influenced by its American equivalent), student demonstrations in Paris, the nightly news bulletins on Vietnam, and the Soviet invasion of Czechoslovakia all fed a generation well able to understand the implications of what they were watching—thanks to the introduction of free secondary education after the Second World War. On both sides of the religious divide in Northern Ireland, bright and articulate young men and women were beginning to loudly voice opinions that their parents' generation could only mutter.

The civil rights movement was inevitable. Compared to Britain, Northern Ireland was solidly stuck in a rigid and uncompromising past. History was lived every day, and to a certain degree it still is. The state was formed on division; Protestants wanted to distance themselves from a united Ireland that was heavily influenced by the teachings of the Catholic Church, and a society far removed from the trappings of empire and loyalty. That a minority of Catholics were left in the new state was a source of constant fear and worry for the new establishment, and this influenced the lawmakers and politicians. Thus, the movement for change in the 1960s was seen by many Protestants as an attempt to overthrow their way of life. The worthwhile idea of bringing to the state long-overdue rights and privileges, which the rest of the United Kingdom enjoyed, was lost in the clamour and fog of alleged revolution, and the push for a united, Catholic, Ireland.

Nevertheless, today it is history that dictates the direction that Northern Irish society is heading in. Each round of talks to bring an end to the decades of friction on parades, flag-flying, and cross-border cooperation inevitably either ends in failure or encounters serious difficulties. Politicians on both sides (at polar opposites on many issues) find it extremely difficult to come to agreement, such is the power of their respective historical backgrounds. The Peace Process still moves on its very rocky path, bumpy as it is, somehow moving on. Old enemies sit together in government, discussing mundane, ordinary things—but the antagonism and bitterness is still there.

My generation grew up in the Troubles, and while bombs and shootings were not a daily occurrence in our part of Ireland, we still felt the heavy hand of history on our society. At school, in the pubs, and at home, Irish history was alive; it was happening all around us, every day. We learned it through our parents and grandparents; The 'Flight of the Earls' and the final subjugation of Ireland under the English, Oliver Cromwell's men on their infamous rampage, the Protestant King William and his battles, the Catholic King James and his own flight, and Pearse and Connolly, with their heroic blood sacrifices in Easter 1916. We learned less about the 'Black North' and their history; that was considered taboo, and rarely spoken about. The Ulster Volunteer Force were now killing Catholics there, a far cry from their initial outing in 1912, but killing all the same. Why would we learn about their heroism during the Battle of the Somme, as the 36th Ulster Division? They were now a 'terrorist' group, killing people like us. They were our own version of the bogeyman.

Many people emigrated, leaving the land of their birth for foreign shores, waiting too long for employment in a country (both north and south) where overseas investment was considered too risky, and where corrupt politicians charmed the aspiring middle classes. Of those that stayed, some found employment, and others didn't. Unemployment was high, and social conditions were poor compared to many other European countries. We knew we were poor compared to them, and we also knew why. The population, which had not fully recovered since the years of the Famine, stayed on its relentless downward slope. Many intelligent and articulate young people left to add quality and prosperity to other lands; indeed, it seemed that every family had an emigrant within their ranks. This brain drain left the country bereft of much-needed talent. Those that remained were talented as well, but they were let down by poor government and no inward investment—the 'lost generation', as they say.

The onset of the Troubles changed everything in Ireland, both in the north and the south. Throughout this book you will read harrowing stories of a generation in Northern Ireland who were radicalised by the upheavals of August 1969. People who would otherwise have led normal and probably mundane lives became 'involved' in one way or another. Many went to prison, many were killed, and many more were maimed for life—physically and mentally. The troubles changed Northern Irish society, radicalised a generation, and polarised that society for generations to come. British and Irish society was affected as well; opinions on the Irish in England rapidly changed for the worse during this period, as the IRA launched several bombing campaigns on British soil. Irish opinion on the north changed as well; many now began to wonder if unification would be good for Ireland, or if it would create another long period of 'Troubles'—this time with bombs in Dublin, not Belfast. The hand of Irish history is a heavy one indeed, and one that many in Northern Ireland still carry.

1

A Beacon of Loyalism, Or a Stillborn Entity?

May this historic gathering be the prelude of a day in which the Irish people, North and South, under one parliament or two, as those parliaments may themselves decide, shall work together in common love for Ireland upon the sure foundations of mutual justice and respect.

King George V on the opening of the new Belfast parliament, 1921.[1]

The Provisional Govt (in Dublin), regard[ed] all the people of Ireland as their nationals and they would define what they considered the proper boundary and fight for that in the event of the North refusing to come in.

Michael Collins in an extract from the minutes of a meeting of the provisional government, 30 January 1922.[2]

What caused the extreme bitterness, hatred and abject violence of August 1969 in Belfast? Was it a product, as many republicans and nationalists would say, of a gerrymandered and unworkable society, created by Unionists in 1921? Was it caused, as Loyalists would attest, by a sullen minority within their midst, determined to destroy their creation?

It is a question that perhaps will never be answered to the agreement of all who live in Northern Ireland. Society lives and breathes history every day here. Belfast, the capital of Northern Ireland, has had an unequal and often tragic share of the problems within this society, and today still bears the scars of more than forty years of sporadic violence, which often threatened to spill over into outright civil war. Here, people of different denominations live in close proximity to each other; walls separate them, and thus leave no room for assimilation. Whole areas go about their daily existence completely unaware of how the 'other side' is living.

The future is uncertain and often problematic, as the 'normalisation' of Northern Irish society trundles along in an atmosphere of mutual distrust and recrimination. However, there are glimmers of change and hope. A generation has come of age in Northern Ireland which has only known peace. It is over to them to release the hand of history from the throat of their society.

This mistrust goes back generations, to the times of Oliver Cromwell in the 1640s and of William of Orange in the 1690s. Events that occurred in these troublesome times left an indelible mark on the Irish psyche. When the south of Ireland pulled away from the rest of the UK in the 1920s, these issues became more defined in the north. Thus, while the south embarked on the road to the Republic (in an attempt to fulfil a dream beginning in the GPO in Dublin, Easter 1916), the northern society stagnated; the past held it in a stranglehold that would be impossible to release.

Nowhere would this stranglehold be more acute than in Belfast. Driven by the insatiable demands of the linen industry, and fed by the influx of victims of the Great Hunger of the mid-nineteenth century, this small town on the banks of the river Lagan grew into a major industrial hub in the United Kingdom.[3] Its dock built some of the biggest ships in the world; its mills produced vast profits for its owners. Housing projects grew up around the mills in order to house the thousands of workers, and in true Victorian fashion it became row upon row of tightly-knitted terraced housing. Eventually, poverty reduced these areas into so-called 'ghettos'.[4] The following description of Belfast is taken from *From Hope to Hatred: Voices of the Falls Curfew*. It is an accurate description of the city of Belfast at a time of transition from war to peace:

Belfast (Beal Feirste, 'mouth of the sandy ford'), the capital of Northern Ireland, is a vibrant, youthful-looking city on the banks of the river Lagan. It only gained city status at the end of the nineteenth century. It has a varied and very successful industrial heritage; the Titanic was built in its impressive docks, and it had a successful and profitable linen industry. The population of the city grew rapidly in the late nineteenth century, when many rural families moved into the city and its environs looking for employment. Many famous authors, musicians, footballers and politicians call Belfast home. Today Belfast is home to a wide, diverse group of nationalities; it has its own 'Gaeltacht Quarter', promoting Irish speech, verse and writing, and has world famous institutions such as Queens University and the Linen Hall Library, a goldmine of historical documents. However, Belfast has also had a troubled and violent past.

A soldier of the 2nd Parachute Regiment describes the Belfast of his youth in Max Arthur's *Northern Ireland Soldiers Talking*: 'When I was a kid, Belfast was divided up into ghettos. Belfast was actually a lot of little Belfast's. They all had their own names, like Shankill or Tiger Bay. My personal one was Sailortown, which consisted of about eight streets divided by one street, Nelson Street. All the streets running off one side were Catholic and all the streets running off the other were Protestant, and you'd have found that people would've gone down Nelson Street on their side to walk round the district on the other. They kept on the outskirts, they'd never walk through. I'm sure there were Protestants born on the Protestant side of Nelson Street who had never been to our town. We used to go to dances and pubs and the pictures, and we used to meet people, and they could tell where you came from. Those little communities were so tight-knit they could tell where you came from just by your accent, in the same city. It was fear that dominated, fear: keep together.'

This fear was innate; it's what young children were taught by their parents. Keep together, don't mix with the other side, and stay away. Mistrust and suspicion were rife in 1960s Belfast. Some of his memories of the activities of the 'B' Specials could however have been tainted with subsequent events and popular opinions of them.

'Of course when they started the civil rights movement it brought it all home to Catholics. Actually, I was quite happy. I mean, I didn't know I was an underdog. People were telling me I was an underdog but I didn't realise it, 'cos I was a merchant seaman, the same as everybody else. The employment situation wasn't all that good but there was always jobs somewhere if you wanted them. But the civil rights thing, Catholic people were watching telly and asking "what are these civil rights?" You see, before 1968 a lot of things were not reported, like the B Specials. Why they had B Specials in the towns I could never understand. B Specials used to carry Sten guns and .38 Webleys, big old fashioned pistols, and it wasn't unknown for them just to take out their pistols and shoot at people. I remember one time when I was twelve I was at a big dance hall above Bellevue Zoo. Something had happened. I think there'd been a fight, and for some reason the B Specials did a raid and locked everybody in. When they were letting us out they asked me: "What religion are you?" If you were a Protestant you would get a smack on the lug and sent home, but if you were a Catholic you'd get a ride in a Black Maria. You know, those were the type of things that happened then.' [5]

Not only Belfast, but Ireland as a whole has had a turbulent history, one which does not just go back to the late 1960s. Even though the British military presence is no longer visible on the streets of Belfast, and nor is there the expectation of imminent violence, there is still an air of trepidation in the centre of the city. An ambulance siren wails; part of normal life in any other major city. However, here people stop and look, anxiety quickly showing in their faces. The people of Belfast still show fear and worry about what has passed, and what might yet come again. [6]

Many Catholics fled the hunger of rural Ireland to the city of Belfast, congregating to the west of the city centre in areas such as the Falls Road, Clonard, and, later on, Turf Lodge and Andersonstown (amongst others). They helped to bring the overall Catholic population up, and at the same time helped to bring old animosities and recriminations to the surface. Fear was also a factor, as many Protestants saw the influx as an attempt to take over. Sporadic violence became a mainstay of these areas, and often occurred along interface lines that are there to this day.

The rump of the old IRA, defeated in the Civil War that engulfed the south in 1922, still held some sort of status in the north; they were seen as the 'protectors' of the vulnerable Catholics. While they were nowhere near their strength during the Irish War of Independence, they were still a potent threat in the eyes of the Protestant parliament at Stormont. Thus, it was easy to allegedly use this threat to bring in draconian laws designed to keep the Catholics in check. The Special Powers Act of 1922 enabled the state to counter any perceived threat from the IRA, while at the same time controlling the sullen, disloyal Catholics. This act was still in force up to 1973, still casting fear and intimidation as it had in its beginnings. It was a sectarian act, which made Catholics fear even the annual parades by Orangemen. Marian Walsh remembers her youth in Conway Street, Belfast, and also remembers the outright sectarian hatred that was a part of daily life.

> The street had always been the scene of sectarian abuse, especially around July, when the Orangemen would march. The bands would stop halfway down Conway Street (just where the peaceline is now) and we would be subjected to 'Kick the Pope' rantings.[7]

There were, however, two major changes that would have far-reaching consequences for the future of Northern Irish society. One of these was the 'Education (Northern Ireland) Act' of 1947; this enabled, for the first time, many children to attend secondary education and thus move on into university. Many historians agree that it was this singular event that gave rise to an educated Catholic class, paving the way for the civil rights organisation of the late 1960s. The main other change was global; it was the 1960s, a decade of revolution and change. In the United States, the Civil Rights Movement was gaining strength and popularity, using its massive profile to change American society from centuries of racism towards the equality of the black community within their midst. Old colonies in Africa began to break away from their European masters, creating their own conflicts and wars in the process. The Soviet Union tightened its grip on Berlin, and the conflict in Vietnam was beginning to outrage and influence a younger generation, completely at odds with the viewpoints of their parents.

All of these ideas and views flowed over a Northern Irish society that was ripe for change. It was fertile ground for new ideas about how society should be equal, just, and fair; moreover, these ideas applied to all members of society, and not just to one grouping. However, many within the ruling elite in Northern Ireland did not view the burgeoning 'Northern Ireland Civil Rights Association' (NICRA) as a vehicle for change. It was viewed as a monster, a front for a pan-nationalist movement that desired to unite Ireland under a republican and Catholic Socialist banner.

One of those who viewed it with acrimony—and sometimes outright hatred—was Ian Paisley, a Free Presbyterian minister. Throughout the 1960s he constantly warned anybody who would listen about the dangers of the Catholics within their midst, the general movement to what he saw as rule from Rome, and of an accommodation with the Catholic Church. He cleverly linked violent republicanism and the bogeyman of the IRA with all Catholics, creating mistrust and fear amongst the Protestant community. As an extremely powerful orator, he became very popular amongst the disillusioned Protestant working class of Northern Ireland, and Belfast in particular.

Jim Shannon, the Democratic Unionist Party (DUP) MP for Strangford at the time of writing, was one such adherent to Paisley's oratorical bellowing:

> As a boy I was a great supporter of Ian Paisley; he was for me the David of the battle, who spoke out fearlessly and strongly against the IRA and Republicans of that time.[8]

Paisley's first real taste of confrontation occurred in 1964. A British general election was underway, and republicans were gearing up for their own election battle. Billy McMillan, an Independent Republican candidate and erstwhile IRA commander, launched his own campaign from an office in Divis Street. The Irish Tricolour—the displaying of which was banned under the Flags and Emblems Act—was proudly hung in the office window.[9] Although this act occurred in a wholly Catholic district, Paisley took apparent offence to it. Patrick Dorrian remembers the occasion:

> During this period, Ian Paisley started a campaign to have an Irish Tricolour removed from the window of a shop on Divis St. Prior to Paisley's intervention, few people had noticed it. Paisley threatened to march a mob up the Fall to take the flag himself; the RUC were sent to do the job for him.[10]

Andrew Boyd, in *Holy War in Belfast*, commented:

> James Kilfedder, the Unionist candidate in West Belfast, complained about the tricolour too, and sent this telegram to McConnell: 'Remove tricolour in Divis Street which is aimed to provoke and insult loyalists of Belfast.', even though Divis Street is in a part of Belfast where few of those people whom Kilfedder described as 'loyalists' are to be seen. He held a conference of his senior police officers on Monday morning and ordered that the flag be removed. His authority to do this was the Flags and Emblems (Display) Act. At the same time, exercising the power given to him by the Public Order Act of 1961, he restricted a Paisleyite protest march to an area within the vicinity of the City Hall. This was a part of Belfast which the minister considered to be a safe distance from Divis Street.[11]

Rioting ensued, with many injuries and extensive damage caused to local properties. The RUC did take the flag, and repeated the feat again when McMillan replaced it—with similar results. More rioting took place, lasting for two days before eventually quietening down.

II

1966 was a year of contrasts in Northern Ireland. Captain Terence O'Neill, Unionist Prime Minister since 1963, was attempting to show a more liberal side to the Unionist governance of the state by extending a hand of friendship across the border to Dublin, and to the Catholic community within the six counties. The previous year he had invited Sean Lemass, his southern counterpart, to Belfast for talks on cross-border initiatives. Catholic schools were visited, and photo opportunities where he shook hands with nuns were plentiful. However, the polarisation of the two communities was on a path that even O'Neill and his semi-liberal agenda could not stop. History was everywhere that year. 1966 was the fiftieth anniversary of the Easter Rising in Dublin, long seen by more-militant republicans as the genesis of the fabled Irish Republic, dormant until the people united to finally rid the island of the British. It was also the fiftieth anniversary of the Battle of the Somme, where the original UVF marched into glorious martyrdom for the cause of the British Empire. Now, in 1966, the UVF reformed. The IRA were still there, although not as apparent. Baroness May Blood remembers:

> As Protestants, we always believed that the IRA was always there, as we were told. The Official IRA was always there and everybody knew that Jim Sullivan on the Grosvenor Road was a member; everybody knew that...[12]

That was enough for men like Gusty Spence, an ex-British Army Military Police sergeant and a leading light in the new UVF. The revived group issued a declaration of war to all alleged IRA personnel—no known republican was safe. In June 1966 they fatally shot Peter Ward, a Catholic barman, as he was leaving a pub just off the Shankill Road. Their real target was Leo Martin, a leading IRA man and a future member of the Provisionals.[13] Peter Ward was not connected to the IRA. However, for the UVF, any Catholic would do—such was the vitriolic hatred of this revived paramilitary force.[14] Although many people, especially in the Protestant community, believed that the IRA was still active, still devoted to the overthrow of Northern Ireland, and still devoted to establishing a socialist republic, the reality was quite different. Led from Dublin, many in the IRA now had little time for militancy, especially in the north. The republican movement was undergoing a period of reorganisation, following on from the failure of its border campaign of 1956–62. This failure encouraged many to follow a path of social protest; housing, fishing rights, and the 'unavailability of higher education to people of modest means' were high on the list.[15] The defence of northern Catholics from attack began to lose support as Northern Ireland enjoyed relative peace. Northern, more traditional republicans thus began to leave the IRA, disgusted at this new turn of events. The rift between IRA members in Belfast (who saw militant action as the answer to British 'occupation') and the Dublin leadership was beginning to take form.

Discrimination in Northern Ireland during unionist rule has been debated widely amongst historians, some coming to the conclusion that Protestants were discriminated against just as much. The common consensus seems to be that Catholics were discriminated against in the fields of employment, housing, and education; however, both sides of the community suffered under a Unionist-led Stormont system, albeit disproportionally.

> Republicans have long promoted the notion that the Protestant community was much better off than the Catholic community. This 'half-myth' retained its potency because Protestants even believed it themselves. The reality was that whatever privileges the Protestant working class was granted were merely 'crumbs from the table' – it simply suited certain people to tell us that these crumbs had to be held on to at all costs.[16]

In *Voice for All: General Overview Report: Northern Ireland*, John Bell gives a detailed description of the discrimination that was prevalent at the time, and how it stemmed from years of mistrust and acrimony:

> In Belfast particularly, the industrial heartland of the north, major industries such as Harland and Wolff shipbuilding and Shorts Brothers aircraft manufacturing overwhelmingly employed Protestants since the end of the nineteenth century for a variety of factors. One reason was that they were traditionally located in Protestant areas such as East Belfast rather than Catholic West Belfast. Secondly, some Protestant employers preferred not to employ Catholics for a number of reasons, one of which was a general belief that Catholics were 'disloyal' to the new six county state, and therefore 'could not be trusted.' Thirdly, a system of unionist and Orange 'clientism' whereby fathers and uncles would often secure jobs for their sons or nephews on apprenticeships in engineering and similar trades in heavy industry invariably led to jobs being passed from Protestant father to son. As well as being less likely to be in employment, Catholics were also much less likely to be represented among the upper echelons of management or in more professional and skilled occupations.[17]

In some ways, then, the Protestant community *was* better off. For example, The RUC was seen as their police force, along with the semi-paramilitary 'B' Specials. The lack of opportunities for Catholics in business and government posts meant that average wages were low; Catholics were less likely to own a property or business, and therefore they had little or no votes.[18] Areas such as housing and employment were also heavily skewered towards the Protestant community. Protest and revolution was in the air, as the Education Act of 1947 began to bear fruit amongst many young Catholics. Patrick Dorrian remembers:

> Agitation from the nationalists (and many liberal Unionists) ensured that they began to protest about the franchise at local government level, which allowed landlords multiple votes in municipal elections but denied votes to tenants.[19]

In April 1967 the Northern Ireland Civil Rights Association (NICRA) was formed in Belfast. It was a coming together of previous groups, such as the Campaign for Social Justice and the Homeless Citizens League.[20] Its main aims were 'One Man, One Vote', an end to the gerrymandering of electoral wards to give a Protestant majority, and an end to discrimination in housing and employment. However, Protestants once again saw the movement as a front for an IRA-led takeover of the state, their fears fuelled on—as usual—by unionist politicians.

> People imagine that Civil Rights was all about reform. Nobody should be fooled by that. Nationalists and Republicans don't want to reform Northern Ireland, they want to destroy it! We could be the most progressive state in the world and the IRA would still be trying to bomb us out of existence.[21]

Many Protestants did join however, seeing the realities of Northern Irish society in a radical and new light, although many would not admit it.

> The biggest mistake the Prods made was not to join in the Civil Rights marches. And even though we didn't, we shouldn't have tried to justify malpractices. We must accept that we were more than aware of the abuses of power which went on in the past; they might not have been done by us, but they were supposedly done for us, and we were only too prepared to keep quiet about them. It was inevitable that some sort of crisis would erupt – whether we like to admit it or not, Northern Ireland was a sick society.[22]

The crisis in the sick society would erupt in August 1969, with devastating consequences for Northern Ireland.

III

The first outing of NICRA took place in April 1968, in protest at the banning of parades, including Republican Club marches at Easter.[23] The organisation immediately began to attract the attention of the Stormont government. In October 1968, a march in Derry City attracted the wrong sort of attention when the RUC baton charged the marchers, leaving many injured.[24] The march was originally banned by William Craig, the Stormont Home Affairs minister (considered a hardliner), in order to allow an insignificant Loyalist protest march to occur. Wallace Thompson remembers:

> Probably from the autumn of 1968 we were shocked at what was happening with the civil rights situation, the first march which was in Londonderry. My gut reaction at that time was that they get what they deserve. We weren't able to take in the enormity of what was happening, we weren't prepared for it at all.[25]

Now the attention of the world—and, more importantly, the British public—was focused on Northern Ireland, thanks to the widespread coverage given to the events by RTE, the republic's state broadcaster. The Unionist anger at these marches was mainly directed at O'Neill and his liberal agenda, but rising anger was also being directed at the Catholic community. Many Protestants saw the rise of NICRA as a front for an IRA insurrection, and many in government also believed this. Many also began to fall behind Paisley and his anti-Catholic rhetoric. Four days later, a group of students in Queens University in Belfast formed People's Democracy, a socialist, left-leaning pressure group with more-radical demands than NICRA. Northern Irish society was becoming more polarised. Wallace Thompson remembers these days of anxiety and fear for the future:

> Clearly from the summer of 1968 you had the civil rights marches, then the Peoples Democracy marches in the New Year we just believed that the world as we knew it was coming to an end. And that was observing it from fifty miles away from Belfast. No, I was young, but I don't think that my father and my grandfather, their generations, were ready for it yet either. Terence O'Neill had spoken of the need for change but we didn't pay enough attention to him. When the illegal marches kicked off and violence increased I as a Protestant and Unionist watched what the government was doing to see whether they were taking a firm enough line against these people who were rising up against everything that I held dear. We were in Londonderry that day, the day it all blew up. We got out pretty quickly, and went home. We believed that our Protestant way of life was being threatened. I didn't sit down and rationalise the demands of the civil rights, as far as I was concerned they were all excuses for what was being foisted upon us.[26]

The next flashpoint in Northern Ireland's descent into violent sectarian chaos was the Belfast to Derry march. Organised by Peoples Democracy (PD), it began on 1 January and was immediately embroiled in controversy.[27] Much of NICRA was against such a provocative march, which was to go through hostile loyalist areas on its way to Derry; they also defied public opinion, as well as the Stormont government.[28] Nevertheless, around fifty students left Belfast and began the long walk to Derry.

Despite numerous attempts at disruption and some violent episodes, the march proceeded, picking up people as well as publicity on the way. At Burntollet, outside Derry, the march was greeted by a loyalist mob containing off-duty 'B' Specials and members of loyalist paramilitary groups. Stones and other missiles had been stashed away the night before to ensure that the attackers had ample ammunition.[29] In *Politics in the Streets: The Origins of the Civil Rights Movement in Northern Ireland*, Bob Purdie discusses the events:

> The attack was brutal and relentless; the unresisting marchers were beaten, knocked down and kicked, prevented from seeking shelter, pursued and further assaulted. There was at least one near fatality when a girl was knocked unconscious and left lying face down in a stream. Several people were taken to hospital...[30]

It was a premeditated, calculated attack, designed to bring chaos to the march and stop it reaching Derry; however, it was not the only attack on the marchers and their demands. In Derry there was severe trouble when Paisley held a counter rally against the marchers; there were bomb scares and further physical attacks. The battered and tired group eventually reached Derry, to a rapturous welcome.

Numerous liberally-minded MPs in London, members of Campaign for Democracy in Ulster (CDU), watched the march from afar with a sense of trepidation.[31] A telegram was sent to O'Neill in Belfast, warning against future violence:

> [We are] disturbed by reports that civil rights marchers in Northern Ireland are being molested by anti-civil rights demonstrators and that police are not giving adequate protection to those taking part in in this peacefull [sic] protest [stop] In view if recent incouraging [sic] events we appeal to you to insure that the right of peaceful democratic protest is not denied to any Ulster citizen.[32]

Now under severe pressure, in his own statement O'Neill heavily criticised the march for adding to an already-volatile situation:

> Some of the marchers and those who supported them in Londonderry itself have shown themselves to be mere hooligans ready to attack the Police and others. And at various places people have attempted to take the law into their own hands in efforts to impede the march. These efforts include disgraceful violence, offered indiscriminately both to the marchers and to the Police, who were attempting to protect them. Of course those who were responsible for this violence were

playing into the hands of those who are encouraging the current agitation. Had this march been treated with silent contempt and allowed to proceed peaceably, the entire affair would have made little mark and no further damage of any sort would have been done to the good name of Ulster. Indeed in turning their backs in peaceful disapproval of these irresponsible and misguided people those who disapprove of them would have shown a maturity which could only have won new respect. The extremism of the Republicans, radical Socialists and Anarchists can only be defeated by the forces of moderation and not by the forces of some other form of extremism.[33]

However, not even he could stop the train of events that were now engulfing the major urban centres of Northern Ireland. On the weekend of 11 January there was severe rioting across the country, and on 3 February O'Neill called an election to counter the rising pressure on his position.

The election was a watershed in many ways. Whilst holding onto his seat, O'Neill saw his overall vote greatly reduced, in part due to a challenge by Paisley and the Unionist Party, split into its relevant moderate and hard-line elements. By April 1969 UVF elements were planting bombs at main waterworks plants in an attempt to pin the blame on the IRA, and there was more rioting across Northern Ireland— Derry being the fiercest. On 23 April, Universal Adult Suffrage was introduced in local government elections, replacing the old point system that was so hated by NICRA.[34] However, this reform was not enough to save the career of O'Neill; after the resignation of James Chichester Clarke as Agriculture Minister because of his opposition to the move, O'Neill resigned. The era of rapprochement (of a sort) with the Catholic community was over. Chichester Clarke replaced O'Neill after defeating Brian Faulkner in the ensuing leadership contest. Clarke would preside over the most violent period in modern Northern Irish history, and—like O'Neill—he would prove to be just as aloof.

As 1968 drew to a close, the atmosphere became tense in Belfast. The geographical layout of the city ensured that if any trouble started it would quickly develop and spread. One such interface was Bombay Street, in the Clonard district; it was Catholic, and a stone's throw away from Cupar Street, Canmore Street, and Lawnbrook Avenue, all of which were 'Protestant' areas.[35] Tensions were always high here, as Jean Canavan (a resident of Bombay Street all her life) remembers:

We went to school in St Galls, just up the top of the road there. You see, when we were kids we were always classed as second class. There was a wee chippie round there [Cupar Street], and we used to go round there. And these kids used to come in, I would say they were around seventeen, we were about eight or nine, and they used to push you back and call you a 'Fenian "B"'. I would then come home and ask my mum, 'what's a Fenian?' But, you know yourself, you kinda knew that there was something wrong. I mean, we couldn't even go and play in the park.[36]

Nevertheless, many people from the Clonard area worked and shopped on the Shankill Road, such was the intermingling of the time. Every day, Protestant workers in their hundreds made their way to 'Mackies', an engineering factory on the Springfield Road—very much in Catholic 'territory'. Danny Morrison, Sinn Fein's Director of Publicity until 1990 and a prominent republican, commented:

> Protestants used to come from the Shankill to certain bars on the Falls Road, and because of their presence there the owners would not let the singing of what was called 'party' songs. For example, you would not be allowed to sing a slightly Republican song if it offended a small section of the Protestant clientele.[37]

Patrick Dorrian remembers his youth in the lower-Falls area, a predominantly Catholic district:

> I was born in west Belfast in 1951, in Slate St, which was close to the Grosvenor Road. The area was pretty much an interface, in so far as across the Grosvenor Road few Catholics lived—as the streets on the south west side of the road were part of the extended 'Village' area of Belfast, which was almost exclusively Protestant and Unionist. There was also a large Protestant community a few streets away towards the city centre ... We were always told to be careful when we were travelling through non-nationalist areas, but this didn't stop me or others travelling to watch Distillery FC, or even visiting Windsor Park to watch Northern Ireland international matches. The most dangerous time of the year was always July, when there seemed to be a 'hormonal' surge in the unionist community and it was not unusual for Catholic youths to be given bad beatings if caught alone in unionist areas.[38]

This close proximity ensured that tensions were always high. A sense of belonging, of almost tribal proportions, would make Belfast one of the most divided cities in the western world. Ultimately this division made Belfast a city on a knife edge, waiting to explode.

Alongside the tensions, poverty was another mainstay of Belfast society for both Catholics and Protestants. Work was scarce, and when it was found was often poorly-paid. The days of the great linen mills and plentiful work at the shipyard were long gone. However, the housing that was supplied for the linen workers remained; long streets of two-up-two-down houses, with a yard out the back and sometimes an outside toilet. Overcrowding was the norm, with three generations of the same family sometimes living in a one or two bedroom house. Pubs were plentiful, and for many they offered the only escape from their difficult lives. Mrs Eileen McAuley—mother of Gerald McAuley, who was killed in Waterville Street in August 1969—remembers the days of trying to find suitable accommodation for her young family, and the subsequent move into her mother-in-law's house:

We couldn't even afford a van or anything so we had to go down to Smithfield and hire a handcart. We got our bits and pieces together and he [Gerry Snr] wheeled them over to his mothers. She put us ... she had a three story house, and she put us right at the top. So I got the three kids to bed and Gerry went over the road to see his friend. I got into bed. At quarter to ten all the lights went out. I got out of the bed and tried the switch... nothing. I'm lying there trembling in the dark. Gerry came in and I said, 'That bulb must have blew.' He said, 'No, that would be my mother. She turns the electric off at quarter to ten.' She used to keep lodgers, you see! [39]

Many families were in Mrs McAuley's position, relying on family members to take them in. Eventually she was offered accommodation, but only after political intervention:

Eventually our case was taken on ... it was actually Gerry Fitt who got us this house. We were that poor we had to sell Gerald's bike that he had got for Christmas for the rent, and then the neighbours were calling us gypsies because we moved in using a handcart! [40]

However, for Mrs McAuley the happiness of being able to settle down in a new house and bring up her family was not to last. Up on the Shankill Road, and the streets running off it, things were not much different.

The homes on the Shankill were as miserable as any on the Catholic side. Some of the houses standing in the 1970s had been condemned as unfit in the 1890s. [41]

Similar in size and nature, houses in the Protestant areas of west Belfast were often in a worse state of repair than those on the Falls Road. However, to the wider world, it was the Catholic areas and their housing issues that were in the spotlight. Patrick J. Roche and Brian Barton explained how poverty and deprivation was as much a Protestant problem as it was a Catholic one:

All denominations clearly suffered poverty and poor housing, and differences between religions were not huge. Slum conditions were well known to both communities. A Building Design Partnership study of Belfast in 1969 found 'gross deficient' standards in most houses in both Catholic Cromac Street and Protestant Sandy Row. The unionist regime may be criticised for not raising standards for all. [42]

Age-old animosities were also coming to the fore during these turbulent months. In *The Red Hand*, Steve Bruce offers an enlightening quote from Sara Nelson, author of *Ulster's Uncertain Defenders*:

Divis Flats may actually be hell to live in but to the Prod watching them being built from his rat infested house, they may seem proof positive to him that his traditional leaders are not even sharing out their new found wealth evenly but are giving it all to his traditional enemy.[43]

Seeing the civil rights movement as a purely Catholic organisation, and being told by senior unionist politicians that it was most likely infested with IRA and republican elements, many in the Protestant community thus began to congregate around Ian Paisley and other hard-line unionists. In May 1969, John McKeague, a controversial and outspoken loyalist, formed the Shankill Defence Association to combat what he saw as the threat of Irish Republican violence on the Protestant community of the Shankill.[44] Known for his anti-Catholic rhetoric, at one stage he was closely associated with Paisley and his Free Presbyterian Church; he eventually left under mysterious circumstances. The more radical and often violent strain of Protestantism was now coming to the surface. Moreover, sectarianism was now the overriding driving force in working class areas of west Belfast.

IV

Ardoyne, to the north of Clonard, was (and still is) a predominately Catholic enclave. The atmosphere here was considerably different, mostly due to the area being surrounded by Protestant districts. There were many interfaces, with Hooker Street, bordering onto the Crumlin Road, being the most notorious. Children growing up in these areas invariably carried the baggage of history with them. Tom Holland recalls:

I can also remember my father sending me to pay the rent to a particular house (again this was before 1969) in an area that was considered 'Protestant'. And I was afraid … to go down to the house. So there were wee indications of something, even at that age, that were showing to me, growing up in that mid-1960s period, that religion was a problem, that we were Catholics, that the Protestants had the power, that there were more of them … there was definitely a fear factor. We, I say Catholics, seemed to be totally surrounded by Protestants. Everything was about … they had everything, they controlled the media, they controlled the TV, they controlled politics.[45]

However much Ardoyne was Catholic, some in Stormont could not see how the local population, after years of alleged discrimination, detested the government and everything it stood for. Housing was a major issue here too. Two-up-two-down houses were once again the norm, and many people lived in abject poverty. None of this seemed to phase O'Neill or his election campaign team, who attempted to win Catholic votes in that crucial election year. Tom Holland remembers:

Coming home from school one day in early 1969, I would have been twelve at the time, I can remember coming down Jamaica Street and seeing a mass of people and the RUC, who were the police at the time, and a mass of cameras, TV cameras. I can remember thinking, 'What's happened?' It was Terence O'Neill, who was Prime Minister at the time, and he was in Jamaica Street. Now Jamaica Street was in the Ardoyne, and the Ardoyne was largely Catholic at the time.

I couldn't understand, I mean, why was the Prime Minister in our street? I didn't obviously know this at the time but the British Labour Party was in power in Westminster at the time, and they had been putting pressure on the Unionists to bring in reforms, and to try and make the north more acceptable to Catholics. So basically O'Neill was on a charm offensive with the Catholic community at that particular time. The house he actually went to, it was a business woman, and her name was McNulty. She lived about twelve doors up from us. Mrs McNulty brought him in, they had tea and talked about whatever they were talking about. Later on that night somebody went up and threw black tar over her door, so there were obviously people in the area who didn't like this visit by somebody who represented everything that was wrong with society in Northern Ireland being welcomed into the Ardoyne, which was mainly Catholic, where there was major unemployment and massive discrimination.[46]

Joe Graham, a lifelong republican and local historian, recalled the event in the book *Ardoyne: The Untold Truth*:

There were only about 20 ardent civil rights activists in Ardoyne at first—people like Liam Mulholland, Patsy Quinn, Rebecca and Frank McGlade, the whole Corrigan family, myself and Martin Meehan. But what brought things into focus in the area was when Terence O'Neill came into the district in January 1969. It was part of his attempt to enlist Catholic support. One local resident invited him into her house and there were pictures in the papers of him having tea with her. This infuriated people because we were conscious of the problems that there were.[47]

The first serious signs of the violence that was to follow occurred in May 1969, outside the Edenderry Inn—a Catholic-owned pub on the junction of Crumlin Road and Hooker Street. What began as a minor incident quickly developed as the police responded to an emergency call made from the pub. Stones were thrown at the police, republican songs were sung, and many local shops were damaged.[48] The trouble continued for a few days before petering out, but the incident was a taste of things to come. Across the Crumlin Road, in places like Disraeli Street and the south side of Crumlin Road itself, Protestants watched in sullen silence.

The government at Westminster also watched these events from the side-lines, as it had done for the past fifty years. Save for a few MPs—who were shocked at what they saw as abject discrimination and sectarianism—parliament allocated very little time to Northern Ireland and its obvious sickness. The first signs that the British government was taking notice came after the demonstrations of 5 October 1968, when police baton charged a civil rights march. Home Secretary James Callaghan called a meeting between Harold Wilson, O'Neill, Brian Faulkner, and William Craig; the purpose of the meeting was to discuss concessions to the civil rights movement. O'Neill was under pressure to reform from Wilson, who stated that the financial arrangements between the two jurisdictions could be jeopardised if reforms were not forthcoming. However, Craig added to the pressure by refusing to act on the proposals.[49]

Whatever O'Neill's failings (and there were many in the eyes of Catholics), he at least made an attempt at modernising a backward and insular Northern Irish society. It was a delicate balancing act; he had to be seen trying to bring much-needed reform, while at the same time assuring the Protestant majority that he was as dedicated to the union with Britain as they were. His dismissal of Craig in December 1968 (because of his opposition to any type of reform) was a brave move, but one that ultimately left him exposed to the more extreme elements within his party and government. Wallace Thompson, who was then living in Ballymoney, recalls his feelings at the time, and his subsequent adherence to the political rhetoric of Paisley:

> I think I remember that I thought that Terence O'Neill was taking the province in the right direction. I remember hearing him at a parade in 1966 and I thought this man is making a lot of sense. But it was the tipping of the balance through the violence that led me to think that Paisley was speaking with clarity. Others spoke with a bit of clarity, like Bill Craig and Brian Faulkner. But Paisley said things that I thought I can agree with that. I felt a kindred spirit with him. He wanted to go the full distance, and represent entirely what we wanted. I remember thinking, 'That's it, I'm a Paisley man.'[50]

O'Neill called a general election in February 1969, in the hope that both Protestant and Catholic moderate opinion would back him and his policy of reform. He won, but it was a hollow victory; his majority within his own constituency was greatly reduced by Paisley, who had decided to tackle O'Neill head on in his own back yard. A British cabinet paper describes O'Neill's position after the election:

> During the weeks that followed the General Election, Captain O'Neill's authority in the Unionist Party gradually deteriorated. He was able to secure the Parliamentary Unionist Party's acceptance of the principle of universal adult suffrage in local government elections at a meeting on 22nd April [1969], but when he saw that the hard-line Unionists in the Party at large were determined to resist reform, he felt that he could no longer reconcile the two wings of the Party and that another leader coming fresh to the situation would have a better chance.

Major Chichester Clarke resigned on 23rd April on the grounds that the timing of the decision on the local government franchise would give rise to disorder; on 28th April Captain O'Neill decided to give up the leadership of the Party and to resign as Prime Minister as soon as a new leader was elected.[51]

The trouble in Derry on 19–20 April—in which Samuel Devenny was severely beaten and critically injured by the RUC—only added to the tension in Northern Ireland. It also severely damaged confidence in the police as a non-partisan force, confidence which Catholics had never had.

By May 1969 O'Neill was gone, and Westminster had to deal with Chichester Clarke. Described as a 'liberal' by Callaghan, there was hope that the long-awaited reforms would be implemented. In a phone call between the two men on 5 May, there was a hint of the Westminster attitude towards Northern Ireland when Callaghan told Chichester Clarke: '... our policy is founded on the belief that we shall get the best solution if Northern Ireland can handle its own problems.' [52] However, that was the issue; Northern Ireland could not solve its mounting problems on its own.

During the summer of 1969 there was frenzied activity within Westminster. The use of the British Army in Northern Ireland was a distinct possibility, as the RUC showed itself to be a partisan force. A series of bomb attacks began, initially believed to be the work of the IRA, but later discovered to be carried out by extreme loyalists.[53] These were aimed at water and electricity installations, and designed to bring pressure on the IRA. The Westminster government announced that troops were to be used to protect vital installations around Northern Ireland, adding to the tense atmosphere.

By July there was serious rioting in many urban centres across Northern Ireland, coinciding with the Protestant marching season. The 'B' Specials were mobilised on 15 July, and the use of CS gas was discussed in view of the seriousness of the rioting, but the RUC were insufficiently equipped.[54] Now it was Chichester Clarke's turn to be under pressure.

After a summer of increasing tension, 12 July passed off relatively peacefully in Belfast. The traditional marches of the Orange Order failed to produce the inter-communal disorder that many predicted; however, the undercurrent of sectarianism and hatred was still there. Danny Morrison remembers:

But it was clear by the summer of 1969 that something was going to burst. At this stage I was working in a bar in Andersonstown, the Whiteford Inn, to supplement my pocket money and to help my studies. Even up 11 July the Orange men who used to march to a field just outside Andersonstown, those who didn't want to march the whole way home, would come in for a drink. I remember serving them on 11 July, thinking 'Jesus, this is amazing,' when you consider the atmosphere. Don't get me wrong, there was intimidation, subtle intimidation.[55]

To many, it was a surprise. For many years these traditional marches were catalysts for violence; marches would invariably come close to Catholic areas and spark random aggression. There was trouble, but it was nowhere near the scale of what was to come.

However, Westminster was still in denial about the approaching storm. Aware of the sporadic outbreaks of violence, they assumed a somewhat-optimistic approach to the situation:

> ...despite the setbacks on 12th–15th July [rioting in many urban centres] there are some signs which are encouraging. The issues are no longer generally seen as the legitimate political grievances of a minority against an unheeding repressive government. The Northern Ireland government is now for the first time firmly committed to the removal of the main grievances and is taking steps to do so.[56]

On 2 August trouble flared up near Unity Flats, a Catholic enclave at the bottom of the Shankill Road. As an interface area, there was sporadic violence here during the summer. A junior Orange Order parade, on its way home from Carrickfergus, became embroiled in trouble outside the flats. The parade passed, but upwards of 1,000 supporters stayed behind. Rumours that the march had been attacked at some point, and that the Irish Tricolour was being waved from the flats, only added to the tension. Stones began to be thrown as loyalist gangs attempted to storm the flats. Hand-to-hand fighting occurred between police and rioters, with the result that a man was hit on the head by a police baton; he later died in hospital.[57] The man's name was Patrick Corry.[58]

The trouble spilled over to the next day, before quietening down when units of the 'B' Specials were deployed. The following statement is the conclusion reached on the trouble by the Scarman Report, set up at the behest of the Stormont government to investigate the violence of 1969.

> The riots of the 2nd and 3rd of August were began and continued by Protestant crowds. They led to loss of life and serious damage to property. They were directed initially against Unity Flats but soon developed into a conflict with the police. They provide evidence not only to the risk to the peace of the province from Protestant violence but also of the determination of the police to protect Catholic lives and property. Although unable to prevent external damage such as the breaking of windows, and on occasions embroiled (once with tragic results) with the residents of Unity Flats, the police did successfully protect the residents from invasion by Protestant mobs.[59p]

There were other incidences of outbreaks of violence that weekend—most notably in the Ardoyne, where Catholic mobs threw petrol bombs at the police and set up barricades across Hooker Street. Catholics began to be burned out of their houses on the south side of Crumlin Road, and the general movement of families into 'safe areas' began on both sides. In *Ardoyne: The Untold Truth*, Charlie Toner remembers:

> There were a couple of hundred of them (Loyalists) marching down the middle of the road (Cambrai Street). They stopped just outside our house and started chanting. Then a petrol bomb was thrown through one of the downstairs windows. My mother and father put it out with water from the buckets. Another petrol bomb was thrown into the off-license. All the windows of the off-license were broken and some of the crowd started grabbing bottles of spirits. Some of our neighbours were trying to stop the crowd but they were threatened and had to leave the scene. We thought the mob were coming into the house and I remember my mother praying on the stairs because she thought we were going to be killed.[60]

Sporadic outbreaks of violence continued, each outbreak adding to an already hostile and incendiary situation.

The impending Apprentice Boys parade in Derry on 12 August was the next focal point. After a summer of rising tensions across the country, many believed that the parade could spark off serious violence. In Dublin, this fear was apparent. At a meeting in the Foreign Office in London between Dr P. J. Hillary, Minister for External Affairs in Dublin, and Michael Stewart, Secretary of State for Foreign and Commonwealth Affairs, these concerns were raised. Stewart confirmed to Hillary that the parade would not be banned, but merely 'controlled'. However, repeated pressure from Hillary failed to get any results about the parade, with Stewart merely repeating that it was an 'internal' matter; the die was cast.

In Derry itself, the atmosphere was thick with anticipation. Many within the civil rights organisation were aware that there was a significant risk of serious violence towards the march from nationalists; they were not far from the truth. After the Belfast to Derry March in January had reached the city, there was severe violence between the RUC and Catholics in the Bogside area. The RUC were alleged to have systematically entered the area and assaulted people and property alike. Witnesses saw police 'break every window in the street', and when they began to protest, the RUC 'threatened them and molested some of their womenfolk.'[61] These reports have to be taken in context; nationalist feelings towards the RUC were hostile to the point of outright hatred, and therefore there is certainly some exaggeration in their reports. However, Scarman concluded in his report that 'there is no doubt that some breakdown of police discipline did occur.'[62]

On 12 August the Apprentice Boys began their march, possibly unaware of the historic events that were about to unfold across Northern Ireland. They were aware that there were attempts to ban the procession, but that it had been decided to allow it to go ahead. The procession marched peacefully through the city until about 3.45 p.m. According to Brian Walker, in *The Belfast Telegraph,* this is when the procession passed Waterloo Place and was subsequently stoned by some nationalists.[63] Police intervened to protect the march, and full-scale fighting broke out between nationalists and the RUC. There was little anybody could do; both sides were spoiling for a fight, and they were soon embroiled in serious rioting. There was also little or no control over nationalists, as Walker states:

> There was no effective stewarding from DCDA [Derry Citizens Defence Association] and the efforts of a few individuals such as John Hume and Ivan Cooper [local leaders within NICRA] were unable to stop the fighting.[64]

The RUC, now completely embroiled, attempted to storm the Bogside and drive the rioters back. Nationalists now erected barricades at all the entrances into the Bogside, and set up camp on top of the Rossville Flats. From here the rioters bombarded the RUC below with petrol bombs and stones, preventing them from entering the area. For three days and nights the rioters battled with the police, with no end in sight. On the evening of 13 August, as palls of smoke were rising from Derry, Jack Lynch, the Irish Taoiseach, went on television to voice the concerns of the Dublin government. He asked for immediate talks with the British on the constitutional future of Northern Ireland and the immediate posting of UN peacekeepers, much to the disdain of the British government. Many viewed his statement as inflammatory, adding to the hopes of the rioters that the south was going to intervene. Field hospitals were set up in Donegal, close to the border, and Irish troops were posted to sensitive areas.

For all the rhetoric coming from Dublin about field hospitals and such, there was talk in government circles of Irish military involvement in the north. In *20th-Century Contemporary History,* Edward Longwill talks in detail about how the violence in the north of Ireland panicked a Dublin government ill-prepared to handle such a crisis:

> On 13 August 1969 the Irish cabinet discussed the developing Bogside crisis. Neil Blaney, minister for agriculture, suggested sending the Irish army across the border in an attempt to provoke United Nations intervention and the consequent deployment of a UN peacekeeping force. After a brief discussion regarding possible outcomes, the cabinet wisely rejected military intervention, although Taoiseach Jack Lynch authorised the formation of a number of infantry groups on the border and the establishment of field hospitals. That evening Lynch made a televised address to the Irish people. He announced the formation of army field hospitals and claimed that his government would 'no longer stand by'.
>
> Directly after the cabinet meeting, all available regular army assets situated near or on the border were mobilised. This culminated in the establishment of an infantry group in the Letterkenny and Ballybofey areas of County Donegal, made

up of nearly 300 combat soldiers, 101 command and support troops and twenty nurses. On 14th August the Ulster Special Constabulary (USC or B-Specials) formed up near the Bogside in preparation for an armed assault. British army intervention prevented USC action, and unrest in the city effectively ended.[65]

Longwill concludes:

The Irish government's contemplation of military intervention never involved the question of partition. Assessments and contingencies developed in response to humanitarian concerns. As Jack Lynch accurately told an emotional Fianna Fáil Árd Fheis in 1970, the Irish army did not have the means to intervene, and his policy in relation to partition was to seek unity by consent. An Irish army incursion into Northern Ireland would have ended in two possible ways: either withdrawal or total destruction. The most likely British response would have been the issuing of a withdrawal ultimatum. Irrespective of the hypothetical, what is certain is that Jack Lynch placed the stability, security and economic prosperity of the Irish state above any potentially ruinous irredentist impulses.[66]

The south was never going to intervene; to do so would have been disastrous for the Republic and the Catholics in Northern Ireland.

The republican movement, not to be outdone by Lynch and his speech, issued a statement of their own through Tomás Mac Giolla, President of Sinn Fein, in Dublin.

The present events in the six counties are the outcome of fifty years of British rule. The civil rights demands, moderate though they are, have shown up that Unionist rule is incompatible with democracy; if the minority thought they could grant them and stay in power they would have done so after the degree of pressure put on them. The question now is no longer civil rights, but the continuation of British rule in Ireland.[67]

He followed this statement with a list of demands:

(a) Universal adult suffrage at 18 for all elections in Northern Ireland.
(b) An impartial boundary commission to draw up fair electoral areas
(c) The introduction of the Proportional Representation system of election
(d) The repeal of the draconic Special Powers Act and Public Order Act
(e) The outlawing of religious discrimination in housing and jobs, and making incitement to religious discrimination illegal
(f) Disbanding of the sectarian B Special Constabulary, and the establishment of independent machinery of enquiry into complaints against the police.[68]

Notwithstanding that these were identical to some of the civil rights organisation's own demands, the Unionist government at Stormont was certainly not going to listen to republicans in Dublin. However, rallying republicans and nationalists to the cause of Northern Irish Catholics by 'using whatever means possible', was another matter:

> We call on all Irish people to rally behind these demands of the Republican Movement, during the next few days, and by holding demonstrations, meetings, rallies, to allow their solidarity with the people of the North in their struggle. They are urged to use the guidelines provided by this statement to do so.[69]

By now Protestants across Northern Ireland were sure that the Irish Army was going to cross the border, and tensions began to rise. Gregory Campbell MP remembers the events:

> It was a strange feeling, watching the rioting. There was a sense of adventure in it, but at the same time it was fearful. Rumours were rife. The Irish Army were deployed to the border adjacent to Londonderry, and rumours suggested (and were believed) that they were actually in the Bogside. It was very exciting for a sixteen-year-old teenager, but also very worrying. We all thought that we were heading straight into a United Ireland. I viewed it as an insurrection, an attempt to destroy Northern Ireland.[70]

In the middle of all the destruction and confusion, Frank Gogarty and Sean Keenan of the Derry Citizens Action Committee (DCAC) appealed for nationalists across Northern Ireland to create diversionary protests, in order to draw the RUC away from the Bogside. His call was received, and answered.

Out of the Ashes:
Belfast Burns

The history of riots and civil commotion in the North of Ireland, and especially in Belfast, prove that so long as the Protestant Unionists think they have the right to dominate and insult the Catholics there can never be lasting peace.[1]

(Andrew Boyd, *Holy War)*

I saw none other than police firing and they were firing at all four flat levels.

(Witness to the death of Patrick Rooney, at his inquest)

The weapon [the Browning machine gun] was a menace to the innocent as well as the guilty, being heavy and indiscriminate in its fire: and on one occasion (the firing into St Brendan's block of flats where the boy Rooney was killed) its use was wholly unjustifiable.

(Violence and Civil Disturbances in Northern Ireland in 1969)

I

The mood in Belfast on 13 August was extremely tense. Catholics along the Falls Road and at other interfaces were fearing the worst. The West Belfast Housing Action Committee, formed earlier in the year, organised a protest march outside Divis Flats against the wishes of NICRA, but in response to the plea for help from Derry. Danny Morrison remembers:

I knew that something bad was going to happen—that was obvious from the Apprentice Boys march on 12 August. The Battle of the Bogside began and I was watching it. I remember the headlines in the *Belfast Telegraph* about the 'B' Specials being mobilised. I think it was the Civil Rights organisation that called a series of protests across the north.[2]

That night, a crowd of around 300 people gathered at the flats, sang songs, waved the Irish Tricolour, and at around 9.30 p.m. proceeded up the Falls Road, towards the newly built Springfield Road RUC station, to hand in a petition of protest about events in Derry. Leading IRA figures Joe McCann and Anthony Dornan were at the head of the march.[3] Gerry Adams was also there, and chaired the meeting.[4] Accounts vary about what happened next; Scarman reported that upon arriving at the station the crowd began to throw missiles.[5] Adams states that the procession was attacked on its way to the station by the RUC.[6] Nevertheless, nationalists and republicans were on the streets in Belfast, and in strength.

The petition was not accepted at Springfield Road Station. The station had undergone a rebuilding programme, and was not fully functional. Thus the crowd decided to march towards Hastings Street RUC station, near Divis Flats. Danny Morrison was one of the marchers.

On the Wednesday night there was a protest outside Springfield Road RUC barracks. The cops opened fire from the roof, they fired over the heads of the people, and maybe there were one or two petrol bombs thrown. It was then decided that the next night there would be marches in as many Nationalist towns as possible, so that the RUC would have to stay and patrol those marches and they would not be sent to Derry. There's photographs of RUC men lying on street corners, exhausted you know, no sleep, and they were continually trying to get into the Bogside, but nobody was letting them in because of what happened to Samuel Devenney.

We also took part in that protest on the Falls Road at Hastings Street barracks. Crowds were milling about, there were all sorts of rumours, and it was starting to get tense.[8]

As the crowd reached Hastings Street station, missiles and petrol bombs were thrown. Armoured cars then came out of the station, with orders to arrest the ringleaders; none were arrested as the crowds scattered.[9]

Crowds now began to gather in other places. In Leeson Street, a crowd of about 200 gathered and began to attack the RUC stationed at the top of the street. According to Scarman, shots were fired at the police. A hand grenade was thrown, and an officer was injured. From then on, Shoreland Armoured vehicles were used by the RUC as it was clear now that there were guns on the Falls Road.[10] By now it was approaching midnight on the 13th, and sporadic fighting was breaking out in other parts of the city. In Ardoyne, residents began to build barricades on Hooker, Brookfield, and Herbert Street, such was the fear in the district. This fear was there since July, when Protestants began to move out of the area and many Catholic families on the wrong side of the divide actually swapped houses with Protestants, who were eager to be with their own.[11]

Back on the Falls Road, things were deteriorating badly. After the debacle at Hastings Street station, the crowd decided to go back to Springfield Road. It was around this time that Isaac Agnews (a car showroom on the Falls Road) was set on fire, and various cars were pulled out onto the street. According to Joe Graham in *Show Me the Man*, IRA volunteers torched the building in an attempt to attract a crowd, and hence draw the police away from Derry:

> At the corner of the Falls Road and Conway ... was a huge Volkswagen car dealership showroom—Isaac Agnew—and it was decided if that was put alight it might bring the Falls Road community out onto the streets and help draw some of the peelers (RUC) from Derry and Ardoyne.... The car used to transport the three volunteers over to the Falls Road was a top-of-the-range type and belonged to a builder who was not a member of the IRA.... The car arrived on the Falls Road and parked in the street opposite the Agnews showroom. The three volunteers stepped out, two carrying petrol and the other some bricks. A few bricks were thrown through the huge window and it shattered, giving access for the petrol carriers to step inside and sprinkle it, while the brick thrower prepared to throw the lit match. With the cars inside containing petrol this acted as an accelerant; the whole four floors went up like a cardboard box, with flames leaping 100 feet into the air.[12]

The New Northern Mill was also set on fire, along with various other properties. Up at Springfield RUC station, things were not much better. As Danny Morrison recalled, petrol bombs and stones were thrown at the station. It was at this point that the RUC opened fire on the crowd, injuring two people. The RUC alleged that they fired into the air; Scarman dismissed this, saying:

> Ugly in mood and aggressive in action though the crowd was, neither the security of the station nor the safety of the police was at such risk to permit 'firing for effect', a euphemism for firing to injure or kill people in the street below.[13]

Rioting carried on in the Falls Road area and in Ardoyne for a number of hours afterwards, finally petering out at around 4 a.m. on Thursday 14th. Whole areas of the Falls Road, Hooker Street, and other roads were full of the debris of a night's violence. However, as serious as the violence was, it was not directed at Protestant areas—it was Catholics versus RUC. Nevertheless, all during the night of the 13th, gangs of Protestants stood and watched the violence from the tops of Conway Street, Percy Street, North Howard Street, and Cupar Street. Anger was building in Protestant areas against the Civil Rights, and their marches for liberties that many of them did not have. They were angry, and ready.

As dawn on 14 August approached, a relative calm descended on Belfast; however, tension was still high. Many Catholic families began the process of moving away from interface areas. Barricades began to be erected, as many believed that there was worse trouble to come. In Stormont there was a sense of panic, as it became obvious that (even with the 'B' Specials mobilised) there was not enough in the Stormont arsenal to control the various outbreaks of violence. As far back as the beginning of the month, Stormont had been in constant contact with Westminster about the prospect of troops being used on the ground in support of the RUC.

In Derry, the rioting raged on. RUC officers were exhausted; there were no replacements; many were injured. Gregory Campbell MP recalls:

> I watched as the Royal Ulster Constabulary (RUC), worn out from constant attacks, collapsed on the streets from exhaustion. The RUC were completely unprepared for what was happening. There were no reinforcements, no equipment to help protect them, and many were injured in the ferocious fighting.[14]

It became obvious that Westminster would soon have to send in troops. However, the implications were extreme; Westminster would have to take control of the Stormont government if troops were used on the streets of Northern Ireland, an event that neither government wanted. After protracted talks, it was agreed that troops could be used only after Stormont had used up all its available security forces, and then it would only be a temporary measure. The troops were to go in 'in aid of the civil power', a solution which was to have far-reaching consequences for the future of Northern Ireland.[15] At approximately 4.30 p.m., a request for the British Army to enter Derry was received by James Callaghan. The request was accepted, and shortly afterwards the Army began replacing the exhausted RUC at the Rossville flats. The Battle of the Bogside was coming to an end.

In Belfast, however, the battles were only beginning. An order for the mobilisation of the 'B' Specials was issued at 3 p.m. on the 14th. This had an immediate effect in Catholic districts of west Belfast. In Ardoyne, barricades were being built at all the flashpoints. Tom Holland remembers:

> What I can vividly remember is the barricades going up at the bottom of all the streets to stop the RUC and 'B' Specials from getting in ... and all the Unionist mobs. The big paving stones from the road were used ... also buses. The local people all went up and stole the buses ... the big red ones.
>
>   This was mainly to keep the RUC Land Rovers out—which would come in firing indiscriminately at people's houses—but it was also to keep the UVF out ... I mean, they had a limited amount of weapons. All the people's windows were also covered up with the wire mesh, or whatever you could get...[16]

Barricades were also being erected along the Falls Road, especially around the Lower Falls area and the Divis Flats. The air hung heavy with anticipation, rumour, and tension, as Marian Walsh describes:

> [The] street seemed eerily quiet even with the mill workers coming down from the Shankill to go to work. Normally people from both sides would exchange pleasantries but not that day. The footballers did not come out at lunchtime. By the afternoon my sister took my 3 young brothers to her friend's house in another part of the city. My dad was at work. He was a steel erector. So there was just me and my mother at home. We watched as some of our neighbours started to board up their windows fearful of another night of trouble. We were wishing my father was home so that we could get ours done. We heard that Ian Paisley was at the Protestant end of Conway St giving one of this inflammatory speeches. Many people started loading furniture onto horse drawn carts and little vans. My mother put a bottle of milk, some pancakes and her family allowance book in a little zipped up brown leather shopping bag—she obviously hoped we would be back home again. But that was not to be.[17]

II

As the sultry afternoon moved into a humid and tense evening, sporadic trouble began to break out. A gang of several hundred Protestants began to move across the Crumlin Road into Hooker Street and Brookfield Street in the Ardoyne, throwing petrol bombs into houses as they went. The difference now—as many suspected—was that the mobs descending from Protestant areas had 'B' Specials amongst them.

In Divis Street, at its junction with Percy Street, a crowd began to gather. Petrol bombs were thrown at Hastings Street police station. Rioting spread up the Falls Road to Northumberland Street and Conway Street. In Conway Street, Protestants began to move towards the Falls Road. By now the RUC were on the ground, and they were heavily involved in the fighting. Shooting began in the street, scattering rioters and adding to an already dangerous situation. Shots were fired back at Catholics by the RUC, according to Scarman, 'for effect'—in other words, at the crowd.[18]

Joe Doyle, a resident of Conway Street at the time, remembers the rioting, the attempts by the RUC to get to the Falls Road, and the wanton destruction of the following Protestant mobs:

> The Falls had about forty people in the area of Conway Street, and shortly thereafter there followed an attack by baton-charging RUC and unionist terrorists. The RUC were beating their batons against their shields; this action was supposed to frighten

us. They made about six different attacks but they did not get onto the Falls. The Unionist terrorists were lobbing petrol bombs into the houses as they followed the RUC down the street, and my home was one of their targets. When the RUC did not achieve their objective by getting onto the Falls Road, they sent down two Shoreland cars; Land Rover chassis and Shorts [factory] body. These were also gun-carrying vehicles. They came down Conway Street firing their guns into the air, and went up to Cupar Street and back to the Shankill area. Everyone thought that they were firing blank shots. Later they were to find out that this was not true.

The second time that they came down they were firing tracer bullets, and their guns were firing at the crowd. Some of the crowd shouted that they were using blanks, but they soon changed their ideas when people began to fall and they could see the blood. During one of these attacks, I was on the Falls opposite Norfolk Street when a Shorland came down Conway Street; a young lad of about fifteen was standing at the corner of Norfolk Street, and the Shorland fired at him. He was a member of the Order of Malta First Aid group. One of the bullets hit the wall and then hit him. I went over to him and the bullet only grazed him on the forehead. I later got him to care as no-one wanted to go to the RVH hospital, as the RUC would have arrested anyone taken there.[19]

By now people in their homes on Conway Street feared the worst. They firmly believed that a Protestant attempt to drive Catholics out of west Belfast was underway. Many attempted to flee the area, as Marian Walsh states:

I could hear the clinking sound of bottles being hit together—these were petrol bombs. The bombers intermingled with armed police men who had their weapons drawn. It was time for me and my mother to get out. As we got closer to the Falls Rd we met my father. He told us to get down to the streets on the other side of the Road but he would not come with us. With only 2 other neighbours—my uncle and a young woman, my father did his best to defend our houses but lumps of coal, broken flagstones and a shovel cannot be a match for petrol bombs, guns and Shoreland armoured vehicles. When my father did eventually leave the Street he had been shot. The bullet took a big slice of the top of his head but he survived.

The first aiders dressed my father's head wound and the wounds of many others. It was rumoured, and turned out to be true, that anyone with injuries attending the local Royal Victoria Hospital was being arrested by the police so the Knights of Malta was providing the only medical help that night and for months to come. It must have been the early hours of the 15th August when we were offered the chance to 'escape' from the area. Someone had arrived at the hostel with a mini-bus which was taking people to St Teresa's Community Hall—a few miles away. The shooting had eased off temporarily so we decided to go for it. A makeshift flag consisting of a red cross on a white piece of sheeting was attached to a brush shaft and stuck out of a window.

It seemed like ages getting up the Falls road towards St Teresa's but when we got there the residents of Andersonstown had come out in force to make tea and tear up sheets for bandages. It was then that we heard that the houses in Conway St had been petrol bombed.[20]

Eamon McGonigle was a resident of Conway Street at the time. Not long married, he was staying at his in-laws' house:

On the 14th August I was in Conway Street at my father in law, Peter Sullivan's, house. Previous to this, there were protest marches on the Falls Road in an attempt to draw the police out and take the pressure of the rioters in Derry. They made their way down to Hastings Street police station, windows in police cars were broken by the marchers. Back in Conway Street, I noticed a crowd of Protestants that were gathering at the other end. One of them broke away from the main crowd, presumably to stoke up tensions with the Catholics. A lot of chanting was happening; Protestants were shouting 'Fenian Bastards' etc. Out of the crowd came the police, in little jeep type cars nicknamed 'Whippets'. They began firing wildly and without aiming.[21]

Conway Street was razed to the ground that night, but the fighting was not over yet. On most of the roads and side streets linking the Falls Road with the Shankill Road, violence was ongoing, sporadic, and deadly. Many of the Protestants who were standing, watching the rioting, or in their homes attempting to avoid it, were also fearful on that fateful evening. Having been fed on a diet of anti-Catholic propaganda for years, they believed that this was the moment, this was the day that the IRA was going to wipe them out. Baroness May Blood remembers:

Now, when the trouble broke out in Belfast that night I was actually on the Falls Road. I was a shop steward at a mill which was just off the Falls Road, and one of my members had been injured.[22]

In Percy Street, the rioting was just as savage. Catholic crowds had gathered in numbers and watched as hundreds of Protestants began to march down the other end of the street. The 'B' Specials were also present and, according to Scarman, they decided that it would be safer to push the Catholic crowd back towards Divis Street.[23] Fearing an onslaught by both the Protestants and the 'B' Specials, the Catholic crowd began to throw missiles and petrol bombs. Corrugated sheets were acquired and held together to form a mobile barricade. A JCB digger was also driven up Percy Street.[24]

In Dover Street there was also hand-to-hand combat. The Arkle Bar public house on the corner of Dover Street and Divis Street was ablaze, as were several other buildings. Patrick Dorrian remembers the events in Dover Street clearly:

I was staying at my aunt's in a house in Hamilton Court—this was actually the gated entry to a council amenity yard. Her husband was the yardman and the house came with the job; the keys to the stores and office, as well as the main gate, were kept in the house. Both the uncle and aunt were going out for the night … Around 8 p.m. I became aware of tumult outside. I went into the yard and could hear shouts and shots. Part of the big store had a gate out to Dover St. I could see through some gaps that there was hand-to-hand combat in Dover St. I then could hear cries for help. On going into the yard, I traced the sounds to a boundary wall between the houses in Dover Street and the council yard. The wall was 18–20 feet high, and on it there were two families—the Livingstones and the Curleys. I then went and brought out first one and then a second extension ladder, and put each one convenient to the families against the walls. Tony Curley started getting his own young family down. One of the young Livingstones came down the ladder first, and ran to join the fray. I was able to assist the younger Livingstones down from the wall and show them how to get out of the yard.[25]

By now vast swathes of the Falls Road area were in serious chaos. Hundreds of people were on the streets, and fires raged all along the interface areas. The RUC were there in Shorelands; foot patrols were also heavily involved. In Scarman, the emphasis seems to be on the defensive nature of the role the RUC played in the violence, but this is disputed by many of the witnesses on the ground. The RUC, backed with elements of the 'B' Specials, launched attack after attack down Percy Street, Dover Street, and Conway Street in order to clear the areas of Catholic rioters. Inevitably Protestant crowds followed the police, launching petrol bomb attacks at Catholic homes along the way.

This is the official account: the RUC were overwhelmed and only attempted to push the Catholics back towards their own areas. Scarman partly absolves the police from any active participation in the rioting; however, things seemed different to the people caught up in the maelstrom, as Joe Doyle remembers:

There was a large crowd of unionists and RUC at the corner of First Street, and the tension was very high. The people on the Falls began to build barricades, and I spoke to an RUC sergeant at the corner of David Street and Conway Street. I told him that we would attempt to keep the people on the Falls back as they were offering no threat, and I asked him to control the unionist crowd and keep them back. I then walked back to Norfolk Street; a small barricade had been built there and, as I reached it, a massive attack took place by the RUC and the unionist terrorists. The RUC were trying to baton the Catholics, and while they were doing so a number of unionist terrorists began to throw petrol bombs from behind the RUC lines.

This confirmed my worst fears—that the RUC and the unionist terrorists were working together to use a scorched-earth policy on the Catholic residents. The first house that went on fire in Norfolk Street was the Boomer's, and in this house lived an elderly couple and their daughter. We were unable to hold off the attack for very long.[26]

To many on the ground attempting to defend the area, it certainly seemed that the RUC were actively engaging with the Protestant gangs in attacking Catholic districts. Fear and rumours spread across the whole area, adding to perceptions of invasions by the Irish Army, widespread murder, and wholesale cleansing of Catholic districts. Age-old perceptions of the RUC as a Protestant force only added to these fears. The Protestant mobs that fought them on the streets and the RUC who were supposedly there to stop the fighting were seen as one unit—the Protestant state.

However, there is ample evidence that the RUC *were* involved in attacks on Catholics that night. For instance, Scarman (while generally clearing the RUC of any malpractice) makes numerous references to aggressive behaviour by the RUC and 'B' Specials. Heavy fire from police armoured vehicles was also reported by witnesses—most notably in Conway Street, where an armoured vehicle was allegedly driven at a Catholic crowd.

Catholics interpreted events in Conway Street and the neighbouring streets as collusion between police and Protestants. They saw the police as attacking those who were trying to defend their homes from invading Protestants who were allowed to burn and loot property with impunity behind police lines. The Tribunal however rejects this interpretation. No doubt the police concentrated their attention on the Catholic crowd because they saw them not only as a threat to themselves but to the whole system of law and order in the city. Nevertheless, the police on duty in these streets were seriously at fault in that, though there in some strength, they failed to control the Protestant mob or to prevent the arson and the looting.[27]

Paddy Devlin, a local MP at the time, recalled this in his autobiography:

Police in uniform, covered in civilian clothes, were recognised amongst Loyalist attackers in Dover Street and I myself saw police armoured cars in Conway Street, standing by as the mobs broke the windows of hastily abandoned Catholic houses before pouring petrol in to burn them. In scenes that had not been paralleled for nearly fifty years, I saw with my own eyes old people and former neighbours flocking out of Conway Street, where my grandparents had once lived at number 32 and my own mother and father at number 80.[28]

The firing from the Springfield Road station, described in Scarman as 'well over the heads' of rioters, was instead focused directly into the crowd. Wounds present on two youths that were injured showed that they were directly hit by bullets.[29] The reckless attempts by the RUC in dealing with the riots, such as the indiscriminate firing into the Divis flats complex, subsequently led to the deaths of a number of people, some of whom were not even involved in the disturbances. It is difficult to say who fired the first shots that night; sporadic firing was being reported from many areas. Nevertheless, when firing did occur it was the general belief amongst the RUC that the IRA was involved, and that they had a plentiful supply of weapons. This was far from the truth.

The IRA in Belfast at this time was a depleted and demoralised organisation. During the 1960s its upper command, led by Cathal Goulding, had pursued a non-military policy, tending to focus on peaceful protest. Hence there was no new build-up of weapons and no training for such an event as was now happening in Belfast and other urban centres. Many had left in protest, with many experienced operators lost as the Marxist elements took over. There was also a general feeling that the ruling body was out of touch with developments in the north and the threat to Catholics there.

Republican elements were also involved in the Civil Rights protests, but not to the degree that many believed. However, many within the Protestant community felt that republicans were in virtual control. Gregory Campbell MP argued:

> The Civil Rights organisation was riddled with Republican elements. They had a major say in the running and planning of the protests. I initially thought little of what was going on, but when banners were unfurled at marches saying 'Smash the Orange State', you began to think. That was when I began to think politically.[30]

The Stormont government was also at pains to present the Civil Rights Movement as 'riddled with republican elements'. On 7 July 1969 a confidential letter was sent to the Ministry of Home Affairs from the Inspector General of the RUC. The push to portray the movement as republican, and communist, was evident throughout the document:

> At grass roots the movement has now crystallised into the familiar 'green' composed of republicans and nationalists, but still, as I have said, containing a vociferous minority grouping of Trotskyites or Revolutionary Socialists.[31]

Paisley was especially mounting a concerted effort to portray the Civil Rights Movement as an IRA-led attempt to destroy the union with Britain. He launched many counter-demonstrations, sometimes at the exact time and place of the Civil Rights marches. Although he was seen by many as a scaremonger, he nevertheless picked up much support from his own evangelical community and working class Protestants across Northern Ireland. Many Protestants in the working class areas of Belfast picked up on his message and believed that an insurrection was on the way.

As violence engulfed the Falls Road, the IRA organised. McMillan began to organise members and weapons for duty on the Falls Road. Weapons were handed out as the rioting intensified. According to witnesses, the total amount of armoury consisted of '1 Thompson machine gun, 1 Sten sub-machine gun, 1 rifle and 6 hand guns.'[32] The IRA fired at police in Conway Street and set up positions on the roof of St Comgall's School, opposite the entrance to Percy Street and nearby Dover Street. Joe Doyle recalled:

> The noise of the houses burning, with the slates crackling, was very frightening as you did not know if it was gunfire, and there was some great acts of bravery by the people that night. I later also learnt that a number of small weapons were brought into the area to defend us. I saw two machine guns, which I believe were ex-RUC, and these weapons were used in a staggered manner by firing up Conway Street and then moving to Percy Street in the lower Falls.[33]

As the Protestant crowd advanced once again down Dover Street, the IRA opened fire, killing Herbert Roy—a twenty-six-year-old Protestant. Scarman states that the shot that killed Roy came from the Gilford Street area; John McQuade MP's testimony alleged that the shot came from high up in Divis Tower. However, it is highly likely that Roy was shot from the roof of St Comgall's by IRA volunteers.

Police reported heavy firing from the vicinity of the school and also from the direction of Divis Flats, where rioters were throwing petrol bombs from the roofs of the various maisonettes. Hastings Street station was under attack by gunfire, and police marksmen were on the roof firing back. Police in armoured vehicles were also firing at the flats. Scarman states that a 'considerable number of rounds of Browning ammunition' were fired at the flats by police, in an attempt to dislodge an alleged sniper.[34] The alleged sniper was never found, although the RUC believed that they had stopped him. The firing resulted in two deaths and unparalleled criticism of the police as an impartial force.

III

The Divis Flats complex was home to some 2,500 people of the Lower Falls area. They were a series of blocks or maisonettes, built to alleviate the chronic overcrowding that was present in the Lower Falls and Divis Street areas. One tower of twenty floors dominated the rest, which were six floors tall. The original plan was to extend the complex up the Falls Road, removing the slum dwellings in the process. The onset of violence stopped that, and the flats themselves became synonymous with the slum areas that they were supposed to replace. However, in 1969 they were mainly well-kept, with local people taking pride in what was infinitely better living conditions than many had before.

On the night of 14 August there was considerable activity within the area of the flats. Divis Street was engulfed in rioting. The RUC believed that there was heavy firing coming from the vicinity, and armoured Shorelands were sent to the general area. From there on in there was chaos. Police witnesses reported shooting coming from the general direction of the maisonettes and also from the tower. At around midnight, a radio message was received by an RUC officer; it simply said, 'Hastings Street Station under fire from low-storey flats opposite station.'[35] A fire crew, dealing with one of the many fires on Divis Street, also reported that they were coming under fire from the flats.[36]

The RUC, who were by now fully convinced that guns were being used in the flats, organised a concerted effort to retaliate. Shoreland Armoured cars began sorties up and down Divis Street. The rioting intensified, with the RUC coming under sustained attack with petrol bombs and missiles. It was at this point that the RUC claimed that they fired shots into the air to disperse the crowds, having come under fire from St Comgall's School.[37] Firing intensified as the Shorelands drove up and down.

In No. 5 St Brendan's Path, Patrick Rooney, a nine-year-old boy, was in the back bedroom with the rest of the family, trying to escape the shooting that was going on outside. The following is a witness statement at the inquest of Patrick's death. Although names are omitted from copies of the inquest, the witness here is almost certainly Patrick's father.

I live with [names withheld]. Patrick Gerard was the eldest. On Thursday 14th August 1969, about 8.30 p.m., a number of people marched up Divis Street in the direction of Springfield Road. They were away about an hour when they returned to Divis Street. I walked up Divis Street as far as Northumberland Street to see what was taking place, and I saw crowds assembled in Dover Street, Percy Street, and Northumberland Street. These crowds seemed to have come from the Shankill Road direction. Then I returned home about 9.30 p.m. I went into my home where I remained afterwards with [name withheld].

Between 9.30 p.m. and 11.30 p.m. ... the opposing crowds threw bottles and petrol bombs at each other. [Names withheld] were asleep in two adjoining bedrooms. At about 11.30 p.m. ... I heard the sound of shots and the shooting continued from that time. [Names withheld] were awakened by the noise and the shooting and they were assembled in a back bedroom. [Names withheld] were with them. I thought that was the safest place to have [name withheld] and [name withheld] when the shooting was taking place. As far as I can recollect I was in my back bedroom with [name withheld] shortly after midnight when the left side of my head was grazed by a bullet. I heard the bullet passing and I felt blood coming from my head.

Just at the same time ... Patrick ... who was standing with his back against the front wall of the bedroom slumped to the ground. I thought he fainted, but when [name withheld] lifted and laid him on the bed I could see blood coming from a gunshot wound in the back of his head. The right side of [name withheld] face and neck was burned and grazed by a bullet also. Prior to the time [name withheld] was shot I saw tracer bullets which were fired at the flats.[38]

One of these tracer bullets went through four walls before it hit Patrick. The RUC denied shooting towards the flats; Scarman claimed in his report that those in the Shorelands, disgusted with what had happened, held some evidence back from his inquiry. Nevertheless, Scarman was satisfied that at least one of the armoured vehicles did shoot towards the flats, possibly in reply to alleged shooting from the Whitehall block.

Although he was shot in the back of the head, Patrick did not die instantly. As the rioting raged on outside, a few witnesses ran out of the flats to summon an ambulance, one of them carrying the child with him.

I saw a boy lying on a bed. Blood was on the pillow. A lot of people were kneeling down saying prayers. I overheard someone say they could not get an ambulance down to the flats because of the shooting. I said I would take the boy out onto the road and get an ambulance. I lifted the boy in my arms, his head was on my right arm ... We went out into Divis Street and into Dover Street. This street was crowded with people, but the people cleared from my way when they saw a boy in my arms. I went on up Dover Street and there saw an ambulance. The ambulance people put the boy on a stretcher and put him into the ambulance.[39]

Patrick later died in hospital. The official police report, filed nearly a month later on 8 September, stated that Patrick was shot as 'gunfire was exchanged between rival groups.'[40] However, it fails to say that one of these rival groups was the RUC. In his testimony, Patrick's father stated:

I heard quite a lot of shooting taking place outside. I am unable to say the direction from which the shots came that entered my flat. There were two bullet holes; one bullet hole through the sunlight above my door and another bullet hole through a window on the left of my front door.

I saw from the front window of my house police armoured cars passing, and tracer bullets were being fired by these cars. I have no doubt that the tracer bullets were fired from whippet (armoured) cars. I have also no doubt that the bullets found in my ... house were fired from the Divis Street direction. I live on the ground floor of the flats. [Name withheld] was shot between 11.30 p.m. and 12 p.m. I saw none other than police firing and they were firing at all four flat levels.[41]

IV

Hugh McCabe was a member of the Queen's Royal Irish Hussars, and was home on leave from Germany. On the night of 14–15 August 1969 he was on the fourth floor of the Whitehall block of flats in Divis Street. Heavy fire was coming from a number of places adjacent to the flats, most notably from a Shoreland armoured car driving up and down Divis Street. McCabe was allegedly shooting at police when he was shot, and he died at the scene.

This death is perhaps the most contentious of the three days in which there was severe violence. The official police version of events was that there was firing coming from the block of flats in which McCabe was shot, but this has been disputed by the many witnesses that were there. The evidence for such shooting was collected by the Scarman Tribunal. In the evidence, a Constable Mahood reported seeing muzzle flashes from the roof of the Whitehall block of flats, near the Divis Street end. He also saw petrol bombs being thrown from the same position. Constable Johnson, who was inside the Hastings Street police station, also heard gunfire; he climbed onto the roof of the station and witnessed gunfire coming from the same position as Constable Mahood did.[42]

Various people involved in the disturbances also witnessed shooting emanating from the flats. John McQuade and Hugh Johnston, of the Shankill Defence Association, testified to Scarman that they saw gunfire coming from the flats.[43] A number of occupants of the flats testified to Scarman that there was no firing from the block of flats that McCabe was killed in, although Scarman seemed quick to dismiss many of them. A Mr Bryan, Mr Wyllie, Mr McGarrigan, Mr Mitchell, and Mr O'Connor all testified that there was no shooting from the flats, although Scarman stated that their observations on the night could have been limited. However, one police officer, a Constable McKittrick, was watching petrol bombers on the roof of the Whitehall flats and did not see any gunfire either, although he did hear shooting.[44]

Thus the killing of Hugh McCabe became shrouded in hearsay and contradictions. Scarman was quick to cite misadventure in his conclusions, stating that they 'consider that the firing which killed Mr McCabe was justified'.[45] The RUC report on his death, echoing the report on Patrick Rooney's death, claimed that 'during the course of riots in the Divis Street area, gunfire was exchanged between rival groups. Police were also fired on and they later returned the fire.'[46] The report was filed on 8 September 1969, and was to become the official line on McCabe's death.

At the inquest into McCabe's death, witnesses told of a chaotic and violent night. Divis flats, not directly in the centre of the area of rioting, was nevertheless attacked by police on a number of occasions during the evening and the night; the police claimed they were returning fire. A very detailed map in the Scarman appendix clearly shows the bullet damage inflicted on the flats that fateful night. One witness described the events leading up to McCabe's death:

There are four storeys to the flats. The position of the flat in which [name withheld] resided was at right angles to Divis Street. From where I was standing I could see Boundary Street and Divis Street quite plainly. The parapet around the flats is about four foot six inches. I do not know how one gets to the roof. Before I got into the apartment I gathered the impression that the firing came from the front of the flats. There was never any firing from the flats. I left the flats to see if it was safe to transport [name withheld] to my house for safety. The 'B' Specials were firing at the flats. When I got back to the flat from which I had been about 40 yards from it someone came in and said someone had been shot dead. It was about 3:30 in the morning when [name withheld] informed me that [name withheld] had been shot and it was he who told me [name withheld] was shot about 12:10 a.m. The flats were sprayed by firing. It appeared to be indiscriminate. We had decided then that if it was safe to leave the flats we would do so. It appeared to us that people would be shot who were in the flats.[47]

A Shoreland armoured vehicle, known as a 'whippet', was making sorties up and down Divis Street. Many witnesses claim that it fired indiscriminately at the flats, although the RUC denied this took place and no officers admitted to the shooting. However, Hugh McCabe's father witnessed the firing:

I was looking over the parapet on the fourth floor in the direction of Divis Street and I turned round and saw [Hugh?] approaching me at a distance of about five yards.... There was then an outburst of machine gun fire; I looked down onto Divis Street and saw that this firing had come from a Whippet [Shoreland] car which had a large figure six painted on the side of it.[48]

Further on in his testimony he goes into more detail:

I should state that before the initial burst of gunfire and after it I saw approximately one dozen 'B' Specials standing at the corner of Boundary Street hanging around with guns in their hands, some of which were rifles and some of which were sub-machine guns. These Specials were spraying indiscriminately up at the Divis Street towers at the same time that the Whippet car had been shooting up the flats.[49]

Hugh McCabe's brother, Seamus, commented:

Now all the police heard gunfire, but their own men were shooting. Now, to my mind, they were firing from armoured cars up at the flats. They were saying Hugh was lying prone, as if he was shooting ... but is somebody is firing heavy machine guns you are going to get down low and the shot that killed him did come from Hastings Street barracks ... from the roof. The RUC had two snipers up there. You can see it there [paragraph from Scarman report]. An RUC man actually conceded that he didn't see any gunfire and that was ignored ... they glossed over that. There was one officer who said he wasn't sure whether it was a Bren gun or a Thompson sub machine gun [allegedly used by Hugh McCabe] that he heard. Now there would be a slight difference between a Bren gun and a Thompson sub machine gun.[50]

As the firing continued, McCabe pushed two women to the ground in order to avoid injury. A moaning sound was heard from around the corner on the veranda, and McCabe went to see who or what it was. That was the last time his father saw him alive. McCabe was allegedly shot by a police marksman based on the roof of Hastings Street police station. However, McCabe was on the roof of the staircase on the side of the flats when he was shot, according to Scarman. Was he taking part in stoning the police, as is alleged?

Scarman's conclusions about the death of Hugh McCabe are general; they do not accuse him personally of firing at police, but agree that the police marksman on the roof of Hastings Street station was correct to return fire to the location of the muzzle shots. Many who have written about these events have also generalised the evidence; if he was shot, surely he must have been shooting. Many have also used the throwing of petrol bombs and the quantity of bottles on the verandas as evidence of wrongdoing on McCabe's behalf. At best this is a generalisation; there was no proof that McCabe was throwing anything from the roof of the flats. At the inquest, one witness described having 'trouble getting past a stack of crates containing petrol bombs' in order to reach the flat that he was in. However, this was after McCabe he was shot.[51] Two witnesses (who came forward some years later) claimed that they were there when McCabe was lowered down from above them after being shot. They were adamant that McCabe was not involved in shooting at police from Whitehall flats that night.[52]

Seamus McCabe has his own opinions on what happened:

You need to remember how tight that area was at the time ... wee streets. To me they conveniently overlooked some facts ... some important facts, and ignored them. My father had gone down [from Whiterock] because the trouble was that bad, to check to see if things were alright ... and he was with my father when the shooting started. He heard someone groaning. And he pushed two women down a flight [of stairs] away from the shooting. You see, many people didn't realise they were firing live rounds. And he said, 'They are live.' So he left the father with the women and he went to see where the moaning was coming from. He got up onto the roof of the stairwell and he got hit up there.

The Whippets, armoured cars, came down and they fired. Now you don't get up on top of somewhere in a white shirt to start firing.

3

Ardoyne

In Ardoyne, tensions were at breaking point. The earlier battles with the RUC and Protestants from the other side of the Crumlin Road were only a forerunner for what was about to occur. The calls for help from Derry on 13 August had been heard loud and clear in the Catholic streets facing the interface; on the same day, Bernadette Devlin made a street speech to rally Ardoyne.[1] The atmosphere was electric, and as rioting began again in Divis Street on the evening of 14 August, the reverberations spread to Ardoyne.

Scarman stated that 'the Hooker Street crowd began the night's rioting'.[2] In *Ardoyne: The Untold Truth*, it is suggested that:

> RUC men, 'B' Specials and a mob of several hundred loyalist rioters surged across the Crumlin Road down Hooker Street and set fire to houses there and in the adjoining Chatham Street and Brookfield Street.[3]

Whatever the truth about the beginning of the night's violence, the whole area had erupted by 11 p.m. Catholic rioters, operating out of Hooker Street, were fighting with RUC and 'B' Specials. Protestant rioters also got involved, and began throwing petrol bombs at Hooker Street. As the two publications mentioned above hold differing opinions as to how this train of events unfolded, and in order to be as neutral as possible, both of these publications will thus be used to describe the events of 14–15 August in Ardoyne and the Crumlin Road areas (along with other sources).

The evening of 14 August had been as tense in Ardoyne as it had been in other parts of the city. During the day, busloads of women and children were moved out of the area into other, safer parts of the city—many of them would never return to the district they called home.[4] The violence of the night before had ensured this, and also that any sort of trouble—however minor—could spark off serious inter-communal rioting on a scale not seen in the area before. Thus, at 5 p.m. an attempt to defuse the situation was made by both Catholic and Protestant clergymen, on the Crumlin Road near Hooker Street junction.[5] However, it seems that their voices fell on deaf ears, as by around 8 p.m. residents of Hooker Street had begun to build a barricade in anticipation of trouble.

Protestants watched from the street corners and roads opposite Hooker Street, and as the evening wore on they became increasingly agitated. Members of the 'B' Specials arrived on the scene and were immediately despatched to Disraeli Street to contain the crowd. Their mood became more aggressive when, at about 10.30 p.m., Catholics behind the barricade in Hooker Street began to stone and petrol-bomb the RUC. The Edenderry Inn, the scene of serious violence the previous May, caught fire; witnesses on both sides were at odds as to who threw the petrol bombs that ignited the pub. Houses along this stretch of the Crumlin Road were also alight by now, and petrol bombs were being thrown back into Hooker Street by a crowd of Protestants in Disraeli Street.[6]

At this point severe street fighting was taking place around the Hooker Street junction, and the RUC decided it was time to try and force the Catholics back up Hooker Street. A baton charge was launched; as Scarman states, about 'two or three such charges' occurred in a short space of time.[7] Scarman does not state why the RUC felt that they had to baton charge Catholics first, considering that by this point there was hand-to-hand combat between Catholics and Protestants on the Crumlin Road; the RUC later claimed that they had come under fire during these sorties up Hooker Street. Nevertheless, the RUC were beaten back on each attempt. A Humber armoured vehicle was brought in for the task, and promptly broke through the barricade in Hooker Street. Protestant gangs invariably followed the RUC into Hooker Street, burning houses as they went. One resident remembered the initial incursion by police:

> I had been looking down Hooker Street and I saw a crowd of people apparently being baton charged towards the Butler Street area by the police. That was practically a common sight in Ardoyne for some time in the Hooker Street area.[8]

Another resident described the Protestant mobs entering her street:

> I remember the night of the 14th–15th August very well. The Paisleyites [supporters of Ian Paisley, invariably Protestant and very militant] came in, smashed all the windows and threw in petrol bombs. I was stuck in the house with two kids. My son had just been born on 7th June that year. I was literally petrified. At one point I was sitting behind the door trying to keep the mob out.[9]

Protestant mobs that entered Hooker Street identified themselves with white armbands. Police later said that the maximum number of people that followed them was about twenty, although this estimate is grossly underestimated. Other witnesses in the area estimated that about 200–300 individuals followed the police. Scarman edged towards the higher estimate, stating 'no less than 100'— but considering the damage to the area the higher figure is more likely.[10] Scarman later stated that Catholics petrol bombed their own houses, perhaps in an attempt to explain the widespread damage in the area.[11] Nevertheless, the rioting was ferocious as Catholics and Protestants fought each other in an orgy of sectarian violence.

As the rioting increased, a number of shooting incidents were reported by the RUC. Head Constable (HC) Patterson stated that the first shooting appeared to come from Butler Street, and the RUC returned fire.[12] However, other witness statements disagreed with the HC, stating that the RUC fired first, and then fired at a small group of people.[13] Whatever happened, this moment changed everything in the Ardoyne. Catholics were now not only protecting their areas from marauding Protestant mobs, but from the RUC and 'B' Specials as well. In their opinion, it was them against the Protestant state.

Sam McLarnon was a native of Ardoyne. Described as a funny, happy man, he was well-known in the area on account of his job as a bus conductor.[14] On the night of 14–15 August 1969, he was in the living room of his house at 37 Herbert Street when he was killed by a single bullet to the head. Initially the RUC denied that they had fired the shot that killed McLarnon, but Scarman found that there was no other explanation. Invariably statements were made that alleged the bullet which killed McLarnon was flattened, possibly by hitting another object before reaching him.[15]

In *Ardoyne: The Untold Truth*, McLarnon's wife, Ann, described the shooting:

Things started to get bad and we brought the kids downstairs. But I thought it was getting too bad to take them out so I put them back up in their cots again. Then Sammy and me were standing at the right hand side of the window [in the living room]. I remember that there was an awful bright light. There must have been a light on down the street because we didn't have a light on in the house. The TV was no on either. There was just this bright light coming from outside the house.

Then I walked away to go into the working kitchen. I came back into the living room again and then the shots came through the window. There were three bullets, very close together. The RUC tried to say at the inquest that they were ricochets but they were head height. They were obviously intended to kill. He was shot through the window. He was pulling down the blind because he must have seen something. The glass actually hit me in the face. Then I ran back into the working kitchen again. When I came out Sammy was on the ground of the living room. I thought he had dived to the ground. But then I realised that he had been shot and I just screamed, 'My husband's shot, my husband's shot'.[16]

It is clear that McLarnon was not involved in any trouble that night, and although the RUC would try to deny that they had anything to do with his death, the evidence was irrefutable; RUC officers were seen outside his house at the time of the shooting. Although Scarman states that he was shot, 'by police fire directed down the street from its junction with the Crumlin Road', his wife alleged that they were standing *outside* the property at the time of the shooting.[17, 18] Whether it was an unfortunate accident or a calculated attack by renegade officers, the results were traumatic. McLarnon's son, also called Sam, explained how it affected his family:

> Sometimes I imagine what it was like when my father was killed, but my mother was there. She saw him lying on the floor. She heard the shooting and saw the bullet holes in the windows. She saw us crying, ran into the street and screamed for help. People shouldn't see those things. No one should see that.[19]

Heavy rioting continued unabated after the shooting of Sam McLarnon, with hundreds of Catholics involved in hand-to-hand combat with the RUC on the Crumlin Road. Protestants watched and once again began to launch their own attacks on the Catholics, throwing petrol bombs and 'assisting the police and intermingling with them', as Scarman noted.[20] Shooting was reported as coming from Butler Street by the RUC, although some witnesses were unsure that this actually happened.[21] However, the RUC returned fire, possibly because of the alleged gunfire but also because of the considerable opposition they encountered from the Catholics in Herbert Street and Butler Street—with more devastating consequences.

Michael Lynch was also a native of Ardoyne, born there in 1940. He had recently returned from London, where he had moved to find work. According to *Ardoyne: The Untold Truth*, he was returning from a night out at the local cinema when he sustained a fatal shot to the chest in Butler Street. The RUC were chasing gangs of Catholics from the Crumlin Road when, as mentioned, they opened fire in the belief that they were being shot at. Joe McDaid, a friend of Lynch's, recounted the events:

> I was up standing at Reid's shop. There was about ten of us standing there. That is where Mickey was, standing with us at Reid's corner. Then I could see that there was shooting. But somebody said, 'They are only bangs'. We thought they were only shooting blanks. But the 'Orangies' and 'B' Specials were shooting into the area. The cops were all gathered around Paddy Cassidy's shop on the front of the road. The 'B' Specials and the other crowd were in the Grove grounds. They were shooting from there. The bullets were hitting Doherty's gable wall and they were sparking off it. But we didn't realise what was happening because somebody said they were blanks, and I didn't know what a real shot sounded like. The next

thing was we saw Mickey falling. All I saw was Michael falling and two people carried him up to [a friend's] house. When Michael Lynch was shot, the only shooting that was happening was coming into Ardoyne from the Grove. Michael Lynch was just standing about. He was no gunman.[22]

The confusing nature of the running battles along the Crumlin Road and in the adjacent streets could have played a major part in Michael Lynch's death. In Scarman it was noted that an attack was made on the Holy Cross Girl's School in Chief Street, off the Crumlin Road, by youths with petrol bombs. The perpetrators were almost certainly Protestant, given the geographic area of the school. Two policemen fired into the air on seeing the attack, and the youths left the scene. RUC officers on the Crumlin Road heard this shooting. Is it beyond the realms of possibility that the shooting which was alleged to have come from Butler Street was, in fact, the discharge of RUC weapons in the Holy Cross Girl's School?

The rioting in the Crumlin Road and Ardoyne area petered out in the early hours of Friday 15 August. Two men lay dead and many were injured—although the true figure will never be known, as many Catholics did not go to hospital for fear of being arrested. The incursions by the RUC and 'B' Specials into Catholic areas of Ardoyne, followed by Protestants determined to burn the Catholics out, have since gone down in folklore, and they certainly added to the appeal of the Provisional IRA only a few months later. The RUC said that Protestants followed them into the Ardoyne; Catholics said that they were all the same mob. Scarman summed up the night, stating the following:

Nevertheless, the riots in the Ardoyne that night were started by the Catholic crowd; Hooker Street had been 'cleared for action' before the riot began and firearms were used by the Catholics as well as by the police. In contrast with the riot of the previous night, it is not open to suggest that the object of the Catholics was to relieve pressure on Londonderry, because, by 5 p.m. on the 14th, the police had been withdrawn from conflict with the Bogsiders and the conflict itself had ended.[23]

He continued:

But equally, the Protestants on the south side of the Crumlin Road must have been ready to resume the conflict started the night before and to crush the Catholics, if they could. For their part, the RUC, advised of possible widespread armed subversive activity, were all too ready to see a community in armed rebellion in the actions of the Ardoyne mobs, especially after they had experienced gunfire from the Catholic side.[24]

Tom Holland recalled the mood in the area and the response of the IRA to the events in Ardoyne:

That sort of climate meant that it was all about defence. Barricade your street, your house, the main road, use the buses, the paving stones, and use whatever you can. There were Republicans about. There were a number of organisations formed around that period, like the Ardoyne Citizens Action Committee (ACAC) and the Ardoyne Relief Committee (ARC). These were basically local Republicans, local people who, in the situation, were trying to help people. Many people who would have been in the IRA at that time were saying that guns were moved out of areas like Ardoyne because there was a new political thinking in the IRA after the Border Campaign—that Republicans needed to try to win over the Protestant working class, to make alliances, and that sectarianism was an obstacle.

But I suppose at best it was very naïve at the time to think that, the way things were bubbling from 1966—to leave enclaves like Ardoyne defenceless. I think there were only two shotguns, and one IRA man decided to move from one street to the next ... to make the enemy think they had more guns than they had. The IRA was ill-prepared, no structure, no organisation, very few volunteers. There was basically very few people with very few weapons.[25]

It is true, as Scarman noted, that the Battle of the Bogside was over; the Army had gone in earlier that day. But for Catholics in Ardoyne, the threat from the forces of law and order was still there. Equally, the fear of being overrun by Protestants from the south side of the Crumlin Road was also there, and to leave themselves defenceless would have been unthinkable. Both Catholics and Protestants lived in fear of each other, the unknown and dangerous neighbour. It only took a spark to ignite centuries-old antagonisms and hatreds. To have the RUC and 'B' Specials in the middle was only going to add to the explosive mixture.

Never Again! Clonard and the Burning of Bombay Street

This street is history, they wanted to knock it down again when the rest of the area was being redeveloped but we all said no. Conway Street doesn't even be mentioned you see, because it was never rebuilt. If this street was not rebuilt you would have never heard of it.

Jean Canavan, Bombay Street, 2014

I

While serious violence was erupting on the Falls Road and in Ardoyne, another Catholic area watched in trepidation. The Clonard district, just to the north of the Falls Road, was in serious danger. Surrounded on three sides by the predominately Protestant Cupar Street, its residents feared the worst. To the south, on the Springfield Road, was Mackie's factory; its workers were almost exclusively Protestant. On the afternoon of 15 August 1969 the sectarian monster that had engulfed other parts of Belfast now spread to the quiet and narrow streets of the Clonard.

Clonard itself was a warren of little streets, built on an area of land that bulges northwards into Protestant territory. It was, and still is, a close-knit community; close enough to the republican heartland of the Falls Road but still able to hold onto a distinct and unique identity. At the part of the district that butts up against Protestant territory is Bombay Street, an area of sixty-three houses that have gone down in republican and nationalist folklore as the abiding memory of the violence of August 1969.

Jean Canavan described Bombay Street, the area's most northerly street and its most vulnerable at the time:

We have lived in Bombay Street all our lives. Not in this house though, it was one across the street. That's where we lived with our parents, that's where we were burnt out. And when we all came back we came back to this side of the street. My grandfather lived in the other house, but now I live in it and my family live here.

We went to school in St Gall's, just up the top of the road there. You see, when we were kids we were always classed as second class. There was a wee chippie round there, and we used to go round there. And these kids used to come in, I would say they were around seventeen, we were about eight or nine, and they used to push you back and call you a 'Fenian "B"'. I would then come home and ask my mum 'what's a Fenian?' But, you know yourself, you kinda knew that there was something wrong. I mean, we couldn't even go and play in the park.[1]

The first sign of trouble on that fateful Thursday came at around 1 p.m. Priests at the nearby Clonard Monastery, an imposing but welcoming church in the heart of the area, received a telephone call announcing that the monastery was about to be attacked. The RUC were informed but they did not attend, as by now they were mainly confined to their stations. A resident priest, Father Mclaughlin, then attempted to organise some form of defence for the church, and allowed two men to position themselves upstairs in a good vantage point.[2]

Fear and panic now began to spread around the district, as rumour and gossip took hold. Catholic families were seen leaving Cupar Street on lorries, and their Protestant neighbours seemed in a state of extreme agitation and excitement. Barricades were erected at the area's most vulnerable entrances. Protestants then attacked a Catholic-owned pub on Cupar Street, taking all its stock and setting it alight. Stone throwing began in earnest between Catholic and Protestant youths at the barricades.

In *The Red Hand*, Steve Bruce describes a Protestant viewpoint of the ensuing night's rioting:

About 500 yards away the lights were being extinguished in Catholic homes in the street. The gas lamps had been smashed and the whole place was in darkness. The invisible barrier that was no man's land had not yet been breached by either side. Each was hesitant, as if afraid of the blackness. Suddenly, flames appeared from behind the enemy lines and Bog Thompson shouted in awe: 'The bastards are fleeing their homes. They are putting them to the torch!' It was the signal for attack. The rest of the night was spent burning rows of houses in Cupar Street, Bombay Street and the surrounding areas. The police were powerless to prevent the raging mass's rampage of burning and destruction. I saw one young fellow smash the front windows of a tiny kitchen house with a flag pole and light the billowing curtains. Soon the place was ablaze.[3]

A taxi driver who was present that evening told the author that he saw middle-aged women rushing around the streets, smashing windows with mops so that petrol bombs could then be thrown in by men following them; the women invariably knew which houses were Catholic-occupied.

The following statement was given by Father Egan, a priest in Clonard Monastery, on the Sunday after the attack on Clonard. It has been used elsewhere, but will be included here because of its valuable historical worth. It is an eyewitness account of a turbulent afternoon and evening.

Were I to speak to you about any other subject other than the one that fills your mind you wouldn't listen to me, and I think it would be a bit unrealistic to speak of anything else except the great tragedy that has befallen our city within the last couple of weeks. Now, men, I'm sure you have heard very many rumours floating around about, I certainly have. Some of these rumours are quite dangerous so I would ask you to discount them. Pay no attention to them.

Tonight, what I will tell you is not a rumour. Tonight, I will tell you what I have seen and what I have heard myself and I will tell you about Clonard, the attack that was made on Clonard, because I know that Clonard is very dear to the hearts of every man present here tonight. We remember—I don't suppose we'll forget it easily—the night of Thursday August 14th. We remember that night and the early hours of the following morning when the Falls Road area was devastated by gunfire and by petrol bombs.

During long periods that night and the early hours of the morning I was standing at a fourth-storey window in the monastery here in Clonard looking out on the scene of desolation, and as I saw the leaping flames reddening the sky and the machine-gun fire breaking the silence of the night, I found myself asking this question: 'Is it possible that only two or three days ago we were assured by Stormont spokesmen that the forces of law and order had everything completely under control?'

Like very many others in the locality I did not retire to bed that night. I stayed up the whole time, said the half past six Mass the following morning and immediately after the Mass, as I was taking up the vestments in the sacristy, a distressed call came. A message saying they were dragging people from their homes in the nearby street. This was seven o'clock in the morning, August 15th.

So, I hastened to the spot to find two police vehicles had drawn up on the street. One of them, as far as I know, was a tender—I am not an expert in these things. The other, I don't know what it was—it was some kind of an armoured vehicle with a large gun mounted on it. And as I approached there was a middle-aged man dressed in a shirt and trousers with raised hands standing on the pavement and he was being searched or questioned by the police.

Whether they were police or B-Specials, don't ask me, I can't distinguish between them. But the man was being questioned anyway and as I approached, the questioning or the searching discontinued. I stood there, watching closely, and while I stood there passers-by, some on their way to Mass and some to work, hastened their steps when they saw the police vehicles. I saluted some of them but they were obviously frightened at the sight of the tenders and the police and they showed a great reluctance to enter into conversation with me with one exception.

A lady deplored the violence that was taking place in the city and she expressed a fervent hope that peace would soon be restored and that a spirit of neighbourliness would prevail. This lady was a Protestant from nearby Cupar Street. While I was there the police took two men into custody. They ordered them into the tender and I did not see any evidence of violence while I was there, anyway, there was no force or violence used. When the police vehicles moved off, the doors of the houses opened one by one and the people came onto the street and a group of women remonstrated with me for having exposed myself to what they called 'grave danger of being shot'. They insisted 'these B Specials would shoot you'. Well, my dearest men, I don't believe there was the slightest danger of my being shot. But afterwards when I thought on that remark, I was appalled to think that this is typical of the lack of confidence which so many of our people have in the forces of law and order.

Later that morning, Friday morning, a voice on the telephone warned the community in Clonard that they had better clear or they'd be burned out. We didn't clear out and we're still here. But anyway, the message came across and a priest in the monastery that you know only too well, not myself, brought this message to the local police station, he phoned the message to them and they promised protection—but no help came. At three o'clock on Friday afternoon the trouble really started when a large mob—I think no other word would describe them—a large mob advanced from the Cupar Street area. I do not say for a moment that were residents of Cupar Street. I do say they came from that area, armed with stones and sticks and petrol bombs. At that time I didn't see any other instrument, but they advanced on the Catholic areas.

At this particular time of day, three o'clock approximately, as you expect, the men of the area were away at work so the defence of the place was left to a handful of teenagers and they did a great job. We were proud of them.

They hurled every missile they could lay their hands on into the faces of the advancing assailants. They did a good job. An urgent phone message went out from Clonard monastery to the local police station asking for protection for the threatened area. The call was received politely but no help came. After making a vain attempt to stop the fighting down there at the junction of Cupar Street, I heard a number of women and girls panicking—they were shrieking and crying all over the place, so I directed them to the monastery. I went with them, brought them in through the kitchen into the monastery where a large number of people had already gathered.

Indeed the people were all over the place. They were up the stairs. They were in rooms where I certainly never saw a female in my life. They were in every place. 'Twas open house. It was at this stage that I heard the first shots ringing out, and moments later looking through a window in the monastery I saw a prostrate figure on the pavement below. The exact spot is at the lamp-post which is directly opposite the old credit union offices in Waterville Street. I dashed down the stairs at once onto the street. A man had arrived there before me. I looked into the face of the boy, whom I didn't recognise at the time. It was Gerald McAuley and Gerald was still conscious. He opened his eyes and I did think he showed signs of recognition as he looked at me. I gave him absolution. I anointed him. I helped to put him on a lorry. Just at that stage an ambulance arrived and we got him onto the ambulance. I was told afterwards he died on the way to hospital.

That was sometime between four and five o'clock, and a father from the monastery accompanied a layman from the locality to visit the local police station appealing for help. There were a number of police officers sitting around. They said their orders were to remain in barracks.

News of the attack spread like wildfire, the attack on the Clonard area, and men came speeding from their work to protect their homes and protect their families and protect their church, and goodness knows they had very, very little with which to protect themselves. Comparatively speaking you could say the men in this area were defenceless. Within the space of an hour I anointed five people out there on the roadway. Fearing a real massacre I got on the phone—and I had to go across the road to do it because our phone was out of order—I got on the phone to with the GCO [*sic*] headquarters of the British forces in Lisburn. The GCO was not available, but the officer who took the call said he would do his best to help and at 7 p.m. in the evening the first group of soldiers arrived and they marched through Clonard Street, Clonard Gardens and took up their position down the Falls Road.

Now you'll understand that soldiers in the Falls Road are pretty useless as far as protecting the Clonard area is concerned, when you are attacked from the rear as we were from the Cupar Street area. So, I sped down the Falls Road. I met the officer in charge of the soldiers.

I tried to explain the position to him. As I talked an officer of higher rank came along and he listened sympathetically and he said that he would try and help. At nine o'clock approximately another group of soldiers arrived and they took up their position at the church to protect the area. They got into military formation and they charged down along these streets, charging the attackers, and the man in charged shouted out an order. He said to the assailants, 'Come out with your hands up and we'll not shoot.' But the command was answered by a litany of obscenities punctuated with uncomplimentary references to the Pope and Fenians and British Tommies.

Instead of coming out with their hands up, they shortly came out with guns blazing and petrol bombs being fired all over the place. More houses were set on fire and at their approach the soldiers turned and ran away. After retiring, the military soon reformed their ranks and they came down along these streets again and they took up their positions, some on the Kashmir Road and some on Waterville Street, but undaunted by the military presence the attackers came along again with their petrol bombs and systematically—I watched it from an upstairs window—systematically they went from door to door in Bombay Street, kicking in some doors, breaking some windows and throwing petrol bombs into the houses.

They stood outside the school, and in full view of the military they broke the windows and threw bombs, fire bombs, into the premises, into the school. Now men, do not for one minute think I blame the military, I do not. They had orders and their order on this particular night was don't fire—so they told me afterwards, because I was amazed at the performance and I asked them about it and they told me their orders were not to fire. I do not blame these men who must act on their orders. I certainly do blame the people who gave the information which resulted in the military getting that type of order. The people who supplied that information are the people who are responsible for most of the destruction done in Bombay Street and in the Clonard area. Obviously, these soldiers didn't know the area. They certainly didn't know they were dealing with ruthless men who had no regard whatsoever for human life or property, as they showed on this particular night under my very eyes. Three times that school beside the monastery was set on fire and three times our local boys went into that school, into the blazing school and with bullets whistling all over the place. I was with them once in the school and I didn't feel a bit brave when you hear these bullets whistling all over the place.

These lads went into there and three times they fought the fire with extinguishers which they got from the monastery. They fought that fire and they put it out and I must say I marvelled at their bravery. Again and again these attackers came during the night and during the early hours of the morning, and outside the monastery and outside the school they chanted, encouraging each other: 'Let's get the so-and-so school. Let's get the so-and-so monastery.' That was the cry during the night. Well, they failed. They did not completely destroy the school, although they did extensive damage to it. They did not damage the monastery at all, although they did succeed in getting one firebomb into the back yard within about two feet from the back door. They did succeed in getting up onto a shed right beside the monastery, with evil intent of course, but they were repulsed. They failed in their evil design that night.

Their failure, my dearest men, was not due to any protection given by the forces of law and order, and let that be recorded. Let it also be recorded that they failed because of the bravery of the local lads who, totally un-prepared and ill-equipped and, comparatively speaking, defenceless, fought against terrible odds and saved this area from complete destruction—you have no doubt in your mind about it. That was the objective that night, complete destruction. Well, my dearest men, there's the story of the attack—savage, murderous attack made on the Clonard area during these days of madness. I gave you the story as I saw it because I knew you'd be interested.

Now, a few more points before I finish. These were terrible days, my dearest men, but some good has already come from these attacks. For one thing, I have noticed that the various communities that were under attack are much more closely knit than ever before. You have young people and elderly people all closely knit together and that's a grand thing like any good Christian community should be.

Now, there's one danger men, and I warn you confraternity men to avoid this danger don't fall into this trap. Already, I have heard people say, 'Father, I can never again act in a normal way with Protestants.' That's a terrible thing to say. You might feel like that and that's understandable but, my dearest men, that's just being emotional. Now, let us think the thing out. The vast majority of Protestants are thoroughly ashamed of what has happened and they wouldn't have hand, act or part in it—now that is true and we must realise that and we must accept that. So we mustn't allow hatred to spring up in our hearts for our Protestant brethren. You have of course the lunatic fringe amongst them. You have the extremists. You have the leaders and you have the leaders of the so-called leaders of this little state who have done nothing at all to deal with those people. That is an abuse which we hope will be remedied. What we are aiming at now, my dearest men, is justice—no more and certainly no less. That's one lesson we must learn from what has happened. We'll demand justice. We're not just begging it, we demand it. It's our right and we'll keep on demanding it until we get it. We don't ask for any more, just a fair deal. No discrimination in the matter of housing or jobs or voting power or anything else, just a fair deal that's all we ask. We don't ask for more. So, I suggest that you pray, my dearest men, that soon we will have a community where everybody, irrespective of his religious beliefs or irrespective of his political ideology, will be able to lead a normal life and will not be unjustly discriminated against, as had happened so often during the past 50 years.

So pray my dearest men. Let's all of us pray that we will have a society where Catholics and Protestants live as they should live together in peace—helping each other as good neighbours should. We must live with each other. It is a mixed society. We must live with each other, but that doesn't mean that we are not going to demand justice, and we pray tonight that God will grant us this justice which is our due.[4]

Father Egan gave a vivid description of the violence that engulfed the Clonard area on 15 August. With Scarman not published until 1972, however, more detail can now be added to the story he told that day.

The Unionist MP for the Woodvale, John McQuade, attended a meeting of Protestant residents just around the corner from Cupar Street on the afternoon of the 15th. Scarman concluded that his appearance at this meeting meant that its original purpose, to ensure that any tensions in the area could be defused, had failed. McQuade had been involved in other activities the night before.

John McQuaid [*sic*] MP for Woodvale led the mob down our (Dover) street. My oldest brother who was 18 at the time and who went on to serve 17 years in jail, brought my father up to the third floor and they were deciding when to get out. They could see McQuaid's men were being very systematic. It was not like a Frankenstein mob with torches and toothless peasants pouring down the street, there was real method to it. It's an interesting experience being burned out of your home by your own MP.[5]

Thus his presence in the Cupar Street area that day can only be construed as inflammatory. He spoke at the meeting himself, dismissing a local 'peace pact' that members of both communities had discussed:

I informed the people that there was no need for any peace pact; if people would obey the law of the land and recognise the constitution there was no other need. I then warned the women and children to go into their homes, and keep off the streets. I told the men that they would have to be prepared to defend them.[6]

Gerald McAuley, the young boy that Father Egan mentioned in his sermon, was from Colinward Street, just off the Springfield Road. His mother described him as an honest, caring boy, ready to help at a moment's notice and with a bright future ahead of him:

When Gerald was fourteen he left school, and he got a start with Johnson and Christie down in Northumberland Street. He was only there two weeks and he came home and said, 'Mammy, Mr So-and-so [she forgot his name] wants you to come down and see him.' So I went down and this man came out to me and said, 'I'll tell you what it is Mrs McAuley. Gerald is a great lad, he and my boys get on exceptionally well. Now we are a family business, we have never taken on an outsider, all down the line. I asked him about going to the Tech [college] in September, and he tells me that he wants to join the Merchant Navy in the south of Ireland.' I said I knew nothing about that![7]

Something else that his mother knew nothing about was that Gerald was in the Fianna, the youth wing of the IRA. On the day of his death he was helping families move out of the district into safer accommodation. Mrs McAuley also described the initial rioting in the Falls Road, her feelings on hearing that somebody had been shot and killed in the Clonard, and the confusing messages she was given:

...the 7 a.m. news came on the radio saying that the wee boy, Patrick Rooney, had died ... had been shot dead by the RUC. I was at home, and I shouted, 'Gerald will you get up for work, you are going to be late!' and he came down. He was wearing a nice pair of cords ... he was a tall chap anyway. Off to work I went. The next I seen of Gerald that day was when him and Tony [a friend] came in, and I was going to give them a couple of French Rolls, and I was going to give him a couple of bob. So away the two of them went, and I made the rolls up.

 The next thing I heard in the evening ... his daddy was working ... up in Sugarfield Street, just up from where Gerald was murdered, was that Gerald had been shot. I went to the City Hospital and pleaded with them to let me in, to see if he was there, and couldn't tell them his name. This guy came in covered in blood and said, 'Good God, what are you doing here?' I said, 'I'm looking for my Gerald, somebody said he's been shot. They won't let me in, will you ask them please?' They said no anyway, mind you they were very busy with all the rioting going on.

 I left there and was on my way back up. I was looking for my daughter, Rita, and I stopped somebody and asked them if they had seen my Rita. 'Yes', they said, 'she is on her way home'. So I came up, and the guy that Rita used to go out with, his mother ... she called me into the house and says, 'C'mon you and I will make you a cup of tea'. Next thing the news came on ... I can still remember that ... saying that a youth of nineteen was in the morgue, and I said to Mrs Burns, 'That's my Gerald.' She said, 'God forgive you, don't say that.' So I came back here and the guy next door took me up to the City Hospital, they couldn't be nicer. These men ... UVF men I think ... came and they were covered in blood. I pleaded with them about my Gerald too ... no good, they knew nothing. This Sister, she was beautiful, she brought me into her office and she said, 'You just settle now. There's a boy in the morgue and he is not your son, he is nineteen.' I just kept saying, 'I know that's my son'.[8]

Eileen McAuley was getting confusing messages because Gerald was so tall he looked older than his fifteen years. She soon found out the awful truth, sadly, in a matter-of-fact way:

I had to go home and Ben brought me back, and as we got to the top of Whiterock they were putting up a barricade. We knew one of them ... Peter ... and Ben got out of the car and whatever he said to them, before we knew it they were throwing all the bits away to let us through. So we went through and went down our street, and my Francis came up to me and said, 'Mammy, the newspaper men were here, and they were looking for our Gerald's photo.' Eventually Gerry came home, and I said, 'Gerry, get you to that morgue, cos I know that that's him.' Gerry and a neighbour from across the street went. Meanwhile [undecipherable] lived over in Fourth Parade, amongst Protestants ... she bought a house over there, and I said to her to come over here. I had led her daughter up to the top of the street, to see her over the road, when this priest came. I can still see him walking up, with a heavy, beated face ... a black beret and a big walking stick. And he just shouted at me, 'Mrs McAuley?' And I said, 'Yes, Father?' He said, 'Your son has died and gone to heaven'. He then got on his stick and walked off down the road ... God's truth! That's how I knew for certain. Then Gerry came back. Apparently they had brought him into St Paul's [Church], and that's how the priest knew.[9]

The realisation that it was her son who had died had a traumatic effect on Mrs McAuley, and left her with disturbing memories which even the passing of over forty years have not diminished:

In them days they used to decorate the rooms with sheets all around, with blue ribbons and a crucifix. Then the body came home. I can and I can't see myself screaming, you know. I was brought upstairs. I said to the man [who brought the body home] that I wanted him upstairs. The man said no, and that the lid was also not to come off the coffin. I remember screaming, 'Why, why, why?' The next thing I remember about it all was waking up and seeing all these bottles of holy water lying around ... I don't know what type it was because it was all green, slimy stuff. I remember coming down the stairs and the coffin was there [points to under the front sitting-room window]. I said, 'Why didn't youse take the lid off him?' And the smell ... they said it was because he died in natural health. And I remember someone saying to me, 'Nelly, you will have to buy some wick candles or something [to get rid of the smell].' I ... I just wanted to see him, and Gerry took me to one side and said, 'Love, you can't see him, just be happy you have got him home.'

... Apparently, Gerald came out of Bombay Street with people. He brought them over to Father McLaughlin and this other priest, who were standing at the side door [of Clonard Monastery] in Waterville Street. One priest took the women and children in, from what I'm told, and he went up the stairs to make arrangements when he heard the shot, and when he looked out Gerald had fell to the ground. He tried to get up when the machine gun was put on him.[10]

Scarman stated that Gerald McAuley was pronounced dead at 4.45 p.m. that afternoon, while the riot was still raging on Bombay Street. Officially, his death was alleged to have been caused by 'a medium or high velocity bullet fired at close range which entered the chest and heart, passing right through the body.' [11] However, Mrs McAuley remembers differently:

His daddy went to the inquest; twenty-six bullets went into him, but Gerry said it was only the one that hit the heart that they count. It was a machine gun that was used on him. That's why I couldn't look at him, he was done from head to toe.[12]

Finding out that he was in the Fianna made no difference to where he would be buried. Mrs McAuley decided that he was to be buried with the family, a decision that she was later to regret bitterly.

I was outside with Father Reid, I forget what we were talking about, and I was brought back inside, and I can see the men standing there opening out the flag. And I said something like, 'No, no. He is going in with my mammy.' Do you know that's the worst mistake that I ever made in my life—depriving that child of that flag? Oh God that hurts. You see, when I see coffins with the flag ... to think, I mean I didn't know [he was in the Fianna]. To me, he was a boy scout—it didn't ring a bell with me. It was a year or so after that it started to hurt ... when I began to realise what I had done to him. I think they gave me that flag ... I can't say whether they did or not.[13]

Gerald McAuley's death had a traumatic effect on the district. Robert McClenaghan remembered the time as a period that changed everything. Now, it was about defence from the Protestants:

We lived just off the Springfield Road, in Colinview Street. The tension was there on 13 and 14 August, and then at night you heard the shooting and that. But 15 August, it was a Friday, and that's when the area starts to get attacked, Bombay Street was burning. To be brutally honest ... it was like an adventure ... you see, we had no sense of the politics. We knew it was dangerous, but at the same time this was something new, completely new.

One of the first people killed ... that I knew personally ... was Geraldo McAuley. We lived in Colinview Street, he lived in Colinward Street. So, this was someone you grew up with, played football with, know what I mean? Hung around corners with and all the rest. And then he's dead. He's been shot ... by the Loyalists. And his only crime, if you like, was helping people ... you know, taking the furniture out and the like. Because the whole of Bombay Street was on fire, and he goes down by Waterville Street, by the Monastery. His death sent repercussions through our whole generation.

For anybody, this is a major event in your life. That was the end of my youth, it changed me. You started realising ... there's something seriously wrong with this place! I mean ... why are people coming in to attack, basically, my family? I wasn't politically aware, all I knew was that we had to defend ourselves.[14]

Danny Morrison also remembered the period as a time that changed everything. If the IRA was something that few Catholic youths thought about at the time, the events surrounding the death of Gerald McAuley made many think again.

On the Monday I went to Gerald McAuley's funeral. A couple of days later I was asked to go to a house, a friend of mine's house, and there was a guy there—I think he was from Cork, but he was obviously involved with the IRA.[15]

Danny Morrison was asked by the IRA to put his skills with radio sets to good use, setting up 'Free Belfast' radio from behind a public house in Leeson Street, off the Falls Road. Thus he was now 'involved'.

Virtually every house was burned out in Bombay Street. Damage was also caused to a number of houses in other streets. Protestant workers leaving Mackie's factory on the Springfield Road found it wise to arm themselves on their way home through the Catholic Clonard, at one point having to fight their way through as Catholics threw stones at them. Inevitably, many of these same workers later got involved in the rioting engulfing Bombay Street.

Jean Canavan has also got plenty of memories of that day; because of their traumatic nature, these memories will stay with her forever:

On the Friday morning I got up and me mammy said to me ... now she was in and out, in and out. I was sixteen at the time so I wasn't thinking about anything like that at the time. And my mammy came in and said to me, 'I want you to make them [the family] a bit of lunch.' And as I was making them ones a bit of lunch, me daddy came running in and said, 'Just turn everything off, youse have to get out!'

So we were all taken over to my aunt's and left the street, but before this ... you see where the peaceline is, there was a road where you could get up and down [to Cupar Street]. And there was a wee fella next door to us ... he was only about four, and his mammy was in an awful state because his father was blind and he worked up in what we called 'the blind shop' in Lawnbrook Avenue. And wee Sean was down at that road, and as I went down to get him they were putting barricades up. There was this man, and he was sitting there with a big rifle shouting, 'Get the young ones!' I just grabbed the child and ran ... that was the Protestants saying that, and it always stayed with me.

We all got out of the street and I think we spent the night in St Paul's hall, and we came back the next day and the street was burnt out ... every house, except a couple up near Clonard Gardens that were not burnt. We ended up having a little caravan up in Moyard,

When the Army came in they used to stay at the bottom of the street, and when the houses were rebuilt they were still there! We welcomed them when they first came, but then they turned on us. We never bothered with them to be honest because my mum was always a Republican ... active in the IRA. You have to remember there was only one IRA then. Now there's too many. My Daddy was a quiet man, awful quiet. I wasn't only burnt out of my house you see, I was burnt out of work as well. I worked in Conway Mill, you left school at fifteen at the time ... there used to be a big, big mill down there. You used to have cars underneath and a big shirt factory above. So I lost my house and job.[16]

Perhaps more than any other district, the burning of Bombay Street was seared into memory of a whole swathe of society in Belfast and Northern Ireland in general. 'Out of the ashes of Bombay Street rose the Provisionals' is an oft-repeated and somewhat erroneous statement; the Provisionals were a manifestation of the failure of the IRA in 1969. However, the seeds were certainly sown there, along with Conway Street, Percy Street, Dover Street, and the rest. Bombay Street is remembered over many other areas because it was rebuilt in the face of many of the Protestants that burned it down. Baroness Blood remembers:

> There was definitely a big movement towards vulnerable Catholic families like in Bombay Street, which was virtually burned out. See, at that time there were Unionist leaders propagating the idea of a 'scorched-earth policy', and that was said openly. I had an aunt who was ferocious about Protestantism, and she moved out of a house on the Springfield Road; her first thought was to set fire to the house as she left. She believed in a 'scorched-earth' policy because Protestant leaders were doing that.[17]

Many Catholics believe this too, and it became violently apparent in August 1969. For the young generation, who were not really interested in politics, the sight of so much damage to the districts they lived in made many think first of defence, and then of revenge:

> So, all we seen was Bombay Street being attacked, the possibility of the Monastery being burned to the ground, and then one of your closest friends being shot dead. So, that changes the course ... the direction of your life from then onward. You also lived behind the barricades, and that created a whole new way of living. Obviously the politics was the IRA splits into the Provisionals and Officials, and what that meant was that there were young men and women at that time running around with guns.
>
> So, can you imagine the double life ... you go to school and try your best but your mind is not into it, then you come home and get changed into your Wranglers, and you are running up to the corner and running around with these people. You became aware of all the politics, you heard whispers between your parents. All of a sudden you are becoming more involved.
>
> But if you take it back to August, it was how unprepared people were, I mean, they were right up to the end of Waterville Street. There was a big possibility of the Monastery being set on fire. And then all these lorries arrive, and try to evacuate ... at least get all the children out of the area, because you didn't know what was coming across the road. If you look at the Springfield Road ... that was the battle ... that was the line. I can remember building the barricades. The older ones hijacked a bread lorry. We got timber, scaffolding, anything at all. At one point they actually put me on the back of a lorry to drive me out of the district, but I went up and climbed down the front of the lorry, and ran into someone's house and closed the front door. So, I then come out and it's like a ghost town. All the doors were open. At the top of the street there were about ten men building a barricade. So I go up and my father was there, and all they were doing was making petrol bombs. If there was a weapon there I didn't see it.

What you have to remember is that they [Loyalists] had the police, they had the 'B' Specials, and they had all the guns. What had we got? We had a few petrol bombs and we had a few hurling sticks.

At that young age I felt that everyone was out to attack my family. My mother's family came from the Pound Loney, so they would have been caught up in the [Falls] Curfew. Then Internment came along and it was almost like ... here comes the state again ... attacking our community. We had to fall back on our own resources. You could no longer trust the police. You could no longer trust the media. And it's as if you were betrayed by the British, who sent in the British Army, and we thought they came in to protect and defend the Catholic community. But what really turned out was they were here to protect British colonial interests.[18]

II

Robert McClenaghan and his generation were deeply affected by the events of August 1969. Death came close to them in those days. The death of Gerald McAuley brought that fact home to many—it could have been any one of them. Defence was now the immediate concern though. For McClenaghan, his life would take many twists and turns, but would always be linked to August 1969 and the death of one of his close friends:

There was so much happening every day after August 1969. Shootings, bombings. And it was as if you grew up very quickly, your whole life was changing. You see, by 1972 you began to see your own friends being killed ... like the bomb in Clonard Street in March 1972. It becomes very real then, it was not a game. And then that's when you have to begin to make choices, do you know what I mean? You could almost see it that at some point you were going to leave the Fianna and join the Army [IRA].

So that was in 1974 when I actually joined the IRA. You see, in Clonard ... the whole area ... there was no one left. They had all gone ... either being arrested, interned, or on the run. So there was this whole generation of seventeen-year-olds left in charge ... left in charge of a whole military area. So instead of us looking to the older people ... people were starting to look at us!

You learned the tactics of guerrilla warfare from a very early age. Even when you were twelve people were operating with weapons ... and your job was to go away and dump them somewhere ... hide them. But now it was us in charge ... and it was us who were saying we have to do this or that. It was only a matter of time though before you realise that I'm either going to get caught or killed. So I ended up in prison in 1976, and that was me until 1988. I got arrested in November 1976 with weapons and explosives, and got twenty years. I was put in the H Blocks, where obviously I would not wear the prison uniform. They took all my clothes off me, so the only thing I had to protect me was the blanket. So I was on the blanket protest.[19]

The youth of the Clonard district grew up quickly, like those in many other areas of Belfast during those days in August. The innocence of youth was lost forever. It was replaced by fear, mistrust, and a determination that such events were never to happen again. An awareness of sectarianism and hatred for each other also began to set in, as Jean Canavan remembered:

Now we're not saying it was all the people over there. There was good people. Now, I actually think they were 'blow in' people; people from different areas. There was a man, Ollie ... he worked for the Housing Executive years ago, and he was away working over in a Protestant area, and a man came up to him and said, 'You and your mate, you better get offside because youse are gonna get done.' I mean there's good people on this side, there's good people on that side. But there's also bad people on this side and vice versa.

   The feelings we had for Protestants after the burnings changed instantaneously. Ian Paisley was the cause of all that trouble. We didn't associate with them, we didn't see them. You could walk by them in the town and not know them after a while.[20]

Bombay Street was rebuilt with help from a number of local sources, most notably a local Irish Language school. The old foundations were reused, ensuring that the new street stood nearly exactly where the old one did. Local people rebuilt the street without governmental assistance. Many that were on social security were allegedly threatened with the loss of their benefits because they were seen to be working.

It was the Irish language people who rebuilt the street. Only for them ... and the young people on the social, along with many others with nothing to do, volunteered to help rebuild the houses. The Government didn't want anything to do with it ... a car park for Mackie's is what was being talked about. A car park for Mackie's meant Protestants moving into Catholic territory ... that's what they wanted ... only for the local people and the Irish language people who saved this area.[21]

Bombay Street stands as a testament to those who rebuilt the street and those residents who moved back in. It is a quiet, unassuming street nowadays. The only reminder of its violent past is the 'temporary' peaceline, which is still there after forty-five years.

'Cromwell's Men Are Here Again!' The Start of Operation Banner

I

Everything had changed in Belfast, and changed forever.[1] Barricades were in place at all the major intersections on the Falls Road and around Ardoyne; lorries, buses, piles of paving slabs, and anything else at hand was used. Fear was in the air and chaos reigned. Public transport was suspended, shops were closed, and crowds of young men stood around at street corners, waiting. Alban Maginness MLA explained:

> It was a time of great tension, one of expectation of something about to happen. Nobody knew what was about to happen though. When it did happen, it was very shocking and traumatic for people. Traumatic for those people who were affected, whose sons were attacked, those who had to flee, and of course those whose families were affected by death and injury. I don't think anybody expected the extent of the trouble. It was a shock seeing so many homes desolated and destroyed. It certainly was like something out of the Second World War.
>
> I was living on the Antrim Road, Brookfield Avenue; we were safe in the sense that we weren't immediately affected. We knew people who were affected. Not only was the Lower Falls affected but so was the Ardoyne. However, the situation in Derry was a lot different than the one in Belfast. The confrontation in Derry was between the people and the police; that wasn't the situation in Belfast. If there was a situation like that in Belfast it was the police, aided and abetted by Loyalist irregulars, attacking the Catholic community. Yes, you could say that it was the pent-up anger of the Loyalist people who vented that anger on the Catholics of Belfast. That changed everything. Although Belfast was sectarianized, this physically divided the city and politically polarised the city even more than it was previously.
>
> That very negative and traumatic period and experience for the whole community is in contrast against the high hopes everybody had on or around 5

October 1968. I found it incredible that in less than a year we had these terrible events. It led to the reintroduction of the gun into Irish politics, and that was a disaster for the whole community—Catholic and Protestant.[2]

The dreams and aspirations of communal unity were dashed in those few disastrous days. Any hopes of Protestant and Catholic working class cooperation—as envisioned by Goulding's IRA in Dublin—were wiped away. Many areas of west Belfast were in ruins. Families on both sides were fleeing the interface areas, and many more were burned out and either looking for other accommodation or (in the case of Catholics), heading south of the border to the safety of the Republic. And the trouble was by no means over.

The IRA was active on a number of occasions, most notably on the Falls Road and to a lesser degree in Ardoyne. However, the general consensus was that they had let the people of nationalist west Belfast down. Weapons were taken out of Ardoyne prior to the violence because of the fear of their use in inter-communal sectarian warfare, but that is exactly what happened. There were a few old and obsolete items in use—enough to convince the RUC of armed rebellion, but nowhere near enough for protection. Now it was the turn of the various defence committees that had sprung up in the most-affected areas to organise the security of the most-vulnerable areas, and to aid in the evacuation of families.

As the morning of the 15th wore on and the movement of people on both sides continued, sporadic trouble began to break out along interface areas. Early in the afternoon, Catholic gangs began to attack Protestants in Percy Street. Andrews Mill, on Percy Street, then became the focus of both sets of rioters as rumours began to circulate of snipers on the roof of the building. Catholic youths attempted to set the building alight, but they were repulsed by Protestants. Baroness Blood remembers:

I was coming down the Falls Road and I was turning off onto the Grosvenor Road, I lived just off it, and ... I couldn't believe it ... people were throwing petrol bombs. I stopped the car and asked someone, 'What's going on?' And they said, 'They are setting fire to Andrews Mill.' I couldn't get my head around it, I mean ... for what reason were they doing this?

I came on down the Grosvenor Road and petrol bombs were flying. There was a priest standing at the Catholic crowd trying to hold them back. I parked the car. I said to one of my friends who lived on the road, 'What's happening?' And she said, 'There's going to be rioting [again], they are going to burn all the Protestants out.'[3]

Pandemonium gripped west Belfast once again, as the previous night's conflagration looked set to be repeated. Shooting began again from both Protestant and Catholic rioters. The RUC, exhausted and depleted from days of serious communal violence, stayed at their bases, either unwilling or unable to attend the latest round of trouble. Houses began to be set alight in Percy Street and along the interface; in Beverley Street alone, out of all the houses that were set alight, all bar one belonged to Catholics. While this new bout of trouble was getting underway, however, a momentous decision had been taken at Stormont and in Westminster. Though it was seen as a temporary measure at the time, this decision was to have long-lasting consequences for the future of Northern Ireland as a whole, and for the Belfast society in particular. The Army had been in Derry since the day before; now Belfast was to have the British Army.

Derry had been in a state of near-anarchy for three days by the time Stormont requested the British Army to enter the city. It was an historic decision, but one that had been discussed in depth by the two governments at various levels for a number of years.[4] The government in Stormont, who were aware that the request for assistance from London would be met with trouble by ministers, had broached the subject in a cabinet meeting on 3 August. High on the agenda was the constitutional implication of such a request—namely, who would be in control.

Stormont wanted control of all aspects of law and order in the event of troops being used; London was having none of it. London wanted control of law and order, something that Stormont rightly saw as the surrendering of her limited sovereignty and the suspension of the Stormont government. In discussions with senior Home Office ministers on 6 August, Stormont made it clear that 'the actions proposed by Her Majesty's Government was surely only proper in the case of a recalcitrant and intractable [Stormont] government which was resisting desirable reforms.'[5] In the face of civil unrest, Stormont believed that that Northern Ireland should be treated like any other area of the United Kingdom, and that troops could be used 'in aid of the civil power.'[6]

London was unimpressed—even after covert threats from Stormont that London 'should consider the situation that might well arise if in fact they did decide to exercise direct rule from Whitehall. There would first of all be a frightening reaction by the Protestant community which could make anything that had happened up to now seem like child's play.'[7] This situation remained when events on the ground dictated the use of troops, effectively leaving them under the nominal control of Stormont.

II

At 5 p.m. on 14 August a company of the Prince of Wales's Own Regiment, 1st Battalion, took over the duties of the RUC in Derry, effectively bringing the Battle of the Bogside to an end. Television images of the time show a surreal scene as members of the RUC—either standing around or sitting down, exhausted—watch on as troops put barbed wire barricades in place. Members of the 'B' Specials (mobilised that afternoon) stand around, their faces covered with handkerchiefs—either as protection from CS gas or for some other, sinister reason. However, the troops were not allowed to enter the Bogside for some time. One soldier recalled the moment his company entered Derry and his initial observations. The author is eternally grateful to Ken Wharton, author of *A Long, Long War: Voices from the British Army in Northern Ireland 1969–1998*, for his help in gathering soldier testimonies.

As the violence escalated we moved closer to Londonderry, and on 13 August Prime Minister Harold Wilson called a Cabinet meeting where the Home Secretary decided to deploy troops onto the streets of the province. Only the night before we were sat on one side of the river, watching Londonderry burning, and I think that it was then that we realised the seriousness of the situation. There was little fear at first, and when the troops moved in on 14 August 1969, we stood on the streets holding the same banners we had used during the war in Aden two years earlier. They said 'Don't cross this line' in Arabic—can you believe that? It was the typical British Army method of using tactics from the previous war. Both the Loyalists and Republicans seemed to welcome the troops, and brought out cups of tea as they stood on the street. The Loyalists saw us as on their side, and the Catholics saw us as an unbiased organisation. They could see that there was this unbiased organisation coming into separate two communities and keeping the peace. They welcomed us just as much as the other side, and if you have a difficult job to do it can be made a lot easier by people being nice and not throwing grenades at you; the hospitable atmosphere was not to last for long, however.[8]

At 5.30 p.m. on 15 August, the Army finally arrived in Belfast in the shape of the 2nd Battalion Queen's Regiment. Stopping on the Shankill Road, they began to fan out down the back streets that separated the Shankill Road from the Falls Road. Many ended up in Springfield Road RUC station, the scene of earlier attacks.

In those dark days, when all law and order appeared to have broken down, our next point of call was to the RUC station on the Springfield Road. When we arrived outside the station we found not a trace of the RUC themselves. They had simply disappeared, unable to cope with the constant anarchy on the streets; the notorious 'B' Specials, however, were still much in evidence. They were still prowling around wreaking havoc, and we spotted an old lady being pushed in a wheelchair by what turned out to be her grandson. She was crying her eyes out and she was covered in blood, and it was explained to me that she had been attacked and beaten up by thugs in the B Specials; they were completely out of control.

I helped push her into the sanctuary of the RUC station, and I just whispered to her, 'You're safe now,' and we took care of her.[9]

Rumours in Belfast were rife as the Army arrived. The IRA was alleged to have occupied numerous houses in the Divis Street area, no doubt with a view to launching fresh attacks on the RUC. Scarman mentioned that armed men were rumoured to be in control of the Royal Victoria Hospital on the Grosvenor Road, but perhaps the biggest rumour of all was spread from the Inspector General of the RUC to General Freeman. He issued the following request, aware that the use of troops could only be agreed to in an extreme case:

> I have to inform you that, following the violence in the city of Belfast last night, renewed clashes are occurring at this time, 11.30 a.m., 15th August 1969. The Commissioner has informed me that all immediately available police have been committed but that he is unable to separate the rioting crowds and has had to fall back to defend his police stations. In the circumstances outlined, I now request further assistance of forces under your command in Belfast city. Information is to hand from a reliable source that an infiltration of members of the Irish Republican Army is about to commence from Eire into Northern Ireland.[10]

Hours later, the troops arrived. The bogeyman of the IRA, dormant since the end of the border campaign in 1962, was enough to warrant intervention of the British Army.

In Ardoyne, as the early hours of the 15th rolled on, the RUC withdrew foot patrols from the Crumlin Road for their own safety. By 2 p.m. the next day, the only armoured vehicle in the vicinity was removed for duties elsewhere, leaving no police in Ardoyne or the Crumlin Road area.[11] Buses were hijacked by Catholics to be used as barricades, in fear of more violence; according to Scarman, many of these were taken under duress, with some bus drivers being pulled from their vehicles.[12] The local bus depot was relieved of a number of buses; these were carefully placed across street junctions to stop incursions by police and Protestant gangs. Rioting then broke out between factions of the opposing crowds. The violence intensified as the afternoon wore on, with shooting being reported early on in the trouble. At about 4.30 p.m., David Linton, a Protestant from nearby Palmer Street, was throwing missiles at Catholics back across the Crumlin Road when gunfire rang out. Mr Linton fell to the ground, fatally wounded by a shotgun blast to his head. According to Scarman, the shotgun was fired from about 20–30 yards away from him—very close.[13]

Rumours of snipers operating in various areas continued, even after police resumed their patrols later on in the evening. Shooting continued late into the night, with police returning fire at a number of targets in the Crumlin Road and Hooker Street areas. The police were bolstered in numbers at around midnight as the initial violence and shootings began to taper off.[14]

Overnight, however, it was the turn of Brookfield Street to add its name to the infamous and growing list of streets that were burned down in Belfast that August.

Rumours began to circulate of a sniper lodged into one of the houses on the road, which were by now all empty because of their proximity to Protestant areas. Scarman states that there was no doubt that Protestants burned down the street, and witnesses testified that an armoured vehicle was stationed at Herbert Street, seemingly ignoring the conflagration.[15]

It was clear by now that the RUC had no control over the situation along the Crumlin Road and into the Ardoyne. The inference that police stood idly by and watched as Protestants torched a Catholic street certainly would have its adherents in the Ardoyne; Scarman blithely states that the police might have 'given the day over to chaos'.[16] They were certainly under pressure, but given their performance in other areas of Belfast the preceding days, and with the benefit of hindsight, it might well have been the case that they were indeed standing idly by.

Troops began to arrive in the Crumlin Road area in the late afternoon on Saturday 16th, with the objective being to separate the two factions. The welcome the Army got from Catholic residents was one of relief and enthusiasm, as in other areas of Belfast that August. The Ardoyne began to calm down, but the damage was done—both physically and mentally.

The Army was seen (at least in the first weeks of their deployment) to be at the very least impartial. They were there to protect Catholics from the Protestant hoards threatening to drive every Catholic across the border. Now that Westminster was involved, surely there would be change, and surely Stormont would go? However, others thought differently. Many Protestants were fearful of the future now that Westminster was directly involved in Northern Irish affairs.

> As a British subject I felt that the Army was welcome into Northern Ireland. But there was also a concern at Stormont position to that because you had that kind of tension between Stormont and Westminster playing out; the constitutional position. The British Prime Minister and the Home Secretary, their comments at the time alarmed me as well; they didn't seem to be terribly supportive, none of them. We were beleaguered, our backs were to the wall and they, our friends, were actually siding with our enemies. Now I am painting the picture as I seen it at the time, now while the Army would have been welcomed I would have seen them as our Army. We had no great difficulty with that but the thing was, why are they here, why can't we control it ourselves? Why weren't the police and the 'B' Specials allowed to do what had to be done? [17]

For the Army, though, it was a steep learning curve. Troops were shocked at some of the sights that greeted them.

> On that first day, one of our lads was shot and wounded by a 12-bore shotgun, but thankfully he fully recovered. I now believe that he was the first British soldier to be shot and wounded during the Troubles, and I also firmly believe that he was

shot by a 'B' Special thug. We managed to stop them in the end, but they were almost uncontrollable.

One abiding and awful memory I have is of seeing literally hundreds of Catholics—women and children in the main—streaming towards us and past us to the safety of the Catholic Church, 50 or 60 yards behind the police station. I simply couldn't believe how many houses were on fire; there was smoke and flames everywhere.[18]

Another soldier remembered:

My first memories, see, were the smoke and the flames and all the screaming going on; there were no RUC about, just mobs, running about throwing whatever they could lay their hands on. It was chaotic, and I hadn't ever seen anything like that in my life before I went to Ireland. There were loads of people, some with bags and cases and prams, and some of the prams had clothes and bedding on them; I even seen a man with a baby's' cot on his back, coming out of all the smoke, his face blackened from all the soot, see.[19]

The relief on the faces of many Catholics was there for all to see. By now, many believed that the RUC, 'B' Specials, and ordinary Protestants were working together to 'remove' them from Belfast altogether. They firmly believed that a 'pogrom' was underway, and troops were welcomed with open arms, cups of tea, and piles of sandwiches. However, some Catholic men were not very impressed, according to many soldiers:

For several weeks afterwards it was something of a honeymoon, as we patrolled around the Falls Road, Divis Street, and around the Grosvenor Road, and we got on famously with the Catholics. We rarely ventured into any Prod areas, but we guessed that—whilst they alluded to be 'British'—they saw us as 'Taig-lovers'. The Catholic men (largely unemployed) were in the main sullen. Sometimes we got a grudging 'Good morning' from them, but the women and the kids were fantastic. 'What about ye, soldier boy?', 'Yerse Mammies will be proud o'youse lads', 'God bless ye, Tommy', and 'Be having a cuppa tea an' a wee biscuit, Tommy' were comments I can remember so well, as the summer turned really hot by the end of August.[20]

The Army is not meant to be political in any way, but for many troops, in those first few days in Belfast, it was hard not to be:

These early days of troops on the streets became known as the 'honeymoon period'. Tea was brewed for the troops in huge quantities by ordinary people, delighted we were there. A patrol of the Catholic Markets area of Belfast

1. The UVF march in Belfast, 1912.

2. The mural of Bobby Sands on the Falls Road—mythology in the making.

3. Stormont—the seat of Unionist power for fifty years.

4. The anti-Treaty IRA meet in Dublin, 1922.

5. The Republican burial plot at Miltown Cemetery.

6. The UDA, formed in the wake of the abolition of the 'B' Specials.

7. Belfast peacelines in 2014.

Above: 8. The Northern Bank emerged unscathed after the rioting in Percy Street.

Left: 9. Eamon DeValera, the leader of the anti-Treaty IRA in 1922 and President of the Republic.

10. Belfast in its Victorian heyday.

Above left: 11. Bernadette Devlin, the co-founder of People's Democracy.

Above right: 12. Danny Morrison.

13. The Falls Road Curfew Mural on the Falls Road.

14. An RUC fortified station in Belfast in the 1980s.

15. Michael Collins leaves Downing Street while people pray for peace, 1921.

Above left: 16. Edward Carson inspects the UVF, 1914.

Above right: 17. Edward Carson—the embodiment of Protestant opposition.

Above left: 18. The 1921 Treaty between the Provisional Government and London.

Above right: 19. The Solemn League and Covenant document—the Unionist's veto on a united Ireland.

20. Percy Street today, with the peaceline in the background.

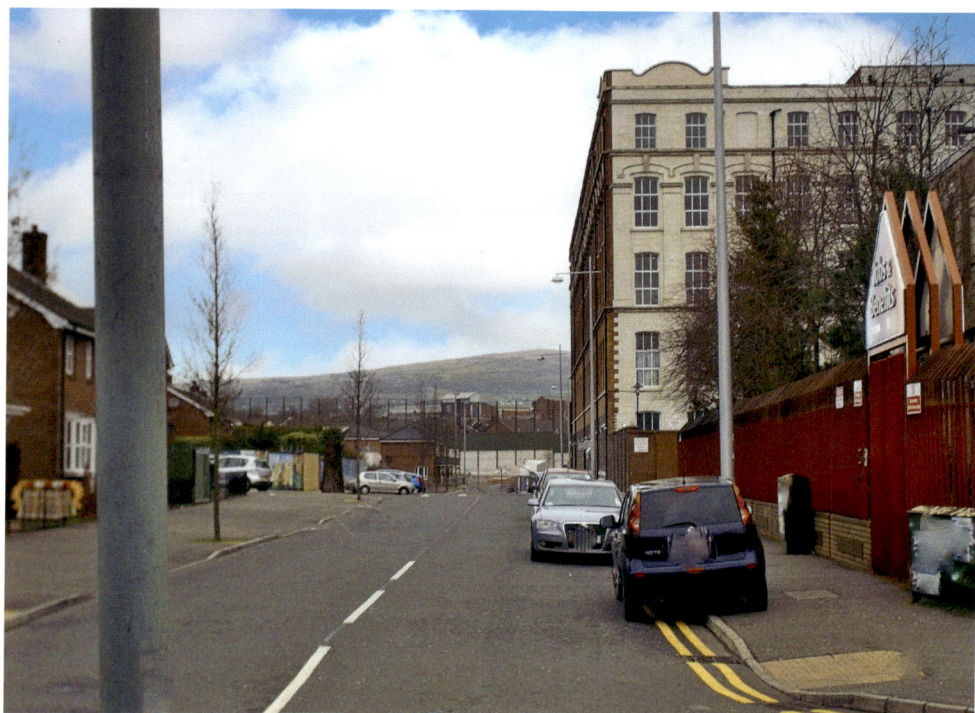

21. Conway Street today.

22. *Right:* Hugh McCabe, 1968.

23. Divis Street today.

24. Dublin city centre in 1916, after the British bombardment.

25. A typical scene of a linen mill in Belfast, c. 1900.

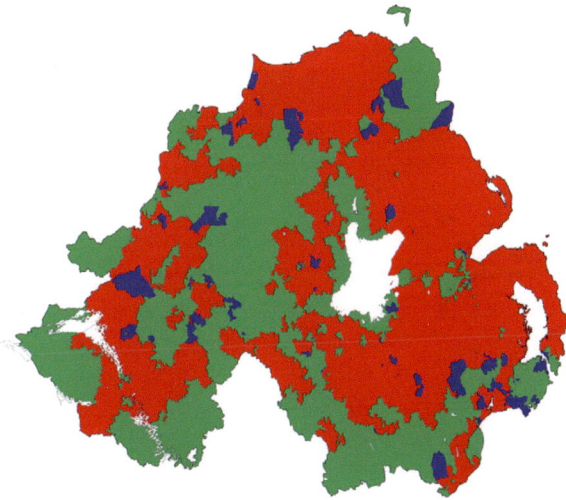

Demographic Breakdown of Northern Ireland

Areas marked in Red are British leaning, and invariably Protestant. Areas in Green are Irish leaning and mostly Catholic. Blue areas denote people who call themselves Northern Irish.

Crumlin Road/ Ardoyne Interface 1969

1) Brookfield Street
2) Hooker Street
3) Butler Street
4) Crumlin Road
5) Disraeli Street
6) Herbert Street
7) Chatham Street
8) Holy Cross RC Church
9) Holy Cross Girls School
10) Holy Cross Boys School
11) Rosebank Street
12) Brookfield Mill

Areas marked in red are businesses and houses destroyed or damaged in the rioting of 1969

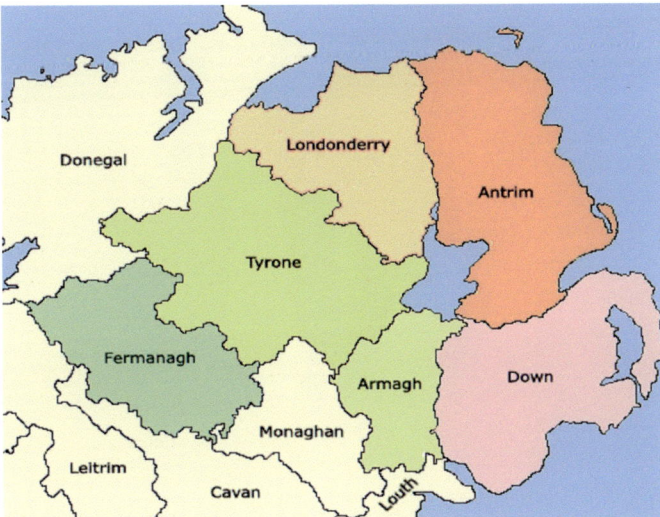

Top: 26. The division between Protestants and Catholics in Northern Ireland.

Above: 27. A map of the Crumlin Road interface, 1969.

Left: 28. The Northern Irish state.

29. The Black and Tans raid Sinn Fein offices, 1921.

30. Sinn Fein prisoners of the Black and Tans, 1921.

31. Imprisoned IRA members, 1921.

32. The opening of the new Belfast Parliament, 1922.

33. A British Army armoured vehicle, 1921.

34. Shankill Road, 1970.

35. The barricades are still in place on Bombay Street in 2013.

36. The Cupar Street peaceline.

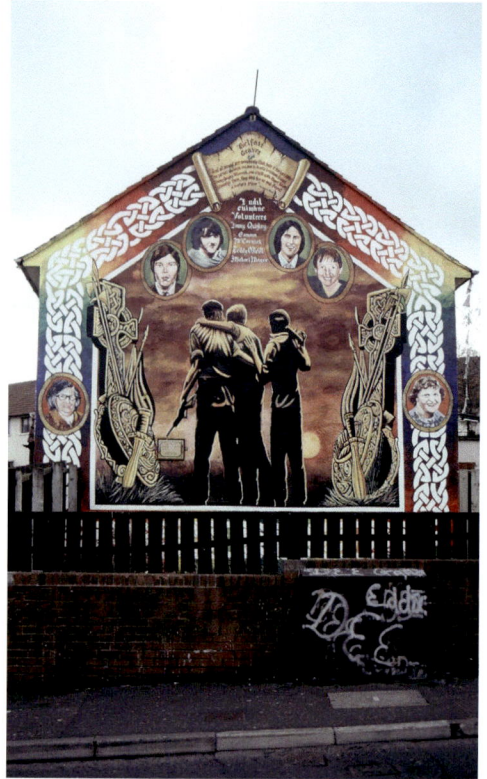

IRELAND

ACCORDING TO THE ACT OF SETTLEMENT
26TH SEPT. 1663 AND SUBSEQUENT ORDERS

Above left: 37. The plantation of Ireland.

Above right: 38. A republican mural in Belfast.

Left: 39. The Declaration of the Irish Republic, 1916.

POBLACHT NA H EIREANN.

THE PROVISIONAL GOVERNMENT
OF THE
IRISH REPUBLIC
TO THE PEOPLE OF IRELAND.

IRISHMEN AND IRISHWOMEN In the name of God and of the dead generations from which she receives her old tradition of nationhood, Ireland, through us, summons her children to her flag and strikes for her freedom.

Having organised and trained her manhood through her secret revolutionary organisation, the Irish Republican Brotherhood, and through her open military organisations, the Irish Volunteers and the Irish Citizen Army, having patiently perfected her discipline, having resolutely waited for the right moment to reveal itself, she now seizes that moment, and, supported by her exiled children in America and by gallant allies in Europe, but relying in the first on her own strength, she strikes in full confidence of victory

We declare the right of the people of Ireland to the ownership of Ireland, and to the unfettered control of Irish destinies, to be sovereign and indefeasible. The long usurpation of that right by a foreign people and government has not extinguished the right, nor can it ever be extinguished except by the destruction of the Irish people In every generation the Irish people have asserted their right to national freedom and sovereignty, six times during the past three hundred years they have asserted it in arms. Standing on that fundamental right and again asserting it in arms in the face of the world, we hereby proclaim the Irish Republic as a Sovereign Independent State, and we pledge our lives and the lives of our comrades-in-arms to the cause of its freedom, of its welfare, and of its exaltation among the nations.

The Irish Republic is entitled to, and hereby claims, the allegiance of every Irishman and Irishwoman. The Republic guarantees religious and civil liberty, equal rights and equal opportunities to all its citizens, and declares its resolve to pursue the happiness and prosperity of the whole nation and of all its parts, cherishing all the children of the nation equally, and oblivious of the differences carefully fostered by an alien government, which have divided a minority from the majority in the past.

Until our arms have brought the opportune moment for the establishment of a permanent National Government, representative of the whole people of Ireland and elected by the suffrages of all her men and women, the Provisional Government, hereby constituted, will administer the civil and military affairs of the Republic in trust for the people.

We place the cause of the Irish Republic under the protection of the Most High God, Whose blessing we invoke upon our arms, and we pray that no one who serves that cause will dishonour it by cowardice, inhumanity, or rapine. In this supreme hour the Irish nation must, by its valour and discipline and by the readiness of its children to sacrifice themselves for the common good, prove itself worthy of the august destiny to which it is called.

Signed on Behalf of the Provisional Government,
THOMAS J. CLARKE,
SEAN Mac DIARMADA, THOMAS MacDONAGH,
P. H. PEARSE, EAMONN CEANNT,
JAMES CONNOLLY. JOSEPH PLUNKETT.

inevitably meant half a dozen stops for a drink and a chat, and several more for the loo. 'Community Relations' became the big Army occupation—organising trips to the sea for kids, dances for teenagers, or soccer matches with the local lads. And we all felt what a jolly good job we were doing.

I think we were aware of the political dimensions.... We all had a feeling there was injustice over housing, jobs, education, and even justice. I think we certainly felt that we were on the side of the Catholics ... there was a huge amount of sympathy for them. That lasted a long time, and it was probably the ham-fistedness of the politicians that put paid to that.[21]

One problem became apparent upon the arrival of the troops on the streets of Belfast, and it was one that soon turned out to be fatal. The Catholic and Protestant areas of west Belfast were separated by a series of imaginary lines or interfaces. Many of these lines divided streets, roads, and even recreational areas. Thus, when the soldiers arrived the sectarian geography was lost on them, and the reliance on the RUC (to show them just exactly where the dividing line was) turned out to be a poor judgement. Many soldiers believed that the line between the two communities was in fact the Falls Road, and that is where many of them were told to line up. Considering the level of violence in Belfast, it was also surprising to see how few troops were actually sent to the city.

As the troops were moving into the Falls Road area, violence was breaking out in other parts of the city—most notably, as we have seen, in the Clonard area. A number of troops left the Falls Road and went into the Clonard district to investigate reports of trouble there. According to Scarman, Col. Napier, who was a member of the party of troops, observed the violence occurring in Bombay Street from a window in Clonard Monastery. A platoon of soldiers was then sent to the Monastery at about 8 p.m.[22]

It was not long before the soldiers became involved in the rioting. CS gas was fired at Protestants attempting to get out of Cupar Street and into Clonard proper. Soldiers were unaware where the boundary was between the two warring factions, and this led to much confusion on the ground. However, as much as the troops attempted to restore order in the district, the sheer numbers of those involved ensured that this was not going to happen. The initial observation of the Army—that the Falls Road was the dividing line between Catholic and Protestant areas—was a fatal mistake, as was the limited numbers of troops initially sent to the area. By the time this error was realised, Bombay Street was burned to the ground.

In the book *Ulster*, The *Sunday Times* Insight Team summed up the feelings of many of the residents of Clonard and the soldiers sent to defend the area at the time:

From that spasm of destruction was born the first of many Catholic myths about the British troops in Ulster. The Army, it was said, had stood by and let Bombay

Street burn. The truth was that [General] Freeland had just enough men to cover Divis Street. The few he could spare, he did indeed send the half mile up the Falls Road to the Clonard area. But, relying on advice from the RUC, they were stationed in Cupar Street to protect the Protestants. Meanwhile, some of the residents of Cupar Street were out attacking the monastery. The only troops anywhere near Bombay Street were a handful of Welsh soldiers. And they did not have the faintest idea which side was which.[23]

It is easy to see why the troops were welcomed onto the streets of Belfast. For days, serious rioting had destroyed hundreds of houses and left hundreds more uninhabitable. Thousands of people were on the move, some genuinely fearing for their lives. For those not into the political ramifications of what was happening around them, the state had failed to make sure that they were safe. They had seen the RUC attack rioters, and they had seen elements of the 'B' Specials move clandestinely through their areas, attacking their homes and their neighbours. Their natural 'defenders', the IRA, were either nowhere to be seen or heavily outgunned and outnumbered. Who could blame them for supporting the Army?

Aftermath: A Return to Normality?
A Future Without Fear?

Where were the IRA, the natural defenders of the Catholic population of Northern Ireland, in those hot sultry days of August 1969? Although the RUC, 'B' Specials, the government and most of the Protestant population believed them to be a major threat, the truth was completely different. Numerous press releases were given out, each one attesting to the perceived threat. The violent outbreaks of trouble in the Falls Road area, and especially in the Ardoyne, were seen by the ordinary Protestant—who had been fed on a diet of anti-Catholic and republican propaganda for years—as a threat to the very fabric of their society. That is why the reaction was so violent.

The events of August took the leadership of the IRA in Dublin completely by surprise. Cathal Goulding belatedly sent men and arms to the border areas; however, the weapons were obsolete and ancient. Many of them did not work— the result of years of scaling back of the IRA's armoury. Limited attacks were made across the border by these units; they had mixed results as the men themselves were unsure as to how to proceed, such was the disorganisation within the group.

To the leadership however, something had to be done; they had to be seen to be active in the defence of the northern Catholics. Goulding therefore issued a statement designed to encourage the northern units of the IRA:

> The Army Council of the Irish Republican Army, acting in its capacity as the Provisional Government of the Irish Republic proclaimed in arms in 1916, and ratified by the universal suffrage of the Irish people in 1918, hereby calls on all Irishmen and Irishwomen, both at home and in exile, to forget the divisions of the past and to stand in unity against the forces of British Imperialism.[1]

Immediately, the blame for the upsurge in violence was put firmly at the door of the British. The socialist policies of non-sectarianism were to play a major role in the ensuing months. The statement continued:

Already northern units of the Irish Republican Army have been in action in defence of their lives and homes of the people who have been attacked by deliberately fomented sectarian forces, backed up by the 'B' Specials with the aim of destroying the natural solidarity and unity of the working class people. These units have played their part in defensive operations in Bogside, Derry, where they have put their discipline and experience at the disposal of the Citizens Defence Association.

Irish people in the 26 Counties. Put every pressure you can on the Dublin Government to support the victimised people of the North. Make Dublin justify its claim to sovereignty over the whole of the national territory. Contribute generously to the relief funds being set up to relieve Catholics and Protestants turned out of their homes. Organise rallies, meetings, demonstrations of support within the coming period. Trade Unionists, farmers, students, people of all political views, let us stand together in this hour of crisis.

The soldiers of the Republic are in the field to serve the people. Let all Irishmen support them so that we may build in our time a united Ireland, and lay the basis for democracy and socialism in our country.[2]

At Stormont, meetings of the Joint Security Committee (JSC, formed upon the arrival of British troops between the Army and RUC) formed their own opinions about the strength and capacity of the IRA, believing that nearly every Catholic was a member.

The Minister in the Senate asked how much was known about the fully-equipped IRA units referred to in the IRA Statement. The County Inspector of Crime Special Branch said that the RUC had known about the existence of such units, about the possibility of an attack on Crossmaglen RUC Station, and about the presence of local IRA units behind the barricades in Belfast and in Londonderry. These local units had been activated prior to the disturbances on Thursday, 14th August. Nothing was known about any new IRA units, nor could conclusive proof be provided that the civilians who started the shooting in Belfast had been members of the IRA, although they were assumed to be so.[3]

In the south, the government took a completely different stance. Reunification under a Dublin government—not a socialist, IRA one—was the only solution to the age-old problem, and this most recent outbreak of violence was just another manifestation of the hatred built up over decades of Unionist rule. The speech by the Taoiseach, Jack Lynch, on 13 August was designed to quell unrest within his own cabinet; the hawks were making noises. He demanded an independent United Nations peace-keeping force to be put in place instead of the British Army.

It is obvious that the RUC is no longer accepted as an impartial police force. Neither would the employment of British troops be acceptable nor would they be likely to restore peaceful conditions, certainly not in the long term. The Irish Government have, therefore, requested the British Government to apply immediately to the United Nations for the urgent despatch of a Peace-keeping Force to the 6 Counties of Northern Ireland and have instructed the Irish Permanent, Representative to the United Nations to inform the Secretary-General of this request. We have also asked the British Government to see to it that police attacks on the people of Derry should cease immediately.[4]

Despite its request for international troops (or because of it), the speech had completely the opposite effect in the north. Troop movements to the border in the guise of field hospitals also did nothing to quell the situation.

On 20 September Lynch made a speech at Tralee in Co. Kerry, outlining his position on partition.

> I would like in clear and simple terms to set out the basis of our thinking and policy. I hope that this will help to reduce those tensions in the North which arise from misunderstandings or apprehensions about our attitude or intentions.
>
> The historical and natural unity of Ireland was also a political unit until this was artificially sundered by the Government of Ireland Act passed by the British Government in 1920. The Act, in effect, provided for the partitioning of Ireland and the creation of a Government of Northern Ireland subordinate to Westminster. Partition was not expected to be permanent even by the authors of this statute—the ultimate aim of 'one Parliament and one Government for the whole of Ireland' appeared in the official summary of the Bill preceding this legislation, and provision was made for a Council of Ireland which, according as powers were transferred to it by the two parts of Ireland, might develop into an All-Ireland Parliament.[5]

No mention was made by Lynch of the fact that many Protestants in the north east wanted this, or that a possible disastrous civil war between north and south was averted by the decision to partition the country.

> I need not explain or justify the fundamental desire of the overwhelming majority of the people of this island for the restoration in some form of its national unity. This desire is not confined to Irishmen of any particular creed or ancestry. I want to make it clear, however, once more, that we have no intention of using force to realise this desire. I said as recently as 28th August that it was and has been the Government's policy to seek the re-unification of the country by peaceful means.
>
> The unity we seek is not something forced but a free and genuine union of those living in Ireland based on mutual respect and tolerance and guaranteed by a form or forms of government authority in Ireland providing for progressive improvement of social, economic and cultural life in a just and peaceful environment.

Of its nature this policy—of seeking unity through agreement in Ireland between Irishmen—is a long-term one. It is no less, indeed it is even more, patriotic for that. Perseverance in winning the respect and confidence of those now opposed to unity must be sustained by good-will, patience, understanding and, at times, forbearance.

The terrible events of the past few months have made it evident to all that, apart from disrupting the unity of Ireland, the 1920 devolution of powers has not provided a system of Government acceptable as fair and just, to many of the people in Northern Ireland. I need not detail these events nor refer to recent objective appraisals of that system of government. But change there obviously must be. We are concerned that the grievances of so many of our fellow Irishmen and women be quickly remedied and their fears set at rest. We also have a legitimate concern regarding the disposition to be made by the British Government in relation to the future administration of Northern Ireland. Our views on how peace and justice can be assured in this small island are relevant and entitled to be heard.

Let me make it clear, too, that in seeking re-unification, our aim is not to extend the domination of Dublin. We have many times down the years expressed our willingness to seek a solution on federal lines and in my most recent statement I envisaged the possibility of intermediate stages in an approach to a final agreed solution.

The proposal for UN troops to act as peacemakers in the north was treated with indifference in London and was seen as interference by Stormont. Chichester Clarke was especially scathing in his reply to the developments:

In this grave situation, the behaviour of the Dublin Government has been deplorable, and tailor-made to inflame opinion on both sides. The moving of Army units, the calling-up of reserves, the absurd approaches for United Nations intervention have all been moves of almost incredible clumsiness and ineptitude. I am glad to say that Dr Hillery returned to his Department in Dublin from his visit to the Foreign Office after what he himself described as a polite but very firm brush-off. These manoeuvres in ordinary circumstances would be merely comic, but in the present inflamed atmosphere they represent a gamble with people's lives. I think that is a very squalid business, and all that the Dublin Government has done is to convince us for all time that we must look elsewhere for our friends. We held out our hand to them as good neighbours. They have behaved much like those hooligans who have used the present Troubles as an excuse to burn their neighbours out.[6]

However, while Lynch was explaining his government's official position, the reality was quite different. Many Catholics in the north believed that Dublin had let them down in not actively intervening in August 1969, and these Catholics now turned to the emerging Provisionals in large numbers. One eyewitness described the feelings in Catholic Belfast as August drew to a close:

> Inside the barricades it is a different story, and I cannot see the Catholics of Belfast taking down the barricades unless and until they are given guarantees that the 'B' Specials will be disbanded and the RUC are taken out of the area. They have lost all trust in the Six County administration. It should also be stressed that there was no political motivation behind this barricade of the Catholic areas in the Falls Road.
>
> It was done for sheer fear and the instinct of self-preservation by people who were under armed attack. There were no IRA units in the area when the attack came.
>
> There may be some IRA men, but they are Belfast IRA men who are living there and who speedily came to the rescue of the Catholic population that night and the next morning.[7]

Protestants believed that Lynch did intervene—through his provocative speech and in sending field hospitals and troops to the border. Many also believed, regardless of the above eyewitness account, that the southern government clandestinely supported the bogeyman of the IRA, and that they were active in large numbers in Belfast.

II

British soldiers were on the streets of Belfast in considerable numbers by the end of October 1969. Their deployment was only supposed to be temporary, but nobody believed that anymore. Peacelines were now a familiar part of the Belfast streetscape, snaking along the backs of houses and dividing streets where Catholic and Protestant children once played, oblivious to the sickness in their society. The peacelines were also only meant to be temporary, but nobody believed that either. Serious violence had subsided by October; there were violent protests on the Shankill Road in the same month, when it was announced that the RUC were to be disarmed; a policeman lost his life as a result. The Army were now becoming heavily embroiled in the complex problems of a sick society. Danny Morrison remembers the turnaround in relations with the Army:

> The other thing was that whenever mobs gathered—for example, in Cupar Street or Kashmir Road—the Brits had what you call 'snatch squads'. But it would be us they arrested. They would come running into a crowd, three or five tough-looking Brits with batons, beat the crap out of you, take you away, and then charge you with riotous behaviour.

People then began to ignore the Brits, wouldn't buy them cigarettes, and the Brits started to get very nasty. At school certain gangs began to form. I was asked to help raise funds for the auxiliaries of the Provo's. I eventually came to sympathise with the Provo's...[8]

Protestants remained behind their barricades as the security situation began to improve, but they were not inactive. For their part, Catholics had launched an attack on their police force, their parliament, and their way of life. There is little or no evidence that the UVF were involved in the August riots, but there were no shortage of local vigilante groups—each one defending their own area, such as the Donegall Road Defence Committee and the Shankill Defence Association amongst others. Many of these small, local groups coalesced to form the Ulster Defence Association (UDA), a direct response to the reorganisation of the IRA on the Catholic side. Lines were being drawn, and Belfast society was polarised along lines of religion like never before.

The growth of support for the newly-formed Provisional IRA grew. The apparent failure of the Dublin-led IRA to defend the Catholics of Belfast was the catalyst for a split in the republican movement, with the more traditional, militant, members joining Sean MacStiofain, Daithí O'Connail, and others in forming the Provisional IRA. In the eyes of those on the interfaces, they became the true defenders of Catholics in Belfast.

Provocation became the norm, as units of the Provisionals began to attack the British Army—who they now saw as an occupying force. The Army launched house-to-house searches, antagonising the local Catholic population to the point where street fights between mobs of Catholics and the Army were almost a daily occurrence. The more the Army cracked down, the more the people resisted. So began the descent into war on the streets of Belfast between Catholics, Protestants, and the Army. It was a three-way fight; with the Army in the middle.

The arrival of troops on the streets—coupled with the continuation of the Stormont government, the setting up of a Joint Security Committee within the confines of Stormont, and Army searches—convinced the local populace that the Army was backing up the status quo. Unionists would remain in power, and the Army would remain to support the RUC. After the traumatic events of those three days in August, Catholics believed that they were now to pay the price. This was another reason why so much support was given to the Provisionals in those early days.

Thus, as the years went by and Northern Ireland settled into a pattern of random killings, explosions, and rioting, the future looked very bleak. The 1970s came and went with very little progress. Direct rule from Westminster became a reality in 1972, after Stormont refused to hand over control of security to London. The McGurks Bar bombing, Bloody Sunday, the Ballymurphy killings, Newlodge, Warrenpoint, Enniskillen... the list went on.

Various peace plans were put forward; all failed, partly due to a Conservative government in London completely focused on security and not taking chances. It took the courage of John Hume and others to make the peace process of today a reality. In 1994 the Provisional IRA called off its twenty-five-year campaign, and was soon followed by a Loyalist ceasefire. These have largely held through often-difficult and challenging times. At the time of writing they are still in place. Just.

Belfast today is unrecognisable compared to August 1969. Gone are the slum dwellings of the Falls and Shankill Roads, the burnt-out potholes on the roads after numerous riots and bonfires. Gone also is the infamous Divis flats complex, replaced by modern housing; only the imposing Divis tower remains. The Unity flats and many of the streets that ran between the Falls and Shankill are gone also. The Army is gone too, the need for them diminishing since the ceasefires of the '90s and the reduction in violence. Only the police remain in their role as security for all of society.

The young generation in today's Belfast have none of the memories of those turbulent times. They have grown up in relative peace, unaware of how their parents and grandparents lived in a time of saturation by the Army, guns on the streets, nightly riots, and daily bombings. They can go to pubs, to clubs, and shopping without the fear of a bombing or shooting incident. Their lives are as normal as living in Birmingham or Manchester.

The generation that saw the violent upheavals of 1969 are also a diminishing breed. Of those who were teenagers at the time, many are now in their late sixties—grandparents and great-grandparents. Many are dead, maimed, or affected in other ways, such is the terrible price of communal warfare. They grew up in a time of Army searches, police raids, riots, bombings, and fear of the unknown. They feared going out to pubs, to the shops, and to the city centre, which was an Army-controlled zone for nearly thirty years; yet they managed to meet, date, have children, and grow old.

The paramilitaries left the stage nearly twenty years ago, but their reputation is still apparent in a society that still bears the scars of its most recent past. Vigilante law and order is prevalent in many areas; beatings and shootings occur, but in no way at the level of the mid-'70s or '80s. It is as if some elements will not let go, and they use the fear of a return to inter-communal violence as a stick to beat their opponents with.

That fear is emphasised by the continued existence of the peacelines. Clonard is still sealed off from the Shankill area as the peace wall snakes its way along what was once Cupar Street, down to Northumberland Street. Dover and Percy Streets are also sealed, as is Conway Street—never rebuilt after August 1969 and now silent and deserted, a far cry from the bustling street of the 1960s. The peacelines are there for generations yet to come; the animosity between the two communities is such that many believe there would be a return to violence if they came down.

Many of the men and women who were involved in or witnessed the August 1969 rioting are now involved in tackling social issues, cross-community groups, or in volunteering for their communities; they are helping to rebuild a society that was ravaged by violence and murder for so long. They help the vulnerable, are involved in housing issues, and help the younger generation to understand the legacy of the conflict. Their war is over. Now it is over to the younger generations to build on their work and ensure that August 1969 does not happen again. Ever.

Appendix 1
'The Plain Truth'

In 1964 the Campaign for Social Justice was set up in Dungannon by Patricia and Conn McCloskey, with the aim of bringing the inequalities within the allocation of housing in Northern Ireland to attention. They released a pamphlet entitled 'The Plain Truth'. According to Cain, this pamphlet:

> ...was to try to publicise what it saw as injustices in the region through a series of booklets, pamphlets, letters, meetings, etc. Much of this material related to perceived discrimination in employment, housing, electoral practices, and public appointments.[1]

The Campaign for Social Justice and various other pressure groups were the forerunners to the formation of NICRA. 'The Plain Truth' is an instrumental document in the understanding of the situation in Northern Ireland in the 1960s. While it is not presented in its full form, the reader can gain valuable information and an insight into the politics of Northern Ireland in the 1960s.

'The Plain Truth'

Since 1920, when Ireland was divided, the Republic of Ireland has been a separate independent state, while Northern Ireland has remained an integral part of the United Kingdom. It is now loosely termed 'Ulster' although there were nine counties in old-time Ulster, three of which are now in the Republic of Ireland. The British Parliament in London first legalised this arrangement by the Government of Ireland Act, 1920. London has since ruled Northern Ireland through its subordinate Parliament at Stormont, Belfast.

Both London and Stormont have always been at pains to present the province as a happy, contented place, whereas in fact it contains a minority which has always been very hard pressed, and indeed denied rights which most of the free world has come to accept as a matter of course.

The outside world was largely unaware of what was going on in Ulster mainly because the British press had always been discouraged from printing stories about it. Some years ago when a British television group had a series of documentaries suppressed, the leader of the reporting team, Alan Whicker, declared 'No country deserves the Government you have here. This is the only place in the world where you can't report honestly without silly people kicking up about what is only the truth.'

Since the 5th October, 1968, when a peaceful Civil Rights march was broken up by the police, the world has been looking at Northern Ireland on television, and reading about her in the press, first with incredulity, and then shock.

Civil Rights activities have been opposed by various groups of militant Protestants. These people already have their civil rights, and do not wish to share them with others. They have caused the recent unrest by opposing democratic demands for change. This opposition has been effected mainly by violent counter-demonstrations, and by arbitrary police bans on Civil Rights marches in certain places, e.g., in the city of Londonderry.

This booklet attempts to explain the situation in Northern Ireland, and to detail the discriminatory injustices from which the minority has been suffering there for almost fifty years. There are roughly one and a half million people living in Northern Ireland, of whom two thirds are Protestant, and who generally support the Unionist Government. The remaining one third are Roman Catholics, who generally support a variety of opposition parties.

Out of a total of 52, the Unionists hold 39 seats in the Stormont Parliament. They are closely linked with the Conservative (Tory) party in Britain. The Unionist Party is a sectarian one. Down the years it has discouraged Catholics from joining and at present only a dozen or so belong to it. It is dominated by the Orange Order, a secret society having many points of similarity with the Dutch Reformed Church in South Africa. Virtually all of the Government, including the present Prime Minister, Major Chichester-Clark as well as most Unionist parliamentarians, are members of the Orange Order.

Six Nationalists, four Labour and three Independent members make up the Parliamentary opposition. Northern Ireland also sends twelve MPs to the London Parliament (Westminster). For many years they were all Unionists, boosting Conservative voting strength there. This is a main reason why the British Conservatives, who were in power most of the time, did not insist that the Stormont Government should modify their repressive and discriminatory policies towards the political minority.

One of these London seats was taken from the Unionists in 1964, and is now held by the redoubtable Gerry Fitt. In April 1969, a twenty-one-year-old Civil Rights leader, Bernadette Devlin, took another seat from the Unionists to become 'the youngest MP in the London Parliament.'

Before Fitt's and Devlin's day, the Republican Party dominated minority politics as far as Westminster was concerned. It took a logical enough view that Irishmen had no place in an English Parliament, and that asking favours of the British, either in their own Parliament or elsewhere, was both degrading and a waste of time. This was the policy of 'abstention'.

Population Control

Outsiders looking at Northern Ireland, and listening to Government claims that it is a democratic State, and that Unionists have been the peoples' choice all along, find it hard to understand why there has never been a change of party control.

It is correct that the Unionists have always had a majority, but mainly because of a ruthless and far-seeing plan to contain their opponents' numbers.

All down the years the percentage of Catholics (anti-Unionists) has been strictly regulated by allowing only the same percentage to remain, and forcing the rest to emigrate by denying those jobs and houses.

At the present time in Northern Ireland the Roman Catholic primary schools contain 51 per cent of all the children (Capt. O'Neill's own figure given in 1968), because the Catholic birth rate is almost twice that of the non-Catholic. If these children were to grow to maturity and remain at home, the Unionists grasp of affairs would be shaken in a very short time. That a good percentage of these potential anti-Tory voters is got rid of is shown by the graph page 3 (Figures from the Government Census, HM Stationery Office, Belfast). It will be noted that the drain occurs principally at voting age.

In 1951 Catholics were 37.7 per cent of the under-30 year's population. Ten years later in 1961 they had fallen to 35.4 per cent of the 10 to 39 years age group, which corresponds to the under 30 year's population of 1951.

In this ten-year period Catholics, although originally only 37.7 per cent of the age group, account for 55.6 per cent of the total decrease of population due to death and emigration. In effect this meant a drop of 16.7 per cent of the total Catholic population under 30 years in 1951. From the Registrar-General's births and deaths report, it can be seen that the death rate is negligible, the main drain is in emigration

The comparative figures for Protestants are: in 1951 Protestants were 62.3 per cent of the under 30 population, ten years later, in 1961 they had risen to 64.6 per cent of the 10 to 39 age group, which corresponds to the under 30 population of 1951. In this ten-year period Protestants, although originally 62.3 per cent of the age group account for only 44.4 per cent of the total decrease of population due to death and emigration.

The official Census shows the Catholic proportion of the total population to have remained static, 33.5 per cent in 1937, and 34.9 per cent in 1961. From 1937 to 1961, the last year in which the Census required a declaration of religion, a total of 90,000 Catholics emigrated from Northern Ireland. For non-Catholics the total was 69,000, or 8 per cent of their 1937 population. The Catholic percentage was 21. The difference in economic opportunity is a regulator maintaining the status quo. This is the formula for these facts, given by two English Quakers, Barritt and Carter, in an impartial survey entitled 'The Northern Ireland Problem'.

Job Discrimination

Reference to the back pages makes it very clear that it has always been Unionist policy, not only to control the numbers, but to keep the Roman Catholics as 'second class citizens' in their own land. They have been rightly referred to as 'the white negroes of Ulster'.

Even the opportunity of menial work is denied first to them. As a result of this they make up by far the greater proportion of the dole queues. The Campaign for Social Justice asked a parliamentarian to request names of all on unemployment benefit in one town so that a percentage figure could be arrived at, but the Government refused this. In a town of half and half Unionists and anti-Unionists which we surveyed, the anti-Unionists predominated on the unemployment register in a ratio of about ten to one. But it is the higher ranks that the politico-religious discrimination is most serious because the lack of opportunity here forces emigration of the best Catholic brains.

In this publication the figures we present are not earlier than 1968, unless otherwise stated.

The Public Boards

The Government administers a large segment of public affairs through its official bodies, the members of which it appoints itself. Where an occasional Catholic is given this important function, not only is he hopelessly outnumbered vote-wise, but also those chosen are often known to be Government collaborators, who would be unlikely to insist on minority rights in a way that members elected by the minority itself would do. The parallel with Mr Ian Smith of Rhodesia choosing tribal chiefs to advise him is surely apparent. Herewith the membership details of the main ruling bodies, with religions:

Electricity Board for N.I., Housing Trust, Craigavon Development Commission, Economic Council, Hospitals Authority, General Health Services Board, Medical Advisory Committee to the Ministry of Health, Pigs Marketing Board, Milk Marketing Board, Seed Potato Marketing Board, Agricultural Wages Board, Youth Employment Service Board, Fire Authority, Child Welfare Council, Ulster Folk, Museum Trustees, Tourist Board, Advisory Council for Education, Council for Education Research, Youth and Sports Council, Industrial Court.

Doctors

The Hospitals Authority administers Northern Ireland's 97 hospitals, practising religious discrimination in the way it chooses the specialist doctors who work in. There are 387 specialists, only 31 of these are Roman Catholic. Of the 387, 61 hold teaching posts at the University. Of the 31 Catholics, three hold University posts. Excluding the University appointees only 8.50 per cent of Hospital Authority specialist jobs go to Catholics. (In general practice doctoring, where the patients are free to choose their own practitioner, one third of the GPs are Catholic, thereby reflecting the general population percentage. Chemists, barristers and solicitors, where free enterprise prevails, show identical trends).

These hospitals are run by management Committees. Total Committee members: 456, 72 are Roman Catholics, i.e., 15.7 per cent. Again the Roman Catholic members are chosen for their 'reliability.' Noteworthy is Londonderry, seven Roman Catholics out of 21. The population of Derry is 65 per cent Roman Catholic. Of the total 50 matrons of Hospitals, only six are Catholic, i.e., 12 per cent.

Government Health Service

Chief Medical Officer and deputy Chief, both Protestants. Medical Referees: Full time, there are eight, all Protestants. Part-time, 50, only six Roman Catholics (Referee figures were obtained in 1969).

There is no Borough or County Chief Dental Officer who is a Catholic. There is no County or Borough Public Health Inspector a Catholic. Of all the sixteen Public Health Inspectors only three are Catholic.

Police

Royal Ulster Constabulary (RUC): Complement, just over 3,000, 10 per cent of which are Catholic, 50 Officers in RUC, six are Catholic: 120 Head Constables, 16 are Catholic. 400 Sergeants, 50 Catholic (1967 figures). Upkeep: £6.7 million* in the coming year, of which over £15 million is pay and allowances.

Ulster Special Constabulary (USC): This is a sectarian part-time force 11,300 strong. All members are Protestant. They are mainly recruited from members of the Orange Order. As recipients of Unionist patronage these constitute a private Unionist army. They have the right to retain their firearms in their own homes. There have been several documented cases of vicious attacks by members of the Ulster Specials on peaceful Civil Rights marchers, and on other anti-Unionists. Specials in mufti have been found in possession of firearms at counter demonstrations to Civil

Rights marches. The Government has recently augmented its full-time police force with well over 1,000 of these men—upkeep: £972,700 in the coming year.

Police Brutality

Up to October 5th, 1968, with some notable exceptions, relations between the police and the minority, were normal. At the first Londonderry Civil Rights march the Royal Ulster Constabulary sealed off the marchers in Duke Street in front and behind and batoned those indiscriminately. Gerry Fitt, MP, was wounded on the head. Edward McAteer, MP, in the groin. A girl was batoned on the mouth. The people were hosed with water cannons. This was all witnessed by two British labour MPs, John Ryan and Mrs Anne Kerr. While this was going on, police not actively engaged were laughing.

At a later date student marchers at Burntollet Bridge received scant protection from the R UC, who fraternised freely with the Paisleyites led by Major Bunting. Students were stoned, beaten with nail-studded clubs, and thrown into a stream. Threats of rape were made on the women (In January 1969, police, some alleged to be intoxicated, broke into houses in Lecky Road, Derry, and, using obscene and sectarian abuse, attacked the citizens indiscriminately with batons and kicks. As a result, 190 formal complaints against the police were documented).

Again, demonstrating its particular brand of 'democracy' the Ulster Government ordered an Enquiry to be carried out by, police officials themselves! The Government has refused to make the results of this Enquiry public.

Religious Discrimination In Rating Abatement

In 1966 the British Government introduced a Rate Rebate plan whereby the rates burden on houses occupied by the lower income groups was eased.

In Northern Ireland this rate rebate was spread over all domestic ratepayers otherwise it 'would benefit too many of the wrong sort' (meaning the poorer Roman Catholics).

In April 1969, in Derry, the police were caught at a disadvantage and were stoned by a mob and some injured. Police later invaded Catholic homes and rendered many men, women (including a semi-invalid) and children hospital cases.

The Schools

School Inspectors. There are 53 Inspectors of County and Voluntary Schools, five are Roman Catholic.

Local Education Committees

These bodies run the schools. There are eight, one for each County and one each for Belfast and Londonderry. Total membership 223. Only 39 are Roman Catholic (17 per cent); there are 36 Protestant and four Roman Catholic clergymen members. Roman Catholics are 35 per cent of the population, but make up 51 per cent of the primary school children.

Religious Discrimination Against Teachers

Like Holland, Germany and the USA, the Roman Catholic Church authorities prefer to educate the children in their own schools. The part upkeep of these schools is a very heavy burden on Roman Catholics, but the fact that they accept it is surely proof that they want things this way.

For educated Catholics schools present some of the few good employment opportunities in Ulster. There is a law in Northern Ireland, unlike the rest of Britain, which prohibits school teachers from being members of County Councils. We claim that this is discriminatory, and is solely to prevent this articulate group in the Roman Catholic community, the teachers, from speaking in local affairs on behalf of the underprivileged.

Post Office

Control of the postal service is directly held by London and discrimination here is widespread. Our figures were collected in 1967. Since the Post Office was divided into Regional Administrations in the mid-1930s there have been eight holders of the post of Director of the Northern Ireland Region. None have been Catholics. The Director heads a Board of Administration consisting of postal Controller, Telecommunications Controller, Staff Controller and Finance Officer.

None of these posts, all of which have changed hands several times in the past thirty years, has ever been held by a Catholic. The other chief posts in the Service here, with a minimum salary of £2,000 plus p.a., are the Head Postmaster, Belfast; Assistant Head Postmaster, Belfast; the Telephone Manager; Deputy Telephone Manager; Three Area Engineers; The Area Accountant; Chief Sales Superintendent; Chief Traffic Superintendent. None of these posts have ever been held by a Catholic.

Outside Belfast, for example, there are thirteen Head Postmasterships. Going back forty years, the holders have never been Catholics with one exception many years ago. There are over 6,000 Post Office employees in Northern Ireland, practically all of whom are recruited locally. On a population basis it is reasonable to assume that at least 35 per cent of these should be Catholic. As one progresses up the grades this percentage gets smaller. Take the Belfast Head Post Office as an example. The basic clerical grade is that of Postal and Telegraph Officer and the rungs of the ladder upwards from that are: Overseerships, Assistant Superintendents, Superintendents, Chief Superintendent. Allowing for mobility among the applicants there are Postmasterships and Head Postmasterships and some occasional transfers outside the manipulative work of the Service such as Welfare Officer Posts.

Religious Discrimination In The Trade Unions

The Northern Ireland Committee of Irish Congress of Trade Unions is the ruling body. Here the Chairman is a Catholic, but none of the other eleven members is.

Full-time Paid Trade Union Officials: Protestants 62; Catholics 16; Catholic Percentage 20. Craft Unions of Manual Skilled Workers: Protestants 35; Catholics 5; Catholic Percentage 12. These comprise the highly skilled and paid Unions. There is a traditional Protestant preponderance here. Other Unions (white collar, professional and unskilled). Protestants 27; Catholics 11; Catholic Percentage 29.

Religious Discrimination In The Business Sector

Because most of the large firms, private and public, are controlled by Protestants, the bias is mainly anti-Catholic. It is very widespread. We give two examples only: In 1966 the Roman Catholic Bishop of the Belfast area, Dr Philbin, claimed that in a specified engineering firm only three or four employees out of the total work force were Catholics (Belfast is 27.5 per cent Catholic). The Bishop could not state the total labour force. Like ourselves in similar circumstances, there was no sympathetic person available to give him information. We estimate it at 3,000 for this factory.

The manager, in a letter to the Bishop, claimed the Catholics 'did not feel at home in a Protestant atmosphere'. As the Bishop pointed out to him, poorly-off discriminated-against Catholics are never in the position of choosing the atmosphere in which they work. Although this factory is in receipt of Government grants the authorities have repeatedly refused to reveal the amounts, or to make a fair employment policy a condition for their continuance.

In another town with approximately fifty-fifty Protestants and Catholics, there is a large textile factory with a pay-roll of about 2,500. In this factory complex there is one Roman Catholic director (who was seconded from London); one Roman Catholic manager; one Roman Catholic under-manager; three Roman Catholic charge hands; one Roman Catholic mechanic: five Roman Catholic supervisors.

In all, only 12 Roman Catholic persons above the lowest grade. There has never been, with possibly one or two exceptions, any Roman Catholics in the despatch department.

The rest are the 'hewers of wood and the drawers of water'. How can it be done so thoroughly? Because, as a matter of policy, this firm does not, nor never has, taken any pupils from the local Roman Catholic grammar school to train for the higher posts. All come from the Protestant grammar school. The academic records of both schools are similar.

Special Powers Act

In April 1963, the South African Minister of Justice, now the Prime Minister, introduced a new Coercion Bill by saying that he 'would be willing to exchange all the legislation of that sort for one clause of the Northern Ireland Special Powers Act'.

This Act, which has been continuously in operation since 1922, empowers the authorities to: arrest without warrant; imprison without charge or trial and deny recourse to habeas corpus or a court of law; enter and search homes without warrant, and with force, at any hour of day or night; declare a curfew and prohibit meetings, assemblies (including fairs and markets) and processions; permit punishment by flogging; deny claim to a trial by jury; arrest persons it is desired to examine as witnesses, forcibly detain them and compel them to answer questions, under penalties, even if answers may incriminate them. Such a person is guilty of an offence if he refuses to be sworn or answer a question; prevent access of relatives or legal advisers to a person imprisoned without trial; prohibit the holding of an inquest after a prisoner's death; arrest a person who 'by word of mouth' spreads false reports or makes false statements; prohibit the circulation of any newspaper; prohibit the possession of any film or gramophone record; arrest a person who does anything calculated to be prejudicial to the preservation of peace or maintenance of order in Northern Ireland and not specifically provided for in the regulations.

Housing Apartheid In Northern Ireland—Ghetto Housing

In towns where the Unionists have a slender majority they consolidate their place by the use of gerrymandered wards. They can convert a paper minority into a majority by this means. This is how it is done. The town is divided into wards, frequently three in number. In the two smaller Unionist wards the electors are thinly spread and allocated the same number of councillors per ward as the anti-Unionists who are crammed into the third ward, and give the same number of councillors. Londonderry is the classical example and is detailed overleaf. This also happens in Dungannon, Omagh, Armagh, Enniskillen and many other places.

The most notorious single ghetto housing estate with regard to size is one owned by Belfast Corporation, called Turf Lodge, where there are 1,175 Catholic families and only 22 Protestant families (1967 figures). There is another Government sponsored body in Northern Ireland, the Housing Trust, which builds homes for letting. It often mixes the religions, and we found in such estates that Protestants and Catholics live together in amity, and have a much healthier attitude to each other. The Trust usually selects better-off people since they make more stable tenants, the neediest being thereby passed over. However, in most towns the bigoted Unionist councils see to it that the balance of power is not upset, even obstructing the Housing Trust if too many Catholics are being accommodated, e.g. Enniskillen and Londonderry.

The Trust is not blameless of occasionally practicing religious discrimination. It has refused enquiring opposition MPs information as to how it selects tenants. More often than not it re-lets to people of the same religion as the old tenants, and not solely on need.

Voting Injustices

In many areas, where they would be in danger from a simple majority, the Unionists manipulate electoral boundaries in a very undemocratic way known as gerrymandering', and thereby keep control. In local government elections there is denial of 'one man, one vote'. Only house-holders and their wives have one vote each. This means that in all of Northern Ireland there are at present a quarter of a million people disfranchised out of a total electorate of less than one million. To prevent control passing from them Unionists refuse to allocate Catholics their fair share of local authority housing—built with public funds, denial of a house meaning denial of a voice in local affairs. Thus Catholics are not in a position to help their co-religionists who are forced to emigrate.

Catholics may be on housing waiting lists for up to twelve years or longer, whilst Protestants can often choose their council house and have it allocated before they are married. Such a case was spotlighted in 1968 at Caledon in Co. Tyrone by Austin Currie, MP, who, after he had exhausted all legal remedies available, himself squatted in a council house. This house had been allocated to a young unmarried stenographer of a Unionist candidate for a Westminster seat, Mr B. McRoberts.

Housing injustices such as this cause great bitterness at local level, and our Campaign is deeply resentful of the unchristian way the least influential and articulate members of the Catholic population have been squeezed out over the past forty-eight years.

British political leaders like Prime Minister Wilson, Lord Butler, Lord Brooke, Sir Alec Douglas-Home and many others before them have been given full details of these injustices, but so far nothing concrete has been done.

Pressure from outside has recently compelled the Unionists to offer 'one man, one vote'. This will be useless unless each vote is of equal value, in other words if there is no gerrymander. It is something of a tragedy that there is no apparent groundswell of Protestant public opinion in favour of this course. It would be hard to imagine the Unionists taking an honourable course in this vital field of public authority housing and voting.

'He Who Pays The Piper Calls The Tune'

The Unionist excuse for denying those who are not householders a vote in local government elections is that they allege they are not paying domestic rates for the upkeep of the local council. But the Minister of Development revealed that only 30 per cent of local expenditure is raised from the rates. The remainder comes from central tax funds, to which all contribute. Despite the fact that Northern Ireland receives more than one third of its yearly upkeep from Britain, the Unionists will not allow Britain to press them to give the Ulster minority civil rights. For example, Viscount Brookborough, a previous Prime Minister, recently called on Unionists to unite in resisting all pressures from Whitehall (the London Parliament).

Electoral Irregularities

There are many voting irregularities in elections. The adage 'vote early and often' is frequently quoted. A South African liberal, writing in the *Belfast Telegraph*, reports how she met an apparently respectable citizen who told her 'I voted thirty-six times.'

This Campaign sent a large dossier detailing electoral irregularities to an official enquiry by the London Parliament in 1965, but so far nothing has been done. We instanced dead people being voted for, a nun being voted for by a civilian, wholesale personation by Unionists, unopened ballot boxes from anti-Unionist areas having been found in an outhouse, intimidation of anti-Unionist voters by a Presiding Officer. We detailed areas where anti-Unionist personating agents were afraid to attend the booths to check on the correct identity of the voters.

Ballot papers in Northern Ireland are numbered. A Unionist official records the voters name as he votes. Even though the voting papers are stated to be destroyed after the count, people fear that some could be retrieved and persons who voted wrongly, subsequently discriminated against. Postal votes are frequently alleged to be destroyed by unsympathetic postmen.

Calculated Neglect Of The West

There are six counties in Northern Ireland, the eastern three, Antrim, down and Armagh are predominantly Protestant; the western three, Londonderry, Tyrone and Fermanagh, predominantly Roman Catholic. The natural capital of the eastern counties is Belfast, of the western counties, the city of Londonderry. Derry is the second city in size in Northern Ireland with a deep sea port and a naval base.

The Unionists have, through the years, continued to consolidate their position by strengthening the economy of the eastern half of the state and encouraging few industries to set up in the western counties.

The extremes to which Unionism will go is exemplified as follows: the then Minister of Commerce, Mr. Brian Faulkner, who held the post for some years, announced, on 21st June 1967, the impending arrival of an East German firm to open a factory in Bangor, Co. Down, where, at that time, official figures gave unemployment as 245 Persons. On the same date 20 per cent of the people of Derry City were unemployed and, in Strabane, Co. Tyrone, the rate was 25 per cent.

In the past few years even more determined attempts have been made to further weaken and depopulate the western three counties in the following ways: there were two separate railway lines to Londonderry. In the interests of economy it became necessary to close one of them. The one to be 'axed' traversed the western region. This has left Fermanagh, Tyrone and practically all of the county of Londonderry with no railway whatever. The other three counties have two separate systems, one running north from Belfast, the other south.

In order to further strengthen the relatively prosperous east, the government of Northern Ireland is building a new city in Co. Armagh. As a further irritant to Catholics it was named after the most famous anti-Catholic bigot, 'Craigavon', Mr Geoffrey Copcutt was engaged as its chief designer. He is an Englishman who came here after planning Cumbernauld New City near Glasgow. After one year's work he resigned saying, 'I have become disenchanted with the Stormont scene.' He suggested the abandonment of the New City and that the development of London-Derry should be concentrated upon in order to give the province a reasonable balance.

The government, in February 1965, accepted the Wilson Plan for economic development. This report outlined four centres for rapid industrial development, all within a 30-mile radius of Belfast, and in western counties virtually nothing.

In February, 1965, the government also accepted the Lockwood Report. Here, Londonderry was rejected as the site for a new university, in spite of the fact that Magee University College, a hundred-year-old institution, is at present providing the first two years of university education in certain subjects. Copcutt in his statement said 'Londonderry is the obvious choice to expand as the centre for higher education outside Belfast. It could prove the most promising way of unifying the present populations and integrating future immigrant communities.'

The Legal Position With Regard To Religious Discrimination

Because of a record of previous discrimination in Ireland, some half-hearted legal provisions to prevent it were incorporated in the Government of Ireland Act,

1920. Half-hearted, because those offered had been rejected in 1893 when they were proposed to safeguard Protestants in a previously united Ireland, where they were in a minority for the whole country. The Republic of Ireland is almost totally Roman Catholic. The relevant sections in the 1920 Act are Nos. 5 and 8. In effect these prohibit Stormont from making any law which would impose disability on any religious group. They are of no practical help, because the Government of Ulster never found it necessary to make laws to penalise Catholics. Using its permanent majority Stormont has always been able to discriminate as it wished.

In 1964, Sir Alec Douglas-Home, like others before him, claimed that the Roman Catholics, who felt they were discriminated against, could seek the protection of the courts, using the relevant sections of the 1920 Act.

This Campaign wrote to him telling him that we had consulted a senior barrister, who told us that the Act could not be used—that it would not even allow discriminated against people to get into court.

We wrote to Sir Alec, asking how this could be done. His unhelpful and evasive series of letters in reply are published by us as a pamphlet, obtainable on request, entitled, 'Northern Ireland, Why Justice cannot be done'.

At a later stage, another Ulster senior barrister claimed that he had found a loophole in the law, which would at least permit aggrieved parties to get into court with a case of alleged discrimination in housing allocation. The barrister informed us that for the litigants to finance their own case up as far as the House of Lords, where their opponents would undoubtedly force it, were they to lose in a lower court, would cost up to £20,000.

Despite the fact that there is a Free Legal Aid scheme for people such as these penniless Roman Catholics, Aid was denied to the litigants.

Full documentation in the Campaign pamphlet 'Northern Ireland, Legal Aid to oppose discrimination, not likely!'

What Legal Safeguards Does The Situation Demand?

In 1968 Britain introduced anti-discrimination legislation, the Race Relations Act. Despite the efforts of a substantial lobby of British Labour and Liberal Members of Parliament, led by Mr. Ben Whittaker, the British Government refused to allow this Bill to apply to Northern Ireland, and to relate it to religious discrimination.

The Labour MPs belong to an 80-strong group of parliamentarians called the Campaign for Democracy in Ulster (President Lord Brockway, Chairman Paul Rose).

In the Stormont Parliament, Miss Sheelagh Murnaghan has been presenting a Human Rights Bill since 1967. She did so for the fifth time on 18:12:68. The Ulster Unionists have always rejected her attempts.

The anti-discrimination clauses of the Government of Ireland Act, 1920, though seen to be ineffective, have never been revised since they were first introduced.

The British Prime Minister is well aware that there is continuing injustice, and it is entirely his Government's responsibility to strengthen the Act.

Unionist Intolerance, Half Truths And Excuses

Unionists claim that their opponents are out to destroy the State, whereas in fact they are merely striving for British standards of justice, as at present obtaining in the remainder of the United Kingdom. The leader of the Parliamentary Opposition at Stormont has never been paid the extra salary his position merits. He is remunerated in the same way as ordinary Members of Parliament. For the past forty eight years the Stormont Parliament has never allowed any Opposition Bill to become law, with the exception of the Wild Birds Act, in 1931. It is not surprising, therefore, that many people think that progress will only be achieved by street demonstrations and civil disobedience.

Unionists claim that Roman Catholics are more bigoted than they. Surely with its monopoly of power the initiative for change must come from the ruling Unionist Party. Instances of Roman Catholic tolerance are:

In Armagh in the 1964 local council elections a Ratepayers group put up candidates. A Catholic was nominated in a Protestant ward. He came bottom of the poll, whereas a Protestant in the Catholic ward topped it. In Dungannon at the last council elections a Protestant topped the poll in the Catholic ward. In the recent Stormont elections, Ivan Cooper, a Protestant, won the seat against Roman Catholics in the mainly Catholic Constituency of Mid-Derry, and Claude Wilton, another Protestant, has just been elected to the Senate by Catholic MPs. Regrettable though it is, it is not surprising that isolated acts of violence and sabotage do occur. It is not always, however, what it seems. Some time ago shots were fired into the house of an extreme Protestant Member of Parliament, Mr John McQuade. It was assumed widely that this was the work of Catholic extremists.

It came out at the trial of murdered Catholics, the Malvern Street trial, sometime later that the attack had been made by extreme Protestants themselves. Many riots in places like Londonderry during the past months have been wrongly attributed to the Civil Rights Movement by the Unionists. With the single exception of Newry, all properly pre-arranged and marshalled Civil Rights demonstrations have been non-violent.

Appendix II
Interviews

In order to give balance, and in view of the concerns of interviewees over the context in which their words would be shown, the full transcripts of these interviews are included in this appendix. There also follows various transcripts from soldiers of the British Army; they give a revealing insight into conditions in Belfast during August 1969 and afterwards. They are used here in their full form to give the reader as broad an insight as possible. The author is grateful to Ken Wharton—author of a selection of books on the soldier in Northern Ireland over the years—for his help and participation.

Squaddie, Infantry Regiment:

It was about five or six days into the tour that we were shipped into Belfast from the Lisburn garrison—in Bedford 3-tonners and land rovers—to familiarise ourselves with the planned patrol territory. We had two magazines (mags) with only five rounds, one locked into the SLR [Self Loading Rifle; the standard NATO and British issue rifle] and one in an ammo pouch, and bayonets in scabbards at our sides, and we had taken off our berets and donned instead steel helmets. We were told that we couldn't return fire in the event of being fired upon. There was a yellow card with all the rules of engagement on; honestly, it was such bollacks!

We arrived at Springfield Road police station (one of the most attacked and beleaguered stations in Belfast) and told that this would be our 'home' later on in the tour, although we had spells at a barracks in Omagh (the site of that terrible atrocity by the 'Real IRA' some years later), the name of which I cannot remember. And there we were briefed by a tall RUC officer (we called them green bottles because of the bottle green of their uniforms) who was about forty-five (we were kids of nineteen and twenty), and we thought how ancient he was at the time. It turned out that he had been fighting against the IRA for almost twenty years! He told us that there were only two kinds of people in his Belfast: Prods and Taigs! He briefed us on a big wall map and showed us the Shankill Road (Prod), Falls Road (Taig), and Crumlin Road (Prod), and Divis Street (Taig), Turf Lodge (Taig), and, of course, the notorious Catholic housing area—the Ballymurphy estate. He didn't even pretend to be neutral, but he was clearly anti-Catholic and this may well have influenced some of us.

For several weeks afterwards it was something of a honeymoon, as we patrolled around the Falls Road, Divis Street, and around the Grosvenor Road, and we got on famously with the Catholics. We rarely ventured into any Prod areas, but we guessed that—whilst they alluded to be 'British'—they saw us as 'Taig-lovers'. The Catholic men (largely unemployed) were in the main sullen. Sometimes we got a grudging 'Good morning' from them, but the women and the kids were fantastic. 'What about ye, soldier boy?', 'Yerse Mammies will be proud o'youse lads', 'God bless ye, Tommy', and 'Be having a cuppa tea an' a wee biscuit, Tommy' were comments I can remember so well, as the summer turned really hot by the end of August.

We weren't overly impressed with the RUC lot—somewhat unfairly, I think— and just thought that the whole bunch of them were useless. The areas we patrolled were very working class, with slum terracing, outside lavs and the like, and it was a lot like the places most of the lads—me included—had been brought up.

Anyhow, we patrolled in shirt sleeves because of the heat and lack of danger. Some of us wore steel helmets (one lad actually fainted from wearing the heavy lid in that heat), but berets were the generally-accepted headgear. Five or six weeks in, and although we had heard shots fired in other parts of Belfast, we had neither fired in anger nor been fired at. Back in England, *The Daily Mirror* ran a campaign to get us to remove our bayonets, which we did, but we sensed that the 'honeymoon' would soon be over. All too soon, the cups of tea, biscuits, and the odd plate of sandwiches stopped! Had they not, what with their attitudes changed, we would have suspected that they would have gobbed in them anyway! [1]

Soldier, 1 Para.

I joined the Paras in 1969, starting my training in April, and I passed out in—I think—September, after which we were sent on leave prior to joining the battalion (1 Para). I had been on leave a few days when I answered a knock at the door to be confronted by a policeman asking for me by name, which I confirmed. He then informed me I was to return to Aldershot as I was going to Northern Ireland.

I duly returned. After the usual briefing and stuff, we found ourselves on a coach to Liverpool to get the ferry to Belfast (passing my home on the way), arriving the next morning. We joined our respective companies, which in my case was 'A' coy, driving about in open-backed 4 tonners which were full of coils of barbed wire. After being shunted about for a few days, still sleeping on camp beds in derelict buildings, with no running water etc., we ended up in an old mill in Northumberland Street (as you probably know, this is a road that joins the Shankill Road & Divis/Falls Road.

We obviously started patrolling both sides of the divide, getting fed and watered by both Prods and RCs—in particular a (Roman Catholic) woman who lived off Divis Street. She started by leaving a tray of sandwiches and a flask of tea out for our patrols twenty-four hours a day, and she eventually passed a front-door key with which we could let ourselves into her house to make our own! And then there was the gentleman who used to supply us with the occasional Ulster fry-up when we were in the OP [observation post] on the top of Divis flats, which was passed to us through the access hatch to the lift gear. Things hadn't deteriorated at that stage, and we were even able to leave our Dennison smocks and denims in the dry cleaners on the Falls Road. It would be much different later in the year, when we returned for a two-year tour and things changed for the worse.

Major Ken Draycott, RRW

The battalion was stationed at Lydd when it all kicked off, and it was due for a posting to West Germany—but in July the Battalion [Bn] was told that we were going to Ballykinler to stand in for 3 LI [Light Infantry]. We had a brief NI training session, but we didn't think too much of it and none of us really thought that it would blow up.

I think that we were expecting a six-week 'holiday', and we didn't even take flak jackets—not that they were even heard of, mind—and we couldn't take the whole thing seriously. I was Sergeant at the time, but I was called upon to do the duties of a Colour Sergeant for the duration of the tour. When we got to Ballykinler we were dumped in a weekend (TA) camp, and the first couple of weeks we relaxed on the ranges and got in some shooting practice. We were able to spend some quality off-duty time in and around Newcastle, Co. Down, around Dundrum Bay, and Clogher, which was just across the water from the camp. It was notable for a pub which doubled as a bookie and stayed open for twelve hours a day, and for the number of drunken squaddies who nearly drowned as they capsized canoes on their way back to camp.

On the night of 13 August we were about to settle down for a meal and I made a quick phone call to the Mrs, and she had seen on the news that troops were going in the next day. I can remember it as though it were yesterday, saying to her, 'It'll never happen; if they call the troops in, it will last thirty years.' [Major Draycott was almost prophetic; it lasted 39]. I went back to my seat, but before the first morsel had passed my lips the CO called the entire Battalion (Bn) to parade on the square in thirty minutes.

We were soon at Violet Street police station on the Falls Road, and I set off to collect food and equipment from Palace Barracks—but every unit in Belfast had the same idea at the same moment! The first night was like bonfire night, with explosions, flames, and gunfire lighting up everywhere. British troops went in with steel helmets, with camouflage scrim, and fixed bayonets. As we had no flak jackets—the British Army had not used them since Korea—I was detailed to go to the QM's store and collect them. I had never seen one before, let alone used one, and I foolishly tried to pick up ten at once; they weighed an absolute ton. They would shortly prove their value.

Sergeant Roy Davies, Royal Regt of Wales

I can lay claim to being the first British soldier on Divis Street on the day that we went onto the streets of Northern Ireland, 14 August 1969. I was driving the Adjutant of the RRW, and we were followed by a convoy of lorries.

In those dark days, when all law and order appeared to have broken down, our next point of call was to the RUC station on the Springfield Road. When we arrived outside the station we found not a trace of the RUC themselves. They had simply disappeared, unable to cope with the constant anarchy on the streets; the notorious 'B' Specials, however, were still much in evidence. They were still prowling around wreaking havoc, and we spotted an old lady being pushed in a wheelchair by what turned out to be her grandson. She was crying her eyes out and she was covered in blood, and it was explained to me that she had been attacked and beaten up by thugs in the 'B' Specials; they were completely out of control.

I helped push her into the sanctuary of the RUC station, and I just whispered to her, 'You're safe now,' and we took care of her. On that first day, one of our lads was shot and wounded by a 12-bore shotgun, but thankfully he fully recovered. I now believe that he was the first British soldier to be shot and wounded during the Troubles, and I also firmly believe that he was shot by a 'B' Special thug. We managed to stop them in the end, but they were almost uncontrollable.

One abiding and awful memory I have is of seeing literally hundreds of Catholics—women and children in the main—streaming towards us and past us to the safety of the Catholic Church, 50 or 60 yards behind the police station. I simply couldn't believe how many houses were on fire; there was smoke and flames everywhere. Our officers told us that we were the police now as all law and order had broken down, and we were to act as policemen—but never to forget that we were soldiers also.

That night, I was on sentry duty outside the front of the station when, all of a sudden, a woman came running towards me in total distress from the houses opposite, pursued by an angry man armed with a carving knife. She got round the back of me, clinging on for protection, and screamed, 'He's going to kill me!' I was armed with an SMG, and I quickly cocked it, pointed it at him, and shouted 'If you come any closer, I'll shoot you!' He was incoherent with rage and his words were largely unintelligible, and he looked at me and then just turned around and disappeared. I pushed this poor wretched woman inside the station for her own protection, and then carried on doing my sentry duty.

'Taffy' Royal Regiment of Wales

My first memories, see, were the smoke and the flames and all the screaming going on; there were no RUC about, just mobs, running about throwing whatever they could lay their hands on. It was chaotic, and I hadn't ever seen anything like that in my life before I went to Ireland. There were loads of people, some with bags and cases and prams, and some of the prams had clothes and bedding on them; I even seen a man with a baby's' cot on his back, coming out of all the smoke, his face blackened from all the soot, see.

Me and three of the lads were patrolling down some of the side streets near the RUC station on the Springfield Road. We heard shouts and whacking noises coming from another street, so we legged it over there and we seen two men in black uniforms hitting this woman with what looked like a hockey stick, and the other fellow had a big stick and they was smacking this woman as she lay on the floor. They stopped when they saw us and then, funny it was, they smiled at us and started whacking the woman again—a girl, really. I was angry but calm, and I cocked my SLR, flicked off the safety, pointed it straight at the bigger of the two, and just said, 'If you hit her again, my friend, I will fucking shoot you right here and now.' They stopped and ran away down the street, stopping only at the end to give us the two-fingered salute, and then they disappeared. I'm thinking, 'Is this why I joined the Army?'

Drummer Richard Nettleton, Grenadier Guards

During my first tour, I found myself stationed at the RUC barracks at Newtownards Road, just down the road from the Harland and Wolf shipyard. Whilst there, we had the unenviable task of patrolling the night-time streets, and I had the pleasure of sitting in the back of a Land Rover, operating the radio. Thankfully, nothing much occurred on these patrols, but the tension was electric; then, one grey, misty morning, there was an incident at the barracks where our Bn was stationed, reported the following day in *The Daily Mirror*.

It would appear that a soldier in the Royal Engineers attached to our Bn went missing whilst on guard, and was later found dead in the grounds. It was reported that he committed suicide, but few believed that. I remember a suspicious-looking 'B' Special standing on guard at the gates of the RUC barracks as we returned in the early hours, saying, 'Well, it's finally started. Mark my words, lads, it'll only get worse from now on.' How right he turned out to be.

Flight Sergeant Reginald Smith, RAF, Ballykelly

At the time of the ambush, the Civil Rights Movement was about 40 per cent Protestant (who had realised that the Catholics were badly treated and wanted a better deal for them). They (the Civil Rights people) organised a march along the Irish M1 which passed through a cutting at Burntollet, with high banks either side. Ian Paisley's second-in-command, a Major Smith (I think), organised truckloads of stones to be delivered to the banks of the cutting, from where his thugs stoned the march as it passed. Members of the RUC looked on or even took part. The head of the Electrical Department at Derry Tech (a Protestant) turned up for work the next morning with a large plaster on his head, where he had been hit by one of the stones.

A reporter for one of the local papers was on the march, which stayed at a school-house that night. During the night he got up to answer a call of nature, and he was confronted three times by men armed with shotguns, patrolling the school 'to protect their own people'—the IRA were back in business, having been effectively dormant for many years; they had lost the support of the reasonable Catholics (and now regained it).The Protestants were now no longer wanted, and the movement became almost entirely Catholic—with the IRA becoming better and better armed, largely from America.

This, of course, bred the loyalist terror gangs who (it must be said) were very quiet for the first few months, most atrocities being carried out by the IRA. The Loyalist terrorists learned from the IRA, and in due time were every bit as bad. The British soldier was, as usual, in the middle, and hated by both sides.

In my opinion, almost every death during the 'Troubles'—Protestant, Catholic or British—can be laid firmly at the door of Ian Paisley. Had he kept his mouth shut and controlled his thugs, the 'Troubles' would not have happened as they did, with so much bloodshed. The IRA would not have had the opportunity to reprogram the Catholic people to support them, and McGuinness and his friend Adams would have stayed in the gutter where they belong.

I do have quite strong feelings on this subject, and I think that the only reason that Ian Paisley is still alive is that he was the best ally the IRA had. Every time he opened his mouth another big trance of moderate Catholics became IRA supporters. I can still remember him on TV nearly every night, with his bigoted views and cries of 'No surrender!' The only reason the Troubles have gone away is that the moderate Irish Catholics have realised that the IRA (far from protecting them) have more or less united world opinion against them, and they have therefore shown the IRA less support than before. Long may this continue.

Soldier of the British Army

In the seventies we would be dealing with bombings and shootings every night. You'd have hardly any sleep, and the only medical help you were given would be a large whisky in the barracks. Some soldiers were killed with us in Northern Ireland, and, well, if you're dead you're dead—there's not a lot anybody can do about it. For people who were maimed or wounded though, there wasn't any help given. Two soldiers on my patrol were injured in an ambush one night. One of them was seriously hurt—they had to remove ¼ of an inch from his leg, and he was discharged from the Army on medical grounds. I met him in Paisley a couple of years ago; he's a forgotten man. He had no help or compensation off the Army, so he's left living on the dole. Once you're out of the Army, the Army doesn't care; it's the same for the Falklands veterans and the ones with Gulf War Syndrome.

After my second tour of Northern Ireland I came home a different man. I'd have recurring nightmares about things I'd seen in Belfast, in fact I still do. One night my wife told me that if I'd had a pistol under my pillow I would have shot my four-year-old son. He wandered into the bedroom, as children do, and I panicked, not knowing where I was or who had come into the room.

Major Ronald Gilpin, Royal Corps of Signals (TA)

I belonged to 40 Ulster Signal Regiment (Volunteers) and had been trained to maintain communications in mainland Europe in the event of an attack by the Red Army, but I found myself needing to be constantly alert in my homeland of Northern Ireland. Living here, you were always cautious about who knew what you were and what you did, and security even after 1969 and as late as 1971 was still pretty lax. Although the IRA had said that they would kill men who were in (or associated with) the British Army, it was not uncommon for us to travel from our homes to TA meetings in uniform.

My uniform was often in the back of the car, open to view, and we would still receive mail with our names and ranks on the outside, and thus our security was open to prying eyes. On one occasion, files listing our personal details, telephone numbers etc. were found in a supermarket trolley, presumably left by a careless officer!

From 1970 onwards, members of the TA in Northern Ireland had to take precautions because the IRA would shoot anybody wearing British Army uniform, and—as we wore the same uniform as the Ulster Defence Regiment (UDR), whose main role was to deal with the terrorist threat—we were targets too. We were allowed to grow our hair longer so that we didn't stand out—a group of three Scottish soldiers were identified as such because of their hair, and they were murdered—it was a dead giveaway. We were forced to use soft-skinned military vehicles and we were not issued with flak jackets.

Major Mick Sullivan, Prince of Wales Own Regiment of Yorkshire

I joined the Army as a teenager in the summer of 1966, and fully expected to be posted to some serious conflicts around the world. What I had not counted on was being asked to keep the peace in my own back yard—on British home soil, in Northern Ireland. Back in April 1969, as a young corporal, it was quite a surprise to find myself being deployed to the province, I must admit. Corporal Sullivan—as I was then—had been in Colchester with the 1st Battalion Prince of Wales Own Regiment, which recruited from York, Bradford, Leeds, and Hull. At first, the deployment to Northern Ireland was intended simply to guard key installations in the province. There was a threat to installations in the province from the Civil Rights Movement, who were stirring up a lot of unrest in order to highlight a problem; and there was a problem. For the first three months, however, I could not sense much of a threat.

County Down was like a home from home, and there was beautiful scenery, glorious beaches to train on, and plenty of local dances, attended by girls who were often pleased to see British soldiers. It was really bizarre; it was all a bit of a phoney war at that time.

Later we moved further north to County Antrim, and by that stage the communist Republican movement had been hijacked by the IRA, who saw an opportunity to stir trouble. The pot had been kept bubbling by them for many years, and they saw the opportunity to put their coals forward. As the violence escalated we moved closer to Londonderry, and on 13 August Prime Minister Harold Wilson called a Cabinet meeting where the Home Secretary decided to deploy troops onto the streets of the province. Only the night before we were sat on one side of the river, watching Londonderry burning, and I think that it was then that we realised the seriousness of the situation. There was little fear at first, and when the troops moved in on 14 August 1969, we stood on the streets holding the same banners we had used during the war in Aden two years earlier. They said 'Don't cross this line' in Arabic—can you believe that? It was the typical British Army method of using tactics from the previous war. Both the Loyalists and Republicans seemed to welcome the troops, and brought out cups of tea as they stood on the street. The Loyalists saw us as on their side, and the Catholics saw us as an unbiased organisation. They could see that there was this unbiased organisation coming into separate two communities and keeping the peace. They welcomed us just as much as the other side, and if you have a difficult job to do it can be made a lot easier by people being nice and not throwing grenades at you; the hospitable atmosphere was not to last for long, however.

Officer from a Welsh Regiment

These early days of troops on the streets became known as the 'honeymoon period'. Tea was brewed for the troops in huge quantities by ordinary people, delighted we were there. A patrol of the Catholic Markets area of Belfast inevitably meant half a dozen stops for a drink and a chat, and several more for the loo. 'Community Relations' became the big Army occupation—organising trips to the sea for kids, dances for teenagers, or soccer matches with the local lads. And we all felt what a jolly good job we were doing.

I think we were aware of the political dimensions.... We all had a feeling there was injustice over housing, jobs, education, and even justice. I think we certainly felt that we were on the side of the Catholics ... there was a huge amount of sympathy for them. That lasted a long time, and it was probably the ham-fistedness of the politicians that put paid to that.

Belfast 1969

Jim Parker, Light Infantry

3 LI was in Northern Ireland. The main body of troop was in a barracks in Belfast; we of Support Company were sent to HQ Northern Ireland in Lisbon. We were billeted in the gymnasium, and if I remember we had to erect our own double bunk beds. I know we spent a short time practicing 'Anti-Riot' drills as the battalion had done in Malaya. Then we were in open 4-tonne lorries, driving into Belfast. We drove through streets littered with debris. Cheering people behind improvised barriers greeted us. Some threw cigarettes at us.

Support Company moved into the church hall on Crumlin Road. My first duty was to stand on the street across the road from the Church Hall. Private Meston—who had served in the Royal Marines and was somewhat older than the rest of us—partnered me. The general public was very glad to see us, and came up to speak and shake hands. Jim Meston would have none of it! When our officer came around he asked if we might move onto the roof of the public toilet, which we did. Later, we moved onto the roof of the fire station, behind the toilet. Thus, except for meals and off-duty sleeping, I spent five days on the fire station roof. My combat trousers were ripped at the knees and backside from clambering about on the slate tiles.

One of the worst things a young soldier can do is 'fiddle' with his weapon. Jim Meston had to go down from the fire station roof for a meal or to go to the toilet. His personal weapon was a GPMG [General Purpose Machine Gun]. It was a weapon I had very little to do with, other than basic training at Shrewsbury over a year before. Jim borrowed my rifle and left me with an unfamiliar gun. However, I remembered one thing about the GPMG—the safety catch could only be applied if the gun was cocked (and ready to fire). I fiddled and pushed the safety catch, and I was surprised that it clicked on and off. I opened the top cover and allowed the ammunition belt to drop free. I checked the breach to ensure it was empty, pulled the trigger, and the working parts flew forward with a clang. I reloaded the ammo belt. When Jim returned I told him he had left the GPMG cocked. For the next seven or eight years he and I have argued this point: he has always denied he left me with a cocked weapon, and I am convinced he did!

Much of the events that occurred on our first tour of the Belfast area have now blurred into several disconnected scenes in my mind, some mixed up with the second tour in 1971. Granny Grover heard I could draw and called me into his office. I was to go out with (I think) the Reconnaissance Platoon and draw what I could see. So off we went in the middle of the night, and plonked in the middle of nowhere. I was given an IWS [Individual Weapons Sight]; this was a night sight, through which it was possible to see in the dark. The vision through this device was green. I had never seen such a sight, and had never used one before. I could not make out anything notable, so I got into my sleeping bag and slept through the rest of the night, until I was woken before dawn to make the return journey. Back at Company HQ I found out where I had spent the night, and borrowed a map. I orientated the map and drew whatever was there. Then I handed the sketch it to Granny, who was 'over the moon' with the result.

Three or four of us were on duty on a wide road, and as the evening drew on a young lady waved at us from her window, a little distance away. We waved back. She remained there for a couple of hours. The next morning a little girl in school uniform, aged about ten, left the house, waved at us, and smiled as she walked past. I didn't know where to look. When our relief arrived, they all did so in a Land Rover; however, none of us could drive. In the end I took the wheel, and drove the vehicle back to the Church Hall in first and second gear.

An Eye-Witness Account of the Events of 14–16 August 1969 in Belfast

I am sending down from Dundalk Military Post some copies of the *Citizen Press*, which is a bulletin got out inside the barricades in Belfast, also copies which you requested of the Protestant Telegraph with a couple of subscription forms which I hope would be worthwhile taking advantage of. Also I enclose a copy of the forms which are given to victims of the Belfast troubles. One is a claims form for compensation for criminal injuries, the other a claims form for compensation for damage to property. You will note that in both forms the person is supposed to report to one of the RUC stations in the area and have this filled in. I am told in Belfast that very few people are making reports. What is being done is that four solicitors are giving their services free to the Relief Services at St Peters Church at the top of the Falls Road, and they will put in the claims in block form.

Belfast today is a powder-keg. The Catholic population with some of their Protestant neighbours are now in enclaves, behind barricades on both sides of the Falls Road and the Ardoyne area at the top of the Crumlin Road. There are nearly 35–40,000 people behind these barricades. These are fully-manned at night from

9 p.m. by men from the different Catholic parishes along the Falls Road and at Ardoyne. No one is allowed in after 10 p.m. unless one can establish one's identity. The British troops remain outside the barricades. The troops are mostly along the Falls Road and at the roads leading on to the Shankill Road, where most of the Paisleyite trouble-makers live. There are also a concentration of troops around the Ardoyne area, and they have also sealed off with barbed wire rows of houses such as Bombay Street off the Falls Road and Hooker street on the Crumlin Road, which were burned out.

The present total of persons who have been burned out reached 1,000. A total of 400 houses have been either burned or partly destroyed, while an area of 2 acres of factories along the Falls Road near Divis Street have been gutted. This was done by the Paisleyite mobs who invaded the area from the Shankill Road district on Thursday afternoon and again on Thursday evening.

The Catholic Parish school of St Galls was also destroyed by fire in Waterville Street. Again forty houses in Kashmir Road in St Paul's Parish were also gutted on the Friday night. It is important that the facts are established as to how this trouble began in Belfast.

The first real trouble in Belfast, as I have now established from different witnesses, started on the Tuesday after 12 July, when the so-called Shankill Defence League held a meeting in Ohio Street, off the Crumlin Road. There were thousands of Paisleyites at that meeting. Tension followed and there was fighting that weekend between Catholics and Protestants in Cupar Street, which runs between the Falls and Springfield Roads in the direction of Shankill Road. The allegation that Catholics at Unity Walk Flats threw stones at the Young Orangemen's Procession which followed the 12th is untrue. Even John McQuade, the Unionist MP, admitted this two weeks ago in the *Belfast Telegraph*.

The facts are that this parade was brought in through the flats, which are a series of 8 or 9-storey buildings. The parade went in through the buildings and where there is a majority of Catholic residents ... A woman was struck on the hand by an Orangeman with one of the decorative spears which they carry or cannon holders, and this led to some trouble, which the police stopped. Catholics were moving out of houses in the Crumlin Road area as early as three weeks ago. This followed threats made to certain Catholic homes in the area by Paisleyites. One woman told me that when she moved out of her home in Crumlin Road, RUC men stood at the street corner and said, 'We cannot guarantee any protection.'

Trouble in Belfast erupted (again) on the Thursday evening, when the 'B' Specials were called out by proclamation of the government all over the Six Counties.

[Catholics believed] the 'B' Specials in Belfast were being put out to get revenge on Catholics in Belfast for what had happened in the Bogside in Derry. My contact tells me that the Specials went to police barracks throughout Belfast and seized the RUC weapons. This is borne out in interviews which I had with a number of people in the Falls Road, who were there when the 'B' Specials came in from the Shankill Road.

For one thing, the 'B' Specials are equipped in districts outside urban areas with Lee Enfield Second World War rifles. In Belfast, they are equipped with .38 revolvers like the RUC. But the 'B' Special forces who invaded the Falls Road area on Thursday night were firing Sterling submachine guns. The parish priest of St Pauls told me:

> I was standing in the street when the first thing was a number of smoke bombs were thrown and then Specials in private cars came driving in from the Shankill Road area down the side-streets. I went into the Presbytery, out of the way, to avoid the shots which were going on. They were firing indiscriminately.

My Special Branch contact also tells me that at one stage, early on Friday morning, 'B' Specials and RUC engaged in a gun battle lasting nearly an hour in Percy Street.

The 'B' Specials finally left the area sometime early on Friday morning, but they were followed by the Orange mobs from the Shankill Road, urged on by people like McQuade, the MP, or by McKeague, the leader of the Shankill Defence League. They rampaged up the Falls Road, burned out houses in Bombay Street, and threw petrol bombs into a number of public houses in the Falls Road. They also smashed windows and threw petrol bombs into factories on the Falls Road, which are now gutted. The reaction to this was described to me as follows:

> The people of the Falls Road on Friday evening, when British troops were beginning to move into position, came out like ants. They dug the paving stones to make barricades, they seized buses, bread-vans, lorries, and blocked all the entrances to their homes from the Falls Road. The Falls Road is now open but all the roads leading from it on either side in the Catholic area are barricaded at both ends.

According to John McQuade, the MP, the explanation of the burnings is given in an interview in the *Belfast Telegraph* of 21 August, a copy of which I send you herewith. The burnings were carried out by IRA men and the Protestants had to look on helplessly, he claims, while IHA men burned out Catholic families.

This is the type of dishonest propaganda which is being put out by the whole Unionist machine, both the right wing, and the centre wing and liberal-wing in the Six Counties at present. It is completely answered by interviews with some of the victims, of the type which I will give here below.

There appears to have been fairly severe gun battles late Thursday night and early Friday morning by a number of people with arms, most of them IRA or old-IRA men and 'B' Specials along the Falls Road area. I spoke to one man who told me that he, with three others armed with a shotgun, a rifle, and two revolvers, held off a force of about 100–150 'B' Specials in Cupar Street on late Thursday night and early Friday morning. They counted seventeen Specials downed. By that the man meant shot, but he could not say whether they had been wounded or killed. One of the four men who took part in this battle is now in a hospital in Dundalk with bullet wounds. This man is looked on as a local hero, and I would not be given his name, but he is reported to have set himself up as a sniper with a rifle in a tree with a packet-full of bullets, and to have held off 'B' Specials throughout the night. It is quite possible that a number of Specials and possibly RUC men are dead. My Special Branch contact had heard reports of this but could not confirm it. It is no secret that a number of Specials who were shot in the 1920–1921 Troubles were secretly buried, and the same thing may be happening again.

Going back to the Specials, it is not yet clear whether they have handed up the RUC Sterling submachine guns which they seized at RUC barracks in Belfast on last Thursday night. This would explain the anxiety shown by the British Military authorities [in getting] 'B' Specials in Derry and Belfast to hand up their weapons. I have made some notes on the 'B' Specials. The only requirement for becoming a 'B' Special is to be a member of an Orange Club. There is no educational or physical test of any kind. The Special is paid a yearly fee when not on duty. He is also paid something for doing weekly training, and he is paid at the full rate of Trainee Policeman when called out on full service. They are allowed to keep their weapons at home. There is some evidence also that 'B' Specials and possibly the police are using Dum Dum bullets. One bullet picked up in Creggan Street in Derry was .38 calibre (and had been nicked across the face). The bullet which killed the nine-year-old boy in Belfast created havoc by the tearing through three walls before it hit the boy in his bed, and was obviously Dum Dum. It is known in Belfast that a number of IRA men have got through to the barricades area. It is also likely that soma arms have come in.

One incident during the attacks at Clonard was that in which a man jumped out of an RUC jeep. He jumped on the top of the jeep and tossed a petrol bomb through a window. The jeep was later used by the Catholics to make a barricade. Catholics who were involved in the fight also told me that on the Friday morning RUC and Specials used an ambulance to get into Leeson Street with firing on both sides.

The centre of activity for the Falls area, as far as life behind the barricades is concerned, centres on St Peter's Catholic School at Andersonstown. There are voluntary workers, young boys, girls, doctors, chemists, professional businessmen all working in different units. There is one special legal section set up to deal with claims for damage or for personal injury. This is being manned by clerical staff and has the assistance of four Catholic solicitors. They will process all claims and submit them in block to the authorities.

The voluntary workers are also compiling a street-by-street register of families who have been burned out of their houses or who have been forced to leave their homes. They will do this by checking at all relief centres of which there are about a dozen in Belfast, all in the Falls area or at Ardoyne. They also are operating a twenty-four-hour service with vans and cars to take out families who are threatened. Two families were taken out at 3 p.m. today out of the Newtownards Road area in East Belfast. This is an area where there has been no trouble reported so far, but there are Catholic families in this strong Paisleyite area who have been receiving threats and notices pushed through their letter boxes.

These families are given one hour to get out. The voluntary workers are very badly equipped. They have no heavy trucks. In one case they are using a small delivery van used by Charrington & Kinahan. This van in question was seized and belonged to a former Lord Mayor of Belfast. This voluntary removal service, if one may call it so, is now standing by for calls from families as far away as Ballymena or Toombridge, where threatening letters are also arriving. Reports that families are coming back are untrue. What is happening is that menfolk, who having left families over the border, are coming back to see what they can pick up in their shattered homes or to see if they can resume work. The voluntary workers at St Peter's are very bitter about the six county state Welfare Service. The state Welfare Service have set up an office at St Peter's in one of the school rooms, but some of the voluntary leaders there told me the State Welfare Service have done nothing We have had offers from all over Ireland.... But we have had nothing at all from our own State Welfare.

The scene at this centre last Friday and indeed last Thursday and Friday must make one ponder deeply. One welfare worker told me of Catholic families in here with children burned, fathers with broken heads, and weeping women—all of them terrified. They are very bitter in Belfast about the Red Cross. They told me that the British Red Cross has not even given us a bandage. We asked for the International Red Cross but we were told that they could only come at the request of the British Red Cross. The Protection Authorities in Belfast on the Paisleyite side are also encouraging some Protestant families to get out. But this has been done purely as a piece of window-dressing. The only one case of a Protestant being burned out was an elderly woman known as 'skinny Lizzie' [on the] Crumlin Road. This old lady had a shop and has been living there untouched for forty years. But she was silly enough during the Troubles when Catholics were being forced out of their homes by an Orange mob last Thursday and Friday to hang out a Union Jack. Catholic workers freely admitted that she had been burned out by Catholics who had been enraged by this gesture.

Witness Statement:

I got the six children and five from the people next door, eleven children in all, into my car and drove them to safety. Then I went back for my wife and the couple next door. The time was 4.30 p.m. Two shots were fired from the crowd of Paisleyites at the end of the street. I knew by the sound of the firing that the shots were .38 bullets, which hit the wall above my head. My wife and three of the children are staying with me at Ladybrook, near Andersonstown. Another of our children is staying with a teacher friend of ours, and two others are with another relative. I went back to see my house but the British Military closed off Bombay Street. It has been plundered and all the houses on either side of it have now been burnt out.[2]

Doreen Gilchrist, Belfast

We used to feed the British Soldiers at the corner of the street. One night our neighbours put money together in a collection and Roy and I went up to the 'The Silver Key' fish and chip shop, at the corner of Duncairn Gardens and Edlingham Street, and bought a bundle of fish and chips for the boys. I have so many stories but this one is a bit of history, and I suppose we never realised just how much until we got older.

Eileen McAuley

I have lived in this wee street fifty odd years now. I am originally from down the town, from near Maddens pub ... that's where I am from. We had great wee neighbours. When me and my husband got married we went to live with my sister; she lived in Ballymurphy. After a while she took off to England, out of the blue. So me and Gerry decided to do the decent thing and went down to the City Hall to tell them. They sent us on to the Housing Executive and they gave us a week to get out ... I had three children at that time and they gave us a week to get out!

We couldn't even afford a van or anything so we had to go down to Smithfield and hire a handcart. We got our bits and pieces together and he [Gerry Snr] wheeled them over to his mothers. She put us ... she had a three story house, and she put us right at the top. So I got the three kids to bed and Gerry went over the road to see his friend. I got into bed. At quarter to ten all the lights went out. I got out of the bed and tried the switch... nothing. I'm lying there trembling in the dark. Gerry came in and I said, 'That bulb must have blew.' He said, 'No, that would be my mother. She turns the electric off at quarter to ten.' She used to keep lodgers, you see!

We eventually moved to a room in Francis Street. We had no gas, and you couldn't cook on the fire because the soot constantly fell down the chimney. I had a little stove and one day the little one below Gerald—Jim—was at my side as I was taking a pot of spuds off. The pot tipped over him. That was it for Gerry; he went down the City Hall and I thought he was going to get arrested! Eventually our case was taken on ... it was actually Gerry Fitt who got us this house. We were that poor we had to sell Gerald's bike that he had got for Christmas for the rent, and then the neighbours were calling us gypsies because we moved in using a handcart!

When Gerald was fourteen he left school, and he got a start with Johnson and Christie down in Northumberland Street. He was only there two weeks and he came home and said, 'Mammy, Mr So-and-so [she forgot his name] wants you to come down and see him.' So I went down and this man came out to me and said, 'I'll tell you what it is Mrs McAuley. Gerald is a great lad, he and my boys get on exceptionally well. Now we are a family business, we have never taken on an outsider, all down the line. I asked him about going to the Tech [college] in September, and he tells me that he wants to join the Merchant Navy in the south of Ireland.' I said I knew nothing about that! Anyway, he asked would I be happy if he continued working and I said I would be delighted.

I was working in C&A at the time with an elderly neighbour, and the 7 a.m. news came on the radio saying that the wee boy, Patrick Rooney, had died ... had been shot dead by the RUC. I was at home, and I shouted, 'Gerald will you get up for work, you are going to be late!' and he came down. He was wearing a nice pair of cords ... he was a tall chap anyway. Off to work I went. The next I seen of Gerald that day was when him and Tony [a friend] came in, and I was going to give them a couple of French Rolls, and I was going to give him a couple of bob. So away the two of them went, and I made the rolls up.

The next thing I heard in the evening ... his daddy was working ... up in Sugarfield Street, just up from where Gerald was murdered, was that Gerald had been shot. I went to the City Hospital and pleaded with them to let me in, to see if he was there, and couldn't tell them his name. This guy came in covered in blood and said, 'Good God, what are you doing here?' I said, 'I'm looking for my Gerald, somebody said he's been shot. They won't let me in, will you ask them please?' They said no anyway, mind you they were very busy with all the rioting going on.

I left there and was on my way back up. I was looking for my daughter, Rita, and I stopped somebody and asked them if they had seen my Rita. 'Yes', they said, 'she is on her way home'. So I came up, and the guy that Rita used to go out with, his mother ... she called me into the house and says, 'C'mon you and I will make you a cup of tea'. Next thing the news came on ... I can still remember that ... saying that a youth of nineteen was in the morgue, and I said to Mrs Burns, 'That's my Gerald.' She said, 'God forgive you, don't say that.' So I came back here and the guy next door took me up to the City Hospital, they couldn't be nicer. These men ... UVF men I think ... came and they were covered in blood. I pleaded with them about my Gerald too ... no good, they knew nothing. This Sister, she was beautiful, she brought me into her office and she said, 'You just settle now. There's a boy in the morgue and he is not your son, he is nineteen.' I just kept saying, 'I know that's my son'.

I had to go home and Ben brought me back, and as we got to the top of Whiterock they were putting up a barricade. We knew one of them ... Peter ... and Ben got out of the car and whatever he said to them, before we knew it they were throwing all the bits away to let us through. So we went through and went down our street, and my Francis came up to me and said, 'Mammy, the newspaper men were here, and they were looking for our Gerald's photo.' Eventually Gerry came home, and I said, 'Gerry, get you to that morgue, cos I know that that's him.' Gerry and a neighbour from across the street went. Meanwhile [undecipherable] lived over in Fourth Parade, amongst Protestants ... she bought a house over there, and I said to her to come over here. I had led her daughter up to the top of the street, to see her over the road, when this priest came. I can still see him walking up, with a heavy, beated face ... a black beret and a big walking stick. And he just shouted at me, 'Mrs McAuley?' And I said, 'Yes, Father?' He said, 'Your son has died and gone to heaven'. He then got on his stick and walked off down the road ... God's truth! That's how I knew for certain. Then Gerry came back. Apparently they had brought him into St Paul's [Church], and that's how the priest knew.

In them days they used to decorate the rooms with sheets all around, with blue ribbons and a crucifix. Then the body came home. I can and I can't see myself screaming, you know. I was brought upstairs. I said to the man [who brought the body home] that I wanted him upstairs. The man said no, and that the lid was also not to come off the coffin. I remember screaming, 'Why, why, why?' The next thing I remember about it all was waking up and seeing all these bottles of holy water lying around ... I don't know what type it was because it was all green, slimy stuff. I remember coming down the stairs and the coffin was there [points to under the front sitting-room window]. I said, 'Why didn't youse take the lid off him?' And the smell ... they said it was because he died in natural health. And I remember someone saying to me, 'Nelly, you will have to buy some wick candles or something [to get rid of the smell].' I ... I just wanted to see him, and Gerry took me to one side and said, 'Love, you can't see him, just be happy you have got him home'.

The priest out of Clonard Monastery never left this house, and there was an old priest ... this priest came from St Paul's and blessed the house for me. And this after him being moved up the country somewhere, to pay his respects. I was outside with Father Reid, I forget what we were talking about, and I was brought back inside, and I can see the men standing there opening out the flag. And I said something like, 'No, no. He is going in with my mammy.' Do you know that's the worst mistake that I ever made in my life—depriving that child of that flag? Oh God that hurts. You see, when I see coffins with the flag ... to think, I mean I didn't know [he was in the Fianna]. To me, he was a boy scout—it didn't ring a bell with me. It was a year or so after that it started to hurt ... when I began to realise what I had done to him. I think they gave me that flag ... I can't say whether they did or not. To me he was in the Boy Scouts, that didn't penetrate with me; that he was involved. I knew about the IRA and all that ... I had cousins and that in the last big campaign. The chap next door was in it as well. The only thing I got back when he died was a big brown envelope with—I think—two sixpences in. His grave is a big Celtic cross, and the Fianna crest and all is on it.

His daddy went to the inquest; twenty-six bullets went into him, but Gerry said it was only the one that hit the heart that they count. It was a machine gun that was used on him. That's why I couldn't look at him, he was done from head to toe. Apparently, Gerald came out of Bombay Street with people. He brought them over to Father

McLaughlin and this other priest, who were standing at the side door [of Clonard Monastery] in Waterville Street. One priest took the women and children in, from what I'm told, and he went up the stairs to make arrangements when he heard the shot, and when he looked out Gerald had fell to the ground. He tried to get up when the machine gun was put on him. Both the Officials and the Provies have claimed him on their rolls of honour. I have always been a Provie, I always went with the people he was with; they all turned Provie after the split. I got a job in St Gall's School, and for years I took the long way around. I couldn't walk up that street. Then one day I had a bad back, and just automatically walked up the street. Never gave it a thought until I got to the top and thought, 'God, I have just walked up that street'. See the way things happen?

I can honestly say that there is never a day ... never a morning when I don't think of Gerald. You just have to go on, make the best of it. He would have been sixty on the 12th October [2014].

Mike Nesbitt MLA, Ulster Unionist Party Leader

I was born just in time to grow up through the Troubles. I lived in Belfast and have some vivid memories of the early days of the violence. I recall a night in 1969 when, aged twelve, my father drove me up the Craigantlet Hills, outside east Belfast, to watch Belfast burning. I could not understand why people did this to each other.

I remember my birthday, when I wanted to get the bus into town after school to buy a new pair of football boots from SS Moore's sports shop in the city centre—but not being allowed to because my father had phoned home to say it was too dangerous.

I also remember my father at dinner at home, telling my mother how worried he was because one side was threatening him for employing Catholics; at the same time, the other side made threats because he employed Protestants. And I remember the day the IRA blew up the family linen business in Belfast city centre.

I was supposed to become the third-generation Nesbitt to walk that piece of land as a linen manufacturer. After the bomb, the business closed, BBC Northern Ireland built on the site, and within ten years I did become the third generation Nesbitt to walk that piece of earth—but as a broadcast journalist, not a businessman.

Paddy Mooney

Where I lived, in Ardmonagh Gardens, a family called Johnston had moved out of Turf Lodge over to England. I'm not sure of the exact date because I was so young, but I do remember one of the sons coming back as a soldier and walking down our street, pointing out all the republican families' houses. From what I remember, the rioters nearly got hold of him at Forsyth's alleyway when he became separated from his patrol. One of the lasting memories I have was just how accustomed I was to the bombs and shooting. When we heard a bomb go off we ran around the back of the flats to see where the smoke was coming from, and we all cheered if it was in the town. When we heard a gun battle it barely stopped our football match. When I told my own son some of the things we lived through, he said we must have been mad or thick! We had some great games to pass the warm summer nights, and my favourite one was Brits and Rioters. The older ones would be the Brits, and us young ones would be the rioters; they used to roll newspaper up inside a sock (that was their baton), and a milk crate with a piece of hanger wire (for the radio and aerial), and we threw tins and grass sods at them. This went on for seven or eight hours per night and was brilliant—except when you got caught, because you got near beat to death.

But what a way to put the days in. Lastly, on a more personal note, in Ardmonagh there was a cul-de-sac; I ran over the grass one day and stood on the neck of a bottle. It went right through my left foot. My own mum and dad were at work, and due to all the hijacking I couldn't get to the RVH. My next door neighbour, June Richmond (God rest her), she carried me down to Henry Taggert barracks, past all the rioters, and she and I were taken in a Saracen down to the RVH, where I got twelve stitches. But it just goes to show how much everyone looked after each other, and your neighbour's door was always open. What a pity those days of looking after each other are long gone.

Tom Holland, Falls Road, Belfast

Coming home from school one day in early 1969 (I would have been twelve at the time), I can remember coming down Jamaica Street and seeing a mass of people and the RUC (who were the police at the time), and a mass of cameras, TV cameras. I can remember thinking, 'What's happened?' It was Terence O'Neill, who was Prime Minister at the time, and he was in Jamaica Street. Now Jamaica Street was in the Ardoyne, and the Ardoyne was largely Catholic at the time.

I couldn't understand, I mean, why was the Prime Minister in our street? I didn't obviously know this at the time, but the British Labour Party was in power in Westminster at the time, and they had been putting pressure on the Unionists to bring in reforms, and to try and make the north more acceptable to Catholics. So basically O'Neill was on a charm offensive with the Catholic community at that particular time. The house he actually went to, it was a business woman, and her name was McNulty. She lived about twelve doors up from us. Mrs McNulty brought him in, they had tea, and talked about whatever they were talking about.

Later on that night somebody went up and threw black tar over her door, so there were obviously people in the area who didn't like this visit, somebody who represented everything that was wrong with society in Northern Ireland being welcomed into the Ardoyne, which was mainly Catholic—where there was major unemployment and massive discrimination.

All of this was over my head; I was a little too young to understand the politics of it all. You also had Ian Paisley emerging at the time, who was warning against any change in the status quo. My father wasn't political though, although I can remember him saying things like, 'There's nothing in this country for Catholics,' and the like. He would have made that remark, but there would be no explanation or anything. So my early years were not political at all.

I was aware there was a difference in society; religion was a problem. My mother died when I was eight, but I remember her bringing me to the Shankill Road for a jumper (this would have been about 1964). I remember her putting it on me and saying, 'That will do,' but I took it off and said I wasn't wearing it because it was red, white, and blue. So, even at that early age there was something ... that I was getting off society. It could—or must—have been religious, because as I said we weren't very political.

I can also remember my father sending me to pay the rent to a particular house (again this was before 1969) in an area that was considered 'Protestant'. And I was afraid ... to go down to the house. So there were wee indications of something, even at that age, that were showing to me, growing up in that mid-1960s period, that religion was a problem, that we were Catholics, that the Protestants had the power, that there were more of them ... there was definitely a fear factor. We, I say Catholics, seemed to be totally surrounded by Protestants. Everything was about ... they had everything, they controlled the media, they controlled the TV, they controlled politics.

Now I can't remember Peter Ward or them other people when I was a kid. I can remember graffiti written on a wall in Ardoyne, saying 'Gusty will be rusty'—now that was in reference to Gusty Spence; he was jailed in 1966. Before there was any IRA you had the UVF, there was no UDA in those days, you had them doing the shootings and bombings well before 1969.

Coming to August 1969 I suppose the best way you could describe it was fear ... a genuine sense of fear in Ardoyne. It became apparent to me at this time that the forces of law and order, the RUC, were also anti-Catholic. What I can vividly remember is the barricades going up at the bottom of all the streets to stop the RUC and 'B' Specials from getting in ... and all the Unionist mobs. The big paving stones from the road were used ... also buses. The local people all went up and stole the buses ... the big red ones.

This was mainly to keep the RUC Land Rovers out—which would come in firing indiscriminately at people's houses—but it was also to keep the UVF out ... I mean, they had a limited amount of weapons. All the people's windows were also covered up with the wire mesh, or whatever you could get ... bits of wood ... because what actually happened on the night of 14–15 August was that they actually burned three streets to the ground. They were Herbert Street, Hooker Street, and Brookfield Street.

Those people who were burned out moved into the local school, the Holy Cross Catholic School, where I originally went. It became a refugee centre for Catholics in Ardoyne. Moreover, in the middle of all this you had Sammy McLarnon and Michael Lynch shot dead. Sammy McLarnon was shot dead in his own home, and Michael Lynch was shot dead standing out in his own street. So there was a real sense of ... we are going to get beat, hammered, there were too many of them, we were surrounded you know, nobody could get in. That sort of climate meant that it was all about defence. Barricade your street, your house, the main road, use the buses, the paving stones, and use whatever you can. There were Republicans about. There were a number of organisations formed around that period, like the Ardoyne Citizens Action Committee (ACAC) and the Ardoyne Relief Committee (ARC). These were basically local Republicans, local people who, in the situation, were trying to help people. Many people who would have been in the IRA at that time were saying that guns were moved out of areas like Ardoyne because there was a new political thinking in the IRA after the Border Campaign—that Republicans needed to try to win over the Protestant working class, to make alliances, and that sectarianism was an obstacle.

But I suppose at best it was very naïve at the time to think that, the way things were bubbling from 1966—to leave enclaves like Ardoyne defenceless. I think there were only two shotguns, and one IRA man decided to move from one street to the next ... to make the enemy think they had more guns than they had. The IRA was ill-prepared, no structure, no organisation, very few volunteers. There was basically very few people with very few weapons. When the IRA became a functioning organisation again after 1969, people then seen a purpose for it, and then that led to the split.

This period would have been my big political consciousness process. Then the British Army came, and they were initially welcomed in places like the Ardoyne because they saw them as stopping people like the UVF, RUC, and the 'B' Specials coming in and shooting people in their own homes. But the British Army coming in was more to do with protecting the Orange State. If the British government were serious at the time then they would have seen that it was not working, that you cannot have a Protestant parliament for a Protestant people. The British government couldn't walk away from their responsibilities at that time. You then had the British Army coming into areas like the Falls Road and Ardoyne, looking for weapons and being aggressive to people. So you began to realise that these people were not here to protect the Catholic population, that they were part and parcel of the regime. You were gradually getting politicised by the regime. The IRA at this stage was on active service. By 1971 I was fourteen, fifteen. By 1972 I joined up, I joined the Republican movement, and along with many, many others ... you know, with my friends. It was a popular thing to do. In my opinion the IRA was a perfectly legitimate thing to do in response to the situation in that period. Then I began my life of being a ... militant republican I suppose. Very, very young;

I acknowledge that, but I felt that the British Army should not be on the streets of our island, they had no right to be there, they were part of the problem, and that partition would have to end. The first time I was jailed, I think I was fifteen. I was only in for a few weeks, for rioting or petrol bombing or something. I got out, then I was back in again when I was sixteen ... for the same sort of thing. The next time I was in was in May 1974—I had just turned seventeen. I then spent the next eighteen years in jail.

It was only while I was in jail, when I began to read widely, that I realised the full magnitude of what had happened to me. I never lost the passion ... the Republicanism. I spent the vast majority of my time in prison resisting British policy. I had 'Political Status' when I was arrested, but I lost it because I tried to escape twice and I ended up in the H Blocks. They took my civilian clothes off me and I refused to wear the prison uniform ... so from 1978 I spent the next four years on protest ... the blanket. Naked on the blanket protest, straight through the Hunger Strikes until we got our clothes ... and our other demands through other means.

Some of the nicest guys that you could ever meet joined the IRA, and they done that out of compassion for their neighbours and their friends and their families. I was released in 1992. It was only when the ceasefires came into play in 1994 that I joined Sinn Fein and began to work politically on the contentious issues to do with the north.

You will not find this story unique; these events happened to hundreds ... no, thousands of people. Certain people today are trying to say that things are as bad in the north as they were in 1969 ... it's an insult to the people ... it's an insult to the historical facts of that period. The '69 period was crucial, it was one of those junctures that ... I remember Terence O'Neill going on television and giving that famous speech ... you know, the one about Ulster being at the crossroads; he was right. Terence O'Neill would probably have been happy bringing in minor reform to try and appease, and he would have went no further. And even if he had wanted to go further, he wouldn't have been allowed. But he had the foresight to look at the situation and say ... 'There's a big explosion coming around the corner if we don't change our ways here,' and, you know, they didn't, and what happened, happened. But, having said that, it's like a lot of other historical things. You can't judge '69 without judging what happened between '21 and '69, but the biggest link is partition. When you look at Irish history, there are two big factors. One is the forced Plantations, when the British, as a policy, planted English and Scots on the good land and gave the native Irish the bad land. The second is that they brought religion into this country.

Patrick Dorrian

I was born in west Belfast in 1951, in Slate St, which was close to the Grosvenor

Road. The area was pretty much an interface, in so far as across the Grosvenor Road few Catholics lived—as the streets on the south west side of the road were part of the extended 'Village' area of Belfast, which was almost exclusively Protestant and Unionist. There was also a large Protestant community a few streets away towards the city centre. [A view of this can be seen in H. Emrys Evans's study of the religious layout of Belfast, which was completed as a piece of research by the Geography Department of QUB].

We were always told to be careful when we were travelling through non-nationalist areas, but this didn't stop me or others travelling to watch Distillery FC, or even visiting Windsor Park to watch Northern Ireland international matches. The most dangerous time of the year was always July, when there seemed to be a 'hormonal' surge in the unionist community and it was not unusual for Catholic youths to be given bad beatings if caught alone in unionist areas.

My first personal experience of this happened in 1963. I transferred from primary school, in the street I lived in, to St Gabriel's on the Crumlin Road. In those days there were few Catholic second-level schools, so if one could get in to one it usually involved travel; for example, the first-year class I was in had boys from the Markets, lower Falls, Andersonstown, and east Belfast. The uniform blazer was burgundy—quite distinctive—and since St Gabriel's was quite close to other non-Catholic second-level schools, its uniform was well-known in local Unionist areas.

I used to cycle to St Gabriel's, but I had to stop because on one occasion we got out early and, as I was cycling home, I was travelling along the Ballygomartin Road at the same time the boys from Ballygomartin school were travelling toward the Shankill. Several recognised the blazer, some shouted 'Fenian Bastard!', and a couple tried to knock me off the cycle. My parents wouldn't let me take the cycle to school after that.

Also in 1963, I witnessed my first example of communal violence. Linfield FC were very successful around that time, winning nearly every local competition. There supporters were drawn from all parts of Belfast, but the Shankill would have been one of their biggest reservoirs of support. During the autumn of 1963, Linfield supporters travelling back from Windsor Park to the Shankill from an evening match crossed Roden St, in the Lower Falls, to pass up through streets there to cross the Fall into the lower Shankill. Some of the supporters, as a show of high spirits, broke the windows of Catholic homes as they passed through.

The following week, after another mid-week match, as the supporters passed through the same streets, local youths were waiting for them; there followed several days of trouble and baton charges in the streets of the Lower Falls.

In May 1964 Alex Douglas Home called a general election. In the six weeks between parliaments, preparations were made for the election. During this period, Ian Paisley started a campaign to have an Irish Tricolour removed from the window of a shop on Divis St. Prior to Paisley's intervention, few people had noticed it. Paisley threatened to march a mob up the Fall to take the flag himself; the RUC were sent to do the job for him. People from the Fall tried to stop them. Cue heavy-handed police action, batons cracked off heads, and three days of rioting. I remember being ushered into my aunt's house while the RUC baton charged people on the street.

Following a period of 'quiet' we had the fiftieth commemoration of the Easter Rising in 1966, with a march from Divis up the Falls. The nationalist celebration seemed to energise Unionists. Paisley caused riots in Cromac Street by marching a crowd through the Markets [a nationalist area]. In the summer, a newly-formed UVF murdered two Catholic men and a Protestant woman, as well as wounding several other people. In Dublin, a Republican group, Saor Eiré, blew up Nelson's Column in O'Connell St.

The Civil Rights Movement started to take root in Northern Ireland in 1968, loosely based on the movement in the USA. Agitation from the nationalists (and many liberal unionists) began protests about the franchise at local-government level, which allowed landlords multiple votes in municipal elections but denied votes to tenants; housing allocation on the basis of religion rather than need; and discrimination in job allocation, based on religious persuasion. At that time student protest was spreading across the world, helped by the growth in televised international news. The students at QUB embraced the new movement with gusto. Paisley saw it as his opportunity to increase his power base, and every time the students organised a demonstration Paisley would organise a counter-demonstration. The RUC would then attack the students rather than the counter-demonstration. When the students organised a march to Derry from Belfast, Paisley's incensed mob eventually were able to ambush them at Burntollet Bridge. Paisley, of course, wasn't there. It was the fuse that lit the civil war.

During the early part of 1969 there was a lot of tension; Unionist politicians wanted internment brought in because they claimed the IRA was fomenting discontent. Three bombs were set off in the spring and the IRA were being blamed, until they found the remains of men whose bomb had exploded prematurely—they were members of the UVF. The summer marches were fractious. By August the place was seething.

On Saturday 9 August, the Apprentice Boys' march in Derry along the city walls saw the marchers attack the nationalists below. Trouble erupted in Derry. The RUC and 'B' Specials were moved in to put manners on Derry. Days of rioting saw many injured and no sign of easing. The Nationalists were under siege. Calls were made for people in Belfast to take to the streets to try and have some of the police drawn back to the city, away from Derry. There was a demonstration outside Divis Tower on the Wednesday night. Rebecca McGlade [wife of Frank McGlade, of the civil rights movement] spoke to the crowd. When the RUC arrived there was stone throwing.

I don't remember much about 14 August except the atmosphere was very tense. The usual evening activities hadn't been cancelled. I was staying at my aunt's in a house in Hamilton Court—this was actually the gated entry to a council amenity yard. Her husband was the yardman and the house came with the job; the keys to the stores and office, as well as the main gate, were kept in the house. Both the uncle and aunt were going out for the night, he to the pub and she to bingo at the local church hall. I was asked to stay in and keep an eye on the house etc.

Around 8 p.m. I became aware of tumult outside. I went into the yard and could hear shouts and shots. Part of the big store had a gate out to Dover St. I could see through some gaps that there was hand-to-hand combat in Dover St. I then could hear cries for help. On going into the yard, I traced the sounds to a boundary wall between the houses in Dover Street and the council yard. The wall was 18–20 feet high, and on it there were two families—the Livingstones and the Curleys. I then went and brought out first one and then a second extension ladder, and put each one convenient to the families against the walls. Tony Curley started getting his own young family down. One of the young Livingstones came down the ladder first, and ran to join the fray. I was able to assist the younger Livingstones down from the wall and show them how to get out of the yard. I then put the ladders away again. When my aunt and uncle returned I informed them about the ladders.

They had seen what was going on outside so we decided to evacuate from the house and move across to Divis maisonettes, where my aunt had friends who let us take shelter in their house. On the way across we were shot at by RUC men, who were driving two-seat armoured cars armed with 30-calibre machine guns. We stayed in the shelter until the next morning.

Robert McClenaghan, Falls Road, Belfast

August 1969 is the thing that probably changed our whole generation, now which sounds dramatic, I was eleven at the time. But ... it's not normal to see people on the streets with guns, people on the streets with petrol bombs, and actually burning your neighbours and killing your friends. We lived just off the Springfield Road, in Colinview Street. The tension was there on 13 and 14 August, and then at night you heard the shooting and that. But 15 August, it was a Friday, and that's when the area starts to get attacked, Bombay Street was burning. To be brutally honest ... it was like an adventure ... you see, we had no sense of the politics. We knew it was dangerous, but at the same time this was something new, completely new.

One of the first people killed ... that I knew personally ... was Geraldo McAuley. We lived in Colinview Street, he lived in Colinward Street. So, this was someone you grew up with, played football with, know what I mean? Hung around corners with and all the rest. And then he's dead. He's been shot ... by the Loyalists. And his only crime, if you like, was helping people ... you know, taking the furniture out and the like. Because the whole of Bombay Street was on fire, and he goes down by Waterville Street, by the Monastery. His death sent repercussions through our whole generation.

For anybody, this is a major event in your life. That was the end of my youth, it changed me. You started realising ... there's something seriously wrong with this place! I mean ... why are people coming in to attack, basically, my family? I wasn't politically aware, all I knew was that we had to defend ourselves. My parents ... they would have been Nationalists, not Republican, so, they were into the Civil Rights. They were into supporting. My uncle Sean was a university student, but also an ex-British soldier who went on to the protests. So that's the political context, but I'm dealing with it as a young person.

So, all we seen was Bombay Street being attacked, the possibility of the Monastery being burned to the ground, and then one of your closest friends being shot dead. So, that changes the course ... the direction of your life from then onward. You also lived behind the barricades, and that created a whole new way of living. Obviously the politics was the IRA splits into the Provisionals and Officials, and what that meant was that there were young men and women at that time running around with guns.

So, can you imagine the double life ... you go to school and try your best but your mind is not into it, then you come home and get changed into your Wranglers, and you are running up to the corner and running around with these people. You became aware of all the politics, you heard whispers between your parents. All of a sudden you are becoming more involved.

But if you take it back to August, it was how unprepared people were, I mean, they were right up to the end of Waterville Street. There was a big possibility of the Monastery being set on fire. And then all these lorries arrive, and try to evacuate ... at least get all the children out of the area, because you didn't know what was coming across the road. If you look at the Springfield Road ... that was the battle ... that was the line. I can remember building the barricades. The older ones hijacked a bread lorry. We got timber, scaffolding, anything at all. At one point they actually put me on the back of a lorry to drive me out of the district, but I went up and climbed down the front of the lorry, and ran into someone's house and closed the front door. So, I then come out and it's like a ghost town. All the doors were open. At the top of the street there were about ten men building a barricade. So I go up and my father was there, and all they were doing was making petrol bombs. If there was a weapon there I didn't see it.

What you have to remember is that they [Loyalists] had the police, they had the 'B' Specials, and they had all the guns. What had we got? We had a few petrol bombs and we had a few hurling sticks.

At that young age I felt that everyone was out to attack my family. My mother's family came from the Pound Loney, so they would have been caught up in the [Falls] Curfew. Then Internment came along and it was almost like ... here comes the state again ... attacking our community. We had to fall back on our own resources. You could no longer trust the police. You could no longer trust the media. And it's as if you were betrayed by the British, who sent in the British Army, and we thought they came in to protect and defend the Catholic community. But what really turned out was they were here to protect British colonial interests.

A fella called John Regan, he was an old IRA person who was involved in the 1950s. They came to arrest him, he lived in our street. So they battered his door down on Internment morning and he wasn't in, so they arrested his father—and his father was in his eighties ... almost blind. They took him out of the house and brought him to the police station, and they left word ... when your son comes home, send him around and we will release the daddy.

So you see your neighbours getting arrested, being pulled out of their houses by their hair, and you think ... I can't put my head in the sand anymore and pretend that there's nothing happening! So when you were at school there was almost like a recruitment going on between all these different organisations. The Fianna was one, that's what Geraldo [McAuley] was in and I felt comfortable ... it was almost like following in the steps of Geraldo. Joining the Fianna seemed to be the right thing to do.

At the start they were just trying to give you a politic, trying to make you understand that it was the British government trying to reassert its policies and reassert its political control—because, if truth be told, if you go back to that August '69 period the state lost control. What was happening in Derry and Belfast meant that the RUC were burnt out. You had Derry on the 12th, then Belfast on the 13th and 14th.... Any police force are meant to defend, but what happens when they crumble, what happens when they join the opposition?

When people talk about the IRA it's like something bad, it wasn't ... it was like something organic ... it was something that grew up in the community, first as a defensive organisation defending against the police, later the British Army, but especially against these bands of Loyalists. If you look at now, in broad political terms, it was the largest movement of people since the Second World War. You really felt under serious threat.

I went in to Mackie's at sixteen in 1974, and I was a first-year apprentice as a lead electrician ... wiring up the textile machines. I would be down trying to wire (or be shown how to wire) up a machine, and next thing there would be, bang, bang, bang on top of the machine. And they would be singing 'The Sash', you know what I mean? Everything around you would be Union Jacks and Ulster flags, the whole sectarian nine yards. And it just made you feel terribly uncomfortable, to the point that I went home to me da' and said, 'I can't cope with this,' and me da said... 'I'll tell you a story son, when I was your age I tried the same thing and I couldn't cope with it either!' The place wasn't even anti-Republican, it was anti-Catholic.

There was so much happening every day after August 1969. Shootings, bombings. And it was as if you grew up very quickly, your whole life was changing. You see, by 1972 you began to see your own friends being killed ... like the bomb in Clonard Street in March 1972. It becomes very real then, it was not a game. And then that's when you have to begin to make choices, do you know what I mean? You could almost see it that at some point you were going to leave the Fianna and join the Army [IRA].

So that was in 1974 when I actually joined the IRA. You see, in Clonard ... the whole area ... there was no one left. They had all gone ... either being arrested, interned, or on the run. So there was this whole generation of seventeen-year-olds left in charge ... left in charge of a whole military area. So instead of us looking to the older people ... people were starting to look at us!

You learned the tactics of guerrilla warfare from a very early age. Even when you were twelve people were operating with weapons ... and your job was to go away and dump them somewhere ... hide them. But now it was us in charge ... and it was us who were saying we have to do this or that. It was only a matter of time though before you realise that I'm either going to get caught or killed. So I ended up in prison in 1976, and that was me until 1988. I got arrested in November 1976 with weapons and explosives, and got twenty years. I was put in the H Blocks, where obviously I would not wear the prison uniform. They took all my clothes off me, so the only thing I had to protect me was the blanket. So I was on the blanket protest.

If you look at all the big players in the Republican Movement today and ask them why they are there, I would say eight out of ten would say August 1969.

We are still dealing today with the legacy of those people who feel they are superior. August 1969, to me, was the start of the beginning of the end of the Orange State.

Bridgett Cuípéir

I was about seven when the troubles started. I remember watching families from burnt-out homes move into flats where I lived. I also remember soldiers being in a school beside us. Us kids used to go to shops for them. They give us money to spend; my friend and I used to go round to see two soldiers, we knew where they stood at the school. The one I liked was called Rudolph, he had a red nose. Then one day we were told we couldn't go and see them again. It broke my heart; I cried for days, and watched out the window for his patrol. Time went on and everything changed as we grew up. I think we all have be affected in some way or another. I still have nightmares and dream that I am back in the days of the Troubles. I've been on antidepressants for years now, like a lot of us.

Jim Shannon MP

I was a young boy at Coleraine Institute School and was fourteen years of age, and yet I can vividly recall the events of August 1969. As a boy I was a great supporter of Ian Paisley; he was for me the David of the battle, who spoke out fearlessly and strongly against the IRA and Republicans of that time. My family and community attended the rally up in Londonderry and Burntollet, and although

I was too young to go I was enthralled at what they told me. In those days the rallies were exciting and not-to-be-missed occasions, but all that changed on 10 December 1970, when the IRA murdered my cousin Kenneth Smyth, a Sergeant in the UDR, along with his best friend Daniel McCormick on a country lane in West Tyrone. The fun changed to sorrow and grief, the laughter was gone, and most of my family moved away from Clady, outside Strabane. Little did I know that was the start of the Troubles that would last thirty years and cast a dark shadow over our lives until the ceasefire. I look back with fondness to the '60s as a teenager, but can be brought to reality in 1969 and how it changed our lives forever.

Seamus McCabe

Basically, Hugh (my brother) was a British soldier who was home on leave. He lived with his wife and children in Divis flats ... in the maisonettes. He ... there was a stairwell, and he got up on top to help people. He was twenty when he died, he would have been twenty-one that November. Mythology would have you know he was on top of Divis flats. His home was along one of the balconies. He came along to see what was happening. For them to say that he was operating ... that he was using a gun ... now he was a trained soldier and he was wearing a white shirt. Now there was a lot of work going on, there was scaffolding.

Now all the police heard gunfire, but their own men were shooting. Now, to my mind, they were firing from armoured cars up at the flats. They were saying Hugh was lying prone, as if he was shooting ... but if somebody is firing heavy machine guns you are going to get down low, and the shot that killed him did come from Hastings Street barracks ... from the roof. The RUC had two snipers up there. You can see it there [in a paragraph from Scarman report]. An RUC man actually conceded that he didn't see any gunfire and that was ignored ... they glossed over that. There was one officer who said he wasn't sure whether it was a Bren gun or a Thompson submachine gun that he heard. Now there would be a slight difference between a Bren gun and a Thompson submachine gun!

The Coroner's report was heavily redacted, as they say, for names and the sort. That [a newspaper which shows his body lying at the bottom of the stairwell] was printed 15 August, his anniversary. A few days later this woman turned up [a picture of a woman in the same paper, who was a witness]. I have had a few letters [from the Historical Enquiries Team] saying that they are investigating further, but that's it.

You need to remember how tight that area was at the time ... wee streets. To me they conveniently overlooked some facts ... some important facts, and ignored them. My father had gone down [from Whiterock] because the trouble was that bad, to check to see if things were alright ... and he was with my father when the shooting started. He heard someone groaning. And he pushed two women down a flight [of stairs] away from the shooting. You see, many people didn't realise they were firing live rounds. And he said, 'They are live.' So he left the father with the women and he went to see where the moaning was coming from. He got up onto the roof of the stairwell and he got hit up there.

The Whippets, armoured cars, came down and they fired. Now you don't get up on top of somewhere in a white shirt to start firing.

There's been numerous books written ... but nobody has actually come and spoke to the family about this. The autopsy proved that it was one bullet that killed him, but the angle that it hit him ... it ricocheted around him, exiting his back. It wasn't instant, he was still alive when they lifted him down off the roof. But the wounds were colossal.

It was just sheer good fortune that it was only my brother and young Rooney that were killed that night [in the flats]. The maisonettes in Divis flats ... you know, they weren't exactly made of solid construction.

The whole case, I mean ... I just want the RUC to come out and say they were wrong, they shouldn't have been firing such heavy-calibre weapons. And they weren't even handed at all ... they were leading a pogrom ... bottom line. They knew what they were actually firing at, so it didn't matter. Again, a trained soldier in a white shirt?

Baroness May Blood

You have to go back to 1968, when that march took place up in Burntollet, near Derry, and that time—and I'm on record as saying this—if Protestants had of taken part ... working-class Protestants, who were every bit as disadvantaged as Roman Catholics, but it was sold as ... by Protestant leaders, as a plot by the IRA to get an all-Ireland. And for that reason, a lot of the leading Protestants who were in the trade union movements, in community development, backed away from it. That was in people's minds, the IRA plot, and I remember saying to my dad at the time, after the trouble at Burntollet, 'Do you think this will go anywhere?', and he said, 'No, no, this will not be allowed to go anywhere'.

Now, when the trouble broke out in Belfast that night I was actually on the Falls Road. I was a shop steward at a mill which was just off the Falls Road, and one of my members had been injured. Now, in those days there was no such thing as 'health and safety'. We were told the Royal [Victoria Hospital] was quite handy to the mill.

So anyway, to cut a long story short I went up to the hospital to see if she was alright, and at that time whole parts of Belfast were alive with rumour. You created a rumour, by the time it got to the end of the next street it was fact! I say that even today. If a rumour started at the top of Peters Hill on the Shankill, by the time it go to the bottom it would be a sworn affidavit!

The rumours grew. I remember going home that night, and really and truthfully the next week was unbelievable—the sense of fear, the sense of tension. We had Mr Paisley arriving and coming to tell us they were coming to get us. I had sisters living up the Springfield Road in a new housing estate called New Barnsley, which was mixed, and Mr Paisley went up and told them that they were coming up to put all the Protestants out of their houses, and that they should get out now and set fire to what was left.

We ourselves lived in the most appalling conditions. Our next-door neighbours were Catholic. We all shared what we had. But the fear in the area that week was unbelievable. You could have touched it. And the Catholics had started to barricade themselves in, and then the Protestants started to barricade themselves in, even though we lived in a mixed area. It was just appalling, and yes they set fire to Bombay Street and some streets in north Belfast, but it just grew and grew. Every day was a different thing, every day there was a bigger thing happening. But Jack Lynch's speech about 'not standing by' was seen by Protestants as that the Irish Army was coming to get them. That gave rise to the thought that we would have to do something ourselves.

That then gave rise to the vigilantes—not the UDA or anything, but vigilantes. The UVF was already there. Gusty Spence had already led a bunch of murderers to kill a Catholic barman in 1966, and he had no excuse for it. But Jack Lynch's speech ... many Loyalist leaders took advantage of that, the Official Unionists, this was right up their street. They had no love for the working class, they couldn't care less about the working class people.

Now, I and a few other trade union people said that we would form a committee to see if we could have meetings to try and hold our little area together and squash all these rumours, because I was having to climb over barricades to go to work. I was climbing over these barricades, meeting Catholic girls, going on up to work all day, coming back, and climbing back behind the barricades. It was a nonsense.

However, the committee didn't work. There were people within the trade union movement who didn't want it to work, so it didn't. By this time the British Army had come in, and this only heightened the fear. Some people thought that it would be over in two or three days; in actual fact it got worse.

So anyway, you had the Protestant vigilantes formed. They used to just parade up and down their own street, first of all to make sure that there was nobody coming to burn us out, and secondly to make sure that nobody was going out to burn anybody else out. But this didn't hold. I remember Protestant bully boys coming to burn our next-door neighbours out. And my dad went out and said, 'Catch yourselves on, this woman is doing no harm, she is trying to rear a family just like the rest of us.' The group of bully boys said, 'That's all right,' and away they went. They came back a fortnight later and burned us out. So I was actually burned out by Protestants!

My mother and father were on holiday, thank God, and I was in the house on my own; the ceiling came down and everything, and all the windows were broken. It was a very scary time. You weren't allowed to speak out; there were Protestant leaders at the time who said, 'If Mr Paisley said it, it must be true.' Gradually, that little area that I was born and reared in for thirty-one years disintegrated.

You had groups coming in at night, taking Catholic families out—nobody knew where they went. You went to bed that night and the next morning the house would be empty. Then somebody said, 'See that, they are taking all the Catholics out, they are going to shoot all the Protestants.' I remember when the Army put on the [Falls] Curfew. Jim and I went out for a walk, and we were escorted home by two police cars! That was the first time that I realised that we lived in the 'Lower' Falls!

I laugh at leading Protestants now, and say, 'Where you around at the time? Did you actually experience the fear that was in working class Protestant areas?' It wasn't in the middle class areas. It was in the working class areas, who were gullible and sucked into the idea that they were coming to get us.

I can remember going down into town and seeing the queues outside the Housing Authority offices, and them saying, 'Right, who wants a house in Lisburn? Who wants a house in Bangor?' The idea was to vacate all those [troubled] areas and just leave them barren. The Catholic community didn't move out, they sat solid. Protestants moved away. Out of the vigilantes, someone had the brilliant idea of forming the UDA [Ulster Defence Association], and I remember being on the Shankill Road the day they first marched. The fear in the Protestant community just transferred onto them, and they became the rulers of the working class areas; unfortunately it is still prevalent today.

There was definitely a big movement towards vulnerable Catholic families like in Bombay Street, which was virtually burned out. See, at that time there were Unionist leaders propagating the idea of a 'scorched-earth policy', and that was said openly. I had an aunt who was ferocious about Protestantism, and she moved out of a house on the Springfield Road; her first thought was to set fire to the house as she left. She believed in a 'scorched-earth' policy because Protestant leaders were doing that. When I went to move my sisters out of New Barnsley, my second one wouldn't move—she was quite content where she was. And then this girl came running up and said, 'Elsie, they are starting to set fire to the end of the row of houses, you better move.' We only got half her furniture out, because she wouldn't move. They were burned out by Protestants because they didn't want to leave the good housing for Catholics.

I worked in a mill that was predominately Catholic, I would say about 75 per cent. When the Troubles started, my job was to keep it outside the gate. We needed the work, we needed to make a living. That was very difficult. I worked in a room with ninety women and two men. Women were sitting together—one husband was in the UDA, one was in the IRA, and on it went like that. Depending on what happened the night before was the way the next day went. It really was a very difficult time.

As Protestants, we always believed that the IRA was always there, as we were told. The Official IRA was always there and everybody knew that Jim Sullivan on the Grosvenor Road was a member; everybody knew that, and the night I was down there, when the rioting started, Jim Sullivan was there in the front row. And that was the association with the IRA that they were coming to get us. Now, when you see people rioting and then see a leading member of the IRA at the front, you will automatically think that. Even though the people behind him weren't. When the Provisionals [IRA] came on the scene, now that's when the Troubles really kicked off.

Protestants have every much shame in all this as Catholics have. You listen to Catholics and they will tell you that it was all the Protestants fault; it wasn't. And in the same token it wasn't all the Catholic's fault. There were people in the middle mixing it; people with a sense of power. The Provisional IRA was running about, every day there was a different atrocity, and on the other side you had the UDA getting stronger and stronger as a bunch of gangsters, and you had many streets living in fear of their own people—never mind the other side.

I remember when all the Catholics were barricaded in on the Grosvenor Road, and all the shops were on our side of the barricades. We used to go up, two or three of us, and the Catholic women would pass a note through the barricade with some money; we would go and do a bit of shopping for them and hand it back through to them!

When the British soldiers first came in they were welcomed as heroes by the Catholics, and I actually had some Catholic girls at my mill going out with some of them. One even got married to a soldier. However, when it all went belly up and soldiers were not welcome anymore, this poor girl was told that she would have to get her marriage annulled—she had to divorce the soldier! All that was going on at a very local level. You had young women being associated with the British Army being tarred and feathered. The powers that be, did they want to know? No. As long as it wasn't British soldiers being killed to any big degree, as long as they weren't coming over here [Britain] planting bombs, they didn't want to know.

Those first few days were very difficult. For a start, you had to get your head around was there any truth in what you were being told? The second thing was if you were going out, were you going to get attacked by the 'other side'? No, we lived cheek-to-cheek with Catholics all our lives, who could you trust? Could you trust them? I mean, women in Sandy Row [Protestants] were very much feared, beating Catholic people to death. It was known as the 'Romper Room', which was a programme on the TV at the time. And there was this room in Sandy Row and anybody suspect ... anybody that dared to go into any one of their bars that wasn't of their religion was immediately taken to the Romper Room and beaten.

If you really analyse what was happening at that time, there was every bit of fear on the Protestant working class side as there was on the Catholic. If you take discrimination—for example, if you were a Catholic doctor, everybody knew that you would never make a consultant. By the same token, working class Protestants never got there either. The same goes for today; there is an elite around grammar schools. It's a nonsense to say that it was one group fighting against another, there were people in the middle mixing it up. If you even tried to become reasonably even-handed you were described as a 'Lundy' [traitor] within your own community. Where did they build the peace lines? Between the two working class communities. There's none on the Malone Road [a mixed, affluent area of Belfast].

Sometimes, when I look back, I say to myself, 'Did we really live through those times?' It was almost like some of the things that you watched happening in Germany. The rumours fed the fear, it was one big rumour machine at the start.

Alban Maginness, MLA

It was a time of great tension, one of expectation of something about to happen. Nobody knew what was about to happen though. When it did happen, it was very shocking and traumatic for people. Traumatic for those people who were affected, whose sons were attacked, those who had to flee, and of course those whose families were affected by death and injury. I don't think anybody expected the extent of the trouble. It was a shock seeing so many homes desolated and destroyed. It certainly was like something out of the Second World War.

I was living on the Antrim Road, Brookfield Avenue; we were safe in the sense that we weren't immediately affected. We knew people who were affected. Not only was the Lower Falls affected but so was the Ardoyne. However, the situation in Derry was a lot different than the one in Belfast. The confrontation in Derry was between the people and the police; that wasn't the situation in Belfast. If there was a situation like that in Belfast it was the police, aided and abetted by Loyalist irregulars, attacking the Catholic community. Yes, you could say that it was the pent-up anger of the Loyalist people who vented that anger on the Catholics of Belfast. That changed everything. Although Belfast was sectarianized, this physically divided the city and politically polarised the city even more than it was previously.

That very negative and traumatic period and experience for the whole community is in contrast against the high hopes everybody had on or around 5 October 1968. I found it incredible that in less than a year we had these terrible events. It led to the reintroduction of the gun into Irish politics, and that was a disaster for the whole community—Catholic and Protestant.

When the [British] Army came in there was a tremendous sense of relief, and there was a sense that the British understood the problem; they were sympathetic to the plight of the Catholic community, and were intent on doing something positive to remedy all that was wrong. I think that was true; I think that was Callaghan's intent. Then of course the whole thing soured. It soured in part because people began to engineer attacks on the Army. There was a deliberate attempt to restart an IRA campaign. The Army did themselves no favours, however. They were a blunt instrument in terms of dealing with a very delicate situation between Catholics and Protestants in Belfast.

The resurgence of the IRA was deliberate. Confrontations with the Army were engineered to bring about a response, and were often brutal. That was the wrong approach, because the Civil Rights Movement between 1967 and 1968 had completely transformed the politics of the north. Indeed, reforms were introduced. Those reforms could have continued very successfully, resolving the situation here, but violence intervened and we lost the opportunity.

In August 1969 everybody was frightened. Families were fleeing the flashpoints and either heading down the south or moving across Belfast to safer areas. Many came up to this area [Antrim Road]. August 1969 reignited militant sectarian feelings and militant sectarian actions on both sides. The thing took off like wildfire; it wasn't hard for it to bed down. It became a war of attrition on both sides.

The more that things went on, the more I became involved in politics to try and help resolve it. I very quickly saw that the only way to do it was through peaceful, parliamentary, democratic means. '69 was a transformative series of events.

Danny Morrison

In 1969, June, I had just finished my O Levels. Now, I had been interested in politics for some time, mostly as a result of my street experiences rather than my family background. My mother's eldest sister's husband had been an MP at Stormont for Republican Labour, a guy called Hugh Downey. My mother's older brother had been a leading member of the IRA in the '40s, and was sentenced to death in '45 or '46 for the killing of a branch man down south. But I don't think that background influenced me.

I grew up in this area, in that next street there, and this was a Presbyterian Church which was worshipped in right up to 1977. In 1969 the Minister here, I think his name was Hill, was actually on our committee until the barricades went up.

...I went on a few Civil Rights marches, a few People's Democracy marches. From 5 October 1968 I followed all the events. That was the attack on the Civil Rights march in Duke Street in Derry. I wasn't on it, but a friend of mine, Martin Taylor, was, and he came back and told me all about it. He later became involved and was interned. He was one of the ones that escaped from the prison ship the Maidstone, he was one of what they called 'The Magnificent Seven'.

So Martin was a good friend of mine, and he told me all about that march and the atmosphere. So I was interested in politics but didn't do anything about it at that stage. But it was clear by the summer of 1969 that something was going to burst. At this stage I was working in a bar in Andersonstown, the Whiteford Inn, to supplement my pocket money and to help my studies. Even up 11 July the Orange men who used to march to a field just outside Andersonstown, those who didn't want to march the whole way home, would come in for a drink. I remember serving them on 11 July, thinking 'Jesus, this is amazing,' when you consider the atmosphere. Don't get me wrong, there was intimidation, subtle intimidation.

I'll give you another example. Protestants used to come from the Shankill to certain bars on the Falls Road, and because of their presence there the owners would not let the singing of what was called 'party' songs. For example, you would not be allowed to sing a slightly Republican song if it offended a small section of the Protestant clientele.

I knew that something bad was going to happen—that was obvious from the Apprentice Boys march on 12 August. The Battle of the Bogside began and I was watching it. I remember the headlines in the *Belfast Telegraph* about the 'B' Specials being mobilised. I think it was the Civil Rights organisation that called a series of protests across the north.

On the Wednesday night there was a protest outside Springfield Road RUC barracks. The cops opened fire from the roof, they fired over the heads of the people, and maybe there were one or two petrol bombs thrown. It was then decided that the next night there would be marches in as many Nationalist towns as possible, so that the RUC would have to stay and patrol those marches and they would not be sent to Derry. There's photographs of RUC men lying on street corners, exhausted you know, no sleep, and they were continually trying to get into the Bogside, but nobody was letting them in because of what happened to Samuel Devenney.

We also took part in that protest on the Falls Road at Hastings Street barracks. Crowds were milling about, there were all sorts of rumours, and it was starting to get tense. Some of the kids my age—I was sixteen—smashed the windows of Isaac Agnews (which was at the corner of Conway Street), and people started to burn cars. I said to my mate Robert, 'We have to head on up the road.'

So we were only a little way up a bit when the shooting started. It was awful, terrible. People were coming up the road saying that people were getting murdered and the like. My ma told me not to go down the road. Houses were starting to get burned down. I had a friend who lived in Conway Street, Joe Doyle. Joe and I and a couple of Protestants from the Shankill and Sandy Row, we had a wee club building pirate radios, and we used to go on the frequency of Radio Ulster when it used to go off air at about quarter to twelve.

We used to just talk about transmitters, valves, capacitors, aerials, and play each other a little bit of music. Joe and his family had to run out of their house in their slippers and pyjamas; their house was burned down. Loads of people were getting burned out of their houses.

The next morning, about seven, my mates, Gregory and Peter Fox, and I belted it down the road. It was frightening, it was like something from the Second World War. We went up Conway Street and found Joe's house burned out. There was still a big gang of Loyalists at the top end of the street, screaming and dancing in the street.

I then decided to go look for Joe and his friends. I went round all the schools in West Belfast. I eventually found Joe, I think it was at St Theresa's. While this was happening the Brits came into Belfast and went up the Clonard, where there was still shooting going on. Bombay Street was burned out that afternoon; Gerald McAuley was shot dead.

I went back down the Falls again and people were saying, 'We have to put barricades up.' There was some criticism about the IRA, like where were they. But the ones that were shouting, 'Where's the IRA?', when the IRA did come on the scene there were very few of them who opened their doors to them. The next day, I think it was on the Saturday, I think it was the headlines in the *Newsletter*, in a picture was the charred remains of Joe's transmitter in the yard of his house, and they said that this was proof that the IRA were involved.

I began to build barricades, a defence committee was set up. A few days later my uncle Harry, the one that was reprieved in the 1940s, came up to my house and was asking me what was going on, and the next thing he opened his coat and there was a revolver. So he was obviously involved in gun running to the area. Now he never liked who became the 'Stickies', he didn't like Cathal Goulding. He was also a good friend of Billy McKee.

On the Monday I went to Gerald McAuley's funeral. A couple of days later I was asked to go to a house, a friend of mine's house, and there was a guy there—I think he was from Cork, but he was obviously involved with the IRA. He said, 'I hear that you know a lot about radios. We need a transmitter, were going to set up "Radio Free Belfast."' I brought my transmitter down to Leeson Street and I recognised the owner of the bar. His name was Paddy Lenihan, and his daughter later went on and became President of Ireland, Mary McAleese.

Above his bar were some GAA clubrooms, and that's where the transmitter was set up. It was when I started going down the Falls to do Radio Free Belfast, that's when I first noticed armed men standing around at barricades. The weapons were all old, German Mausers, probably from the First World War, .303s etc.

By mid-September the Catholic Church, along with the British Army, very powerfully convinced the people that the barricades needed to come down, normality would be returned, and that they would protect the area. It was all so exhausting, the barricade duty. I mean, some people worked. I was a student—eight hours at school after barricade duty.

The barricades were taken down but there were a lot of people who didn't want them taken down, I mean people down the Falls. The barricades were taken down, and in the October the Loyalists did the exact same thing again. They came into Coates Street, behind Hastings Street barracks, and burned down about twelve or fourteen Catholic houses. The Brits stood by. But you see, earlier there had been allegations that the Brits had stood by and let them burn down Bombay Street, they definitely ran away.

The other thing was that whenever mobs gathered—for example, in Cupar Street or Kashmir Road—the Brits had what you call 'snatch squads'. But it would be us they arrested. They would come running into a crowd, three or five tough-looking Brits with batons, beat the crap out of you, take you away, and then charge you with riotous behaviour.

People then began to ignore the Brits, wouldn't buy them cigarettes, and the Brits started to get very nasty. At school certain gangs began to form. I was asked to help raise funds for the auxiliaries of the Provo's. I eventually came to sympathise with the Provo's [after the split]. Then serious rioting began in Ballymurphy in 1970 and they fired gas, so I was up at those riots. 27 June was another big date. Again, Loyalists were marching; there was gunfire in Crumlin Road. Then it was the Curfew.

A few days after the Curfew, again, someone asked to see me. So I went round to Jimmy Green's house. Jimmy is dead so this is why I can mention this. In Jimmy Green's back garden someone said to me, 'Look, we need someone to hold weapons. Would you be prepared to hold arms for us?' This was just after the Curfew. So I said okay, as long as the guns were for defence purposes only—I was still a pacifist.

My parents were away for a weekend so I arranged for the two guys to come to my house. It was like something out of the 1920s; they had this guitar case. We went upstairs in my house and decided to put them under the floorboards on the landing. We lifted the carpet, sawed through the floorboards, and took the guns out of the guitar case. One of them was a .303, one was a Sterling submachine gun, a 9-mm Luger, two hand grenades, and about 400 or 500 rounds of ammunition. However, the rifle wouldn't fit into the hole we cut. We put the whole thing back together again, wondering what we were going to do. We obviously couldn't take them back to where we had lifted them from. So I said, 'Let's just put everything underneath my bed'. I had my own bedroom, with bunk beds for my sister's British Army boyfriend to sleep in whenever he was visiting us.

I put them under my bed and surrounded them with novels; I cleaned my own room, so I knew my mother wouldn't go in there. So Greg, whenever he stayed, would be sleeping above an IRA arms dump, which I found very ironic. To be honest, I probably got a wee kick out of it as well. I held the guns for six months, and they came in January 1971 and asked me to be prepared to move the stuff out. One of the guys who came was an older man who was later caught with explosives down south, and who did a lengthy sentence in Portlaoise [prison]. Earlier he had been caught here with a car bomb and did a sentence here. The other guy, he was a young lad, much younger than me, and I was seventeen at this stage. He was a guy called Jimmy Quigley, who was later to become my friend and who was later killed by the British Army in September 1972. That was '69 to me, I don't want to go into much detail about the rest

Gregory Campbell MP

Well, I was sixteen when the fighting started in Londonderry. I was a shop assistant in the centre of the city and I remember it vividly. Before all this happened, Northern Ireland—in my eyes—was a peaceful and content country. People seemed content, and there was no trouble. Then you had the Civil Rights marches and all that. It seemed to come out of nowhere, the trouble in August 1969. The previous winter there had been trouble at a Civil Rights march, but even then it was a bolt out of the blue.

I was in no way political before August 1969. My parents split up when I was very young, but even they were not politically-minded. My background was very similar to a lot of other people in Londonderry at the time; a two-up, two-down terraced house. It was a very working class upbringing. But, just like many others across Northern Ireland at the time, I became very interested in politics after the events in August.

I was working the day of the Apprentice Boys march. On my lunch break I went to see what was happening. The entrance to the Bogside was only a couple of hundred yards away from the shop. It was a strange feeling, watching the rioting. There was a sense of adventure in it, but at the same time it was fearful. Rumours were rife. The Irish Army were deployed to the border adjacent to Londonderry, and rumours suggested (and were believed) that they were actually in the Bogside. It was very exciting for a sixteen-year-old teenager, but also very worrying. We all thought that we were heading straight into a United Ireland. I viewed it as an insurrection, an attempt to destroy Northern Ireland.

I watched as the Royal Ulster Constabulary (RUC), worn out from constant attacks, collapsed on the streets from exhaustion. The RUC were completely unprepared for what was happening. There were no reinforcements, no equipment to help protect them, and many were injured in the ferocious fighting. That was the game changer for me. It all changed after 13 August. The Civil Rights organisation was riddled with Republican elements. They had a major say in the running and planning of the protests. I initially thought little of what was going on, but when banners were unfurled at marches saying 'Smash the Orange State', you began to think. That was when I began to think politically. Everything changed after those few days in August 1969.

Marian O'Neill Donaghy

I was nearly fifteen years old in 1969. I remember Friday the 15th; I was in my grandmother's with my friend. She lived in Scotch Street in the Pound Loney. I lived in Andersonstown, but my mum and all her family were from the Falls Road. When I left my gran's house to get the bus home, there was what seemed like a lot of people running everywhere with their furniture, and there was a very strong smell of smoke. I could hear shots being fired but I didn't know where they came from. We couldn't get back down the Falls Road so we started walking home, when a small minibus with families in it picked us up. When arrived back at the house in Andersontown, I couldn't believe what I saw. My mum's sister, her husband, and five children were screaming and crying. They had no shoes or belongings, only their dog, and they had been burnt out of their house in Cupar Street. They had nothing left or nowhere to go, so they came up to us; I believe they walked the whole way.

My aunt married a Protestant but he changed to Catholic; they lived at the top of Cupar Street, nearly at the Shankill Road. The next day, my dad's brother, his wife, and their children fled the Falls Road and came to our house as well, because they all felt safe there. The people of our area opened up the Holy Child's School, and all the families were put there until they could get help. Most of the families moved down south. My dad's brother and his family went to Shannon and never came back. My aunt and uncle from Cupar Street were eventually given a flat in Divis, and not long after that they lost two of their children to illness. After 1969, when they brought the troops in, things started to escalate, and the Troubles really did start. As I got to my late teens and early twenties, it got a lot worse; living through it wasn't easy, but we all just got on with it, and it became normal to us. But I'll never forget 1969; we who were fortunate enough survived it.

Joe Doyle

On the nights before 13 August, Billy Wilson was in our house right up to midnight. On one of these nights (I think that it was the 13th), a unionist crowd had gathered up the street at the corner of First Street. They had bottles and were banging them with stones, and the noise was being used to intimidate the people in the street. The people took no notice of it, but the RUC were aware of it and they were also present. They did nothing about it, and Billy was very annoyed at that. On 13 August 1969 Clonard Monastery was expected to be one of the main targets of Unionist terrorists, and a number of men were asked to go to defend it. On arrival the priests were asked if they would accept armed help, not that they had any to offer them, and the priests said no. On 14 August, when the defenders arrived, the priests asked them if they had anything to defend them with, i.e. arms. Their views had changed overnight.

One person who lived in our street had a shotgun, but a few days before he was asked by a police inspector to get his gun out of the area. The inspector was a Catholic and during the 1969 Pogrom he was moved to Derry. Rioting had been going on in the Derry area for a number of days and it over spilled into Belfast. The tension on the Falls had been very tense as the police were in the area in very heavy numbers, and riots developed. It must be remembered that there were no personnel trained in the use of guns in the Falls area, and there was no known supply of arms to be got. The IRA had been nearly disbanded in the early 1960s and to us was non-existent, and we were alone. The only people who had any experience of arms were ex-British forces who lived in the area. They were well-known to the RUC and did not have any arms. In fact, some of them blew off as soon as they could. On the night before the main attack, the RUC raided the Bombay Street area and they seized the only gun in that area.

Our main problem was not being able to trust the people of the area as some of the marriages were mixed. One man who lived in our street, a Mr Y, would have been seen on 12 July walking towards the Shankill to march in the unionist parades. Before this, no one took notice of things like that, but it came to us all of a sudden. On 14 August the atmosphere was very tense, and the unionist mill workers, who were finished at six in the evening, said that they hoped that there would be no trouble as they walked by us on their way home. We later found out that there was a meeting of unionists at the corner of Conway Street and Fourth Street, at which planning for their actions that night had taken place.

Some of the residents at our end of the street began to board up their houses as they thought that there was going to be trouble, and the truth was that some of them trusted the RUC to stop any trouble. Later that night they got their answer. One of the residents who worked for a tea company got all his house contents out in a van and disappeared. The majority of the men in the street stayed. There was a large crowd of unionists and RUC at the corner of First Street, and the tension was very high. The people on the Falls began to build barricades, and I spoke to an RUC sergeant at the corner of David Street and Conway Street. I told him that we would attempt to keep the people on the Falls back as they were offering no threat, and I asked him to control the unionist crowd and keep them back. I then walked back to Norfolk Street; a small barricade had been built there and, as I reached it, a massive attack took place by the RUC and the unionist terrorists. The RUC were trying to baton the Catholics, and while they were doing so a number of unionist terrorists began to throw petrol bombs from behind the RUC lines.

This confirmed my worst fears—that the RUC and the unionist terrorists were working together to use a scorched-earth policy on the Catholic residents. The first house that went on fire in Norfolk Street was the Boomer's, and in this house lived an elderly couple and their daughter. We were unable to hold off the attack for very long. I later made my way to the Falls Road, as I thought that we may be getting assistance from somewhere. I stopped a car on the Falls and the driver, who had a lady with him, said that he was an Australian priest; later it dawned on me that the driver could have been a British or RUC spy. We were never used to thinking on these lines.

The Falls had about forty people in the area of Conway Street, and shortly thereafter there followed an attack by baton-charging RUC and unionist terrorists. The RUC were beating their batons against their shields; this action was supposed to frighten us. They made about six different attacks but they did not get onto the Falls. The Unionist terrorists were lobbing petrol bombs into the houses as they followed the RUC down the street, and my home was one of their targets. When the RUC did not achieve their objective by getting onto the Falls Road, they sent down two Shoreland cars; Land Rover chassis and Shorts [factory] body. These were also gun-carrying vehicles. They came down Conway Street firing their guns into the air, and went up to Cupar Street and back to the Shankill area. Everyone thought that they were firing blank shots. Later they were to find out that this was not true.

The second time that they came down they were firing tracer bullets, and their guns were firing at the crowd. Some of the crowd shouted that they were using blanks, but they soon changed their ideas when people began to fall and they could see the blood. During one of these attacks, I was on the Falls opposite Norfolk Street when a Shorland came down Conway Street; a young lad of about fifteen was standing at the corner of Norfolk Street, and the Shorland fired at him. He was a member of the Order of Malta First Aid group. One of the bullets hit the wall and then hit him. I went over to him and the bullet only grazed him on the forehead. I later got him to care as no-one wanted to go to the RVH hospital, as the RUC would have arrested anyone taken there.

I then went to the Edel Quinn building in Sultan Street, which was being used to take in homeless people, and found a lot of confusion there. There were a number of priests there, and this was the first time that I ever heard a priest curse. During the night a number of us went to Conway Street to take out a number of elderly people, and there was still some firing going on. My next door neighbour and I tried to get some vehicles to form a barricade at the corner of Cupar Street from a place beside the De La Salle brother's house, which was beside the Falls library— and there was only one lorry there. The lorry was taken and placed as a barricade at Cupar Street, and this all happened under gunfire. My neighbour was later murdered by a hit-and-run driver, those so-called 'joy riders' who stole cars and drove them at very high speeds, outside the Bee Hive bar, at the top of Broadway on the Falls Road.

The noise of the houses burning, with the slates crackling, was very frightening as you did not know if it was gunfire, and there was some great acts of bravery by the people that night. I later also learnt that a number of small weapons were brought into the area to defend us. I saw two machine guns, which I believe were ex-RUC, and these weapons were used in a staggered manner by firing up Conway Street and then moving to Percy Street in the lower Falls. Firing a few shots there and then going to the Bombay Street area gave the RUC the impression that there was a widespread use of arms. This tactic worked. About six attacks took place altogether by the Shorelands, and a number of injured were removed to a field hospital—which had been set up in a matter of minutes in the lower Falls. Any transport available was used to convey the people there, and soon an eerie silence—except for an odd shot—could be heard in the area. It broke my heart to see my home go up in flames, and that there was nothing that I could have done.

Mr M, who lived in no. 21, was a Protestant married to a Catholic, and escaped that night from his home by lying in the entry all night. In the Divis flats area, a nine-year-old boy, the son of Nelly Rooney, was murdered by the RUC, who had fired a Browning machine gun mounted on a Shorelands into their flat in the Divis flats complex. The child was standing at his bedroom wall when a bullet entered his brain. The clock on the Falls baths was broken and stopped at two minutes past two, and that time always reminded me of that horrible night. One incident that stood out in my memory was the death of a woman called Mrs Crawford. She was shot outside no. 68 Rossnareen Avenue. On that particular day, everyone was told to keep off the streets as there was going to be lot of shooting. The Crown forces were in the estate, and I was in the house when I heard the shooting. I went out to see what was happening and I found this lady lying at the side of a lorry. Mrs Crawford was shot in the back of her head, and we got her away to hospital. Mrs Crawford died a few hours later. She had been dressed in cloths that were easily mistaken for the same type as worn by the Crown forces.

During my period of time working in the Grove Baths, a police sergeant came into the swimmers every few weeks. He was a very friendly person. Six weeks after I lost my home, I met him in the Grove Baths and I said to him that they did a great job in Conway Street. He said that they had the IRA up from Dublin on the Falls Road. I asked them where exactly where they on the Falls Road. He said, 'They were there.' I said that that was funny because I was on the Falls Road that night, that I lived in Conway Street, and saw no IRA. At this he turned as white as the tiles on the walls. From that day on, I never saw him again.

By the morning of the August 15 there was nothing more that we could do, so we made our way to St Teresa's school on the Glen Road as it had been set up to receive the homeless people. There was hundreds of people there, from elderly people to babies in arms. All the Catholic area of Belfast started to put up barricades to keep out all of the guns of the RUC, the Crown forces, and unionist terrorists. On arrival at St Teresa's we were very tired. We all tried to get some sleep, and it was very difficult to do so. My transmitter was out the back of our house in the shed before the house was burnt down, and it was handed over to the RUC the next day by the unionists. The unionist *Newsletter* had a headline that stated that an IRA transmitter had been found in Conway Street. I went to the RUC the next day and told them the truth. I also went to the *Newsletter* the next day and got a retraction printed. Billy Wilson went to the RUC as well and he confirmed my story. Belfast at this time was a very dangerous place, as there was large bombs going off every night and many people were being shot and murdered. The retraction was printed in The *Newsletter*'s Sunday paper; it was three short lines in the inside pages.

Over the next few weeks I helped out with the ambulance patients coming in from the troubles further down the road. Most came in at night, and because of this I tried to get some sleep during the daytime. As there were hundreds of people there, it was nearly impossible. On one occasion we went out to get some residents of Durham Street, who were in danger of unionist terrorists. It was fortunate that we did so, as the home that we were going to had three men at the door trying to get in. They ran off when we came and made their way into the unionist Sandy Row area. Unfortunately, we did not have a gun with us, or they would have got their best answer.

Some of the people on the Falls thought that they would stop the Pogroms by the unionist terrorists, and there was a short settling-in period by them. They were working with the RUC, but some of the Catholic population saw what was going on and went against the Crown forces as well. There was nothing else that we could have done, and this brought death back onto the streets of the Catholic areas. After ten weeks, the Crown forces cleared all the barricades away and they were supposed to look after the security of the areas. They were not able to look after themselves, never mind the Catholics. The 'B' specials were disbanded, and the so-called Ulster Defence Regiment was set up. Catholics were asked to join and very few did, as most thought it was only another means for Britain to keep its continued hold on Ireland. This regiment was disbanded, and a new regiment—under the name of the Royal Irish Regiment—was formed in July 1992. Although the people did a great job looking after the areas, unionist terrorists were still able to come into Catholic areas and murder—almost at will. There was some retaliation by some Catholics, and the Catholic Church never stood by the ordinary people. The Church always followed the British line.

Endnotes

Introduction

1. *Northern Ireland. The Plain Truth*. Taken from www.cain.ulst.ac.uk/events/
   crights

Chapter One

1. www.alphahistory.com/northernireland '*King George V opens Northern
   Irish Parliament June 1921.*'
2. http://www.difp.ie/docs/1922/Northern-Ireland/256.htm Document No.
   231 Volume 1 (30 January 1922) '*Extract from the minutes of a meeting of
   the provisional government*'.
3. 'The Great Hunger' (*An Gorta* Mor in Irish) occurred during the years
   1845–47. It was the continuous failure of the potato crop that drove nearly a
   million people to starvation and another million to emigration. During these
   years other crops and livestock were exported from Ireland. Many historians
   now argue that there was no famine, as other foodstuffs were available; thus
   the British establishment was responsible. The problem was that the potato
   was the staple diet of the poor; once this failed, there was no other means of
   getting food. Many now call it the 'Irish Holocaust'.
4. Many Catholics and Protestants hated the description of where they lived as
   'Ghettos', as it implied that they lived in squalor. In fact, many of the houses
   in these ghettoes were well-looked-after, and decorated on a regular basis by
   their inhabitants. The lack of basic amenities such as hot water, indoor toilet
   and damp proofing made this a difficult job at the best of times.
5. Max Arthur, *Northern Ireland Soldiers Talking* (London: Sidgwick and
   Jackson, 1988), p. 2.

6. Andrew Walsh, *From Hope to Hatred: Voices of the Falls Curfew* (Stroud: The History Press, 2013).

7. Marian Walsh Interview, 9 October 2013.

8. Jim Shannon Interview, 27 March 2014.

9. The *Flags and Emblems Act 1954* gave the Royal Ulster Constabulary the power to remove any flag or emblem from any property if they considered the emblem to be in a breach of the peace. The Union flag, or Union Jack, was legally exempt from this order, meaning that it could be flown from anywhere. Thus, it was mainly the Irish Tricolour that was considered a breach of the peace, and they were taken down at every opportunity, causing extreme unrest amongst Catholics.

10. Patrick Dorrian interview, January 2014.

11. http://cain.ulst.ac.uk/othelem/docs/boyd69.htm (accessed 14th May 2014).

12. The IRA was certainly the bogeyman of Protestant Northern Irish society. They were a perennial nightmare in the minds of Unionist politicians, ready to appear and launch an attack at a moment's notice. This notion was bred into Protestant children as soon as they were old enough to understand. Inflated membership figures flattered the depleted IRA, but served their purpose well.

13. Interview with Baroness May Blood, House of Lords, 11 January 2014.

14. Richard English, *Armed Struggle: The History of the IRA* (London: Macmillan, 2003), p. 99.

15. Gusty Spence was charged with the murder, convicted, and sentenced to life imprisonment. He escaped in 1972 while attending his daughter's wedding, but was captured four months later. Back in prison he renounced the growing sectarian violence outside and educated many young Loyalists on the futility of violence. He was released in 1984, having served 18 years of his sentence. He was prominent in the Loyalists' move towards a ceasefire in 1994, subsequently reading out the declaration at a press conference later that year. He died in 2011. He had always denied the murder of Peter Ward.

16. Brian Hanley, Scott Millar, *The Lost Revolution: The Story of the Official IRA and the Workers Party* (London: Penguin, 2009), p. 75.

17. Michael Hall. *Ulster's Protestant Working Class: A Community Exploration* (Newtownabbey: Island Publications, 1994), p. 13.

18. John Bell, *Voice for all. General Overview Report: Northern Ireland* (Institute for Conflict Research, July 2008), p. 8.

19. It is important to remember here that traditionally, Catholics did not support the state of Northern Ireland. Thus, many Protestants felt that putting Catholics in positions of authority was dangerous and counterproductive.

20. Patrick Dorrian Interview, October 2013.

21. *The Campaign for Social Justice* was created in January 1964 in Dungannon, County Tyrone, by Patricia McCluskey and her husband, Dr

Conn McCluskey. They had initially created a *Homeless Citizens League* to highlight what they had seen as the injustices towards Catholics in social housing.

22. Michael Hall. *Ulster's Protestant Working Class: A Community Exploration* (Newtownabbey: Island Publications, 1994), p. 16.

23. *Ibid.*, p. 23.

24. *Republican Clubs* were an attempt to bypass the Stormont government ban on Sinn Fein until 1974.

25. Gerry Fitt, MP for West Belfast, was one of the injured on the day. Legend has it that he stuck his head in front of a police baton in order to gain maximum publicity.

26. Wallace Thompson Interview, Stormont Hotel, Belfast, January 2014.

27. Wallace Thompson, January 2014.

28. *Peoples Democracy* was a radical student group, formed in Queens University in October 1968 as a reaction to an attack on the NICRA march in Derry. They were more reactionary than NICRA, but somewhat faded from view as the troubles engulfed Northern Ireland. Leading members included Bernadette Devlin, Michael Farrell, and Eamonn McCann.

29. Bob Purdie, *Politics in the Streets: The Origins of the Civil Rights Movement in Northern Ireland* (Belfast: Blackstaff Press, 1990), p. 213.

30. Bob Purdie, p. 215.

31. According to the '*Conflict Archive on the Internet*' (Cain), '*The Campaign for Democracy in Ulster* (CDU) was established in early 1965 by a group of British Labour Party MPs. The chairperson and prime mover of the group was Paul Rose (MP). The CDU investigated allegations of religious discrimination in Northern Ireland. The CDU was especially active in pressing for reforms during the late 1960s. However, the group only achieved limited success and was not able to influence the Labour government under Harold Wilson before the outbreak of violence on 5 October 1968.' (www.cain.ulst.ac.uk/othelem/organ/corgan.htm)

32. CAB/9/B/205/8 *Telegram to the Right Honourable Capt. Terence O'Neill from Paul Rose MP, Stan Orne MP, Hugh Jenkins MP and Patrick Byrne of the 'Campaign for Democracy in Ulster'*, 2 January 1969.

33. PRONI CAB/9/B/205/8 '*Press Release*' www.cain.ulst.ac.uk accessed 12 January 2014.

34. It was one reform, delayed until the next council elections, that was too little too late. Many Unionist MPs showed their true colours by aggressively campaigning against the reform.

35. Cupar Street was in fact a 'mixed' street up until 1969, with Protestants and Catholics living together fairly peacefully for decades.

36. Interview with Jean Canavan, Bombay Street, Belfast, 5 January 2014.

37. Interview with Danny Morrison, 5 January 2014 in *An Culturlann*, Belfast.

38. Interview with Patrick Dorrian 29 October 2013.

39. Interview with Mrs Eileen McAuley, 5 January 2014, Colinward Street, Belfast.

40. Mrs Eileen McAuley, 5 January 2014.

41. John Conroy, *Belfast Diary: War as a Way of Life*, (Beacon Press: Boston, 1987), p. 111.

42. Patrick J. Roche and Brian Barton (eds) *The Northern Ireland Question: Nationalism, Unionism and Partition* (Aldershot: Ashgate Publishing Ltd, 1999) www.cain.ulst.ac.uk/issues/discrimination.

43. Steve Bruce. *The Red Hand: Protestant Paramilitaries in Northern Ireland* (Oxford: Oxford University Press, 1992), p. 28.

44. Born in 1930 in County Antrim, McKeague was a clandestine and somewhat obnoxious character. He was heavily involved in the initial rioting in August 1969, leading gangs of Loyalists into Catholic areas to attack and burn Catholic homes. Many allegations surrounded him concerning his alleged homosexuality and involvement in several rapes of young boys. He was shot dead in 1982, in his shop on the Albertbridge Road in east Belfast, by the *Irish National Liberation Army,* after threatening to name prominent figures in the Kincora Home scandal, where young boys were allegedly abused.

45. Interview with Tom Holland, 3 January 2014 in Sinn Fein offices, Falls Road, Belfast.

46. Tom Holland.

47. *Ardoyne: The Untold Truth*, (Ardoyne Commemoration Project, Belfast: Beyond the Pale, 2002), p. 18.

48. *Violence and Civil Disturbances in Northern Ireland in 1969*, (HM Stationary Office: Belfast, 1972)

49. PRONI CAB/129/141.

50. Wallace Thompson Interview, January 2014.

51. NA CAB/129/141 *'Memorandum by the Secretary of State on Northern Ireland, 5th May 1969'.*

52. PRONI CAB/129/141.

53. The alleged repeal of the *Special Powers Act* was delayed by Stormont because of these bombing outrages.

54. PRONI HA/32/3/1 *'Conclusions of a Meeting of the Cabinet Security Committee,'* 31 July 1969.

55. Interview with Danny Morrison, 5th January 2014 in An Culturlann, Belfast.

56. NA CAB/129/144 *Memorandum by the Secretary of State for the Home Department, Northern Ireland, 28th July 1969.*

57. *Violence and Civil Disturbances in Northern Ireland in 1969.* p. 53.

58. According to the *Irish Republican News,* 20 August 2009: *'On Saturday August 2 1969 a Junior Orange parade was due to pass the flats on the way to catch a train to Bangor. Before the parade was due the footpaths*

at Unity Flats were filled by a mob led by the notorious John McKeague and the Shankill Defence Association he had formed in 1969. As soon as the Junior Orange had passed McKeague's men surged towards Unity Flats. There appears to have been about a dozen police on duty at the entrances to the flats but according to residents these police joined the SDA mob in their attack. The residents held off the attackers, police and Shankill men, in desperate hand-to-hand fighting. A rumour had meanwhile spread that the Junior Orange parade had been attacked on its way past the flats with the result that crowds of people poured down the Shankill to await the parade's return. Before that happened, shortly after 6pm according to the Scarman report, the crowd launched another assault on Unity Flats but were repelled by police. Other police were in the courtyards of the flats fighting with residents, one of whom, 61-year-old Patrick Corry, subsequently died from his injuries - three skull fractures. Fighting continued until about 3am.'

59. *Violence and Civil Disturbances in Northern Ireland in 1969*, p. 59.
60. *Ardoyne: The Untold Truth*, p. 21.
61. www.rte.ie/archives/exhibitions/1031-civil-rights-movement-1968-9/1039-peoples-democracy-march-belfast-to-derr/319689-derry-police-accused-of-breaking-windows-day-5 (Accessed 27th January 2014).
62. *Violence and Civil Disturbances in Northern Ireland in 1969.*
63. www.belfasttelegraph.co.uk/opinion/northern-ireland-troubles-battle-of-the-bogside (Accessed 29th May 2014).
64. www.belfasttelegraph.co.uk/opinion/northern-ireland-troubles-battle-of-the-bogside
65. Edward Longwill, *20th-Century Contemporary History*, Features, Issue 4 (Jul/Aug 2009), *Troubles in Northern Ireland*, Vol 17.
66. *Ibid.*
67. NAI 2000/6/657, *Republican Statement on Northern Crisis*, 13th August 1969.
68. NAI 2000/6/657.
70. *Ibid.*
71. Interview with Gregory Campbell MP, March 2014.

Chapter Two

1. www.philipjohnston.com/quotations
2 Danny Morrison.
3. Simon Prince, Geoffrey Warner, *Belfast and Derry in Revolt: A New History of the Start of the Troubles* (Irish Academic Press: Dublin, 2012), p. 208.
4. Gerry Adams, *Before the Dawn* (Heinmann: Great Britain, 1996), p. 102.
5. *Violence and Civil Disturbances in Northern Ireland in 1969*, p. 121.

6. *Before the Dawn*, p. 102.

7. The following text concerning Samuel Devenney's death is from 'We Shall Overcome' ... The History of the Struggle for Civil Rights in Northern Ireland 1968–1978: 'It was during Chichester Clarke's term of office that the first murder occurred. On Saturday, April 19th, civil rights supporters held a sit-down demonstration in Derry which was attacked by a Paisley-led counter demonstration. In the violence which followed the RUC took the side of the loyalists and severe rioting occurred throughout the city. The RUC led a number of raids into the Bogside, injuring a total of 79 civilians. During one raid they broke down the door of 42-year-old Samuel Devenney's house and in front of his children beat him senseless despite pleas for mercy from his daughter. When the baton blows had stopped Devenney was a crumpled heap on his living room floor, an innocent victim of police violence. Three months later he died in hospital in Belfast where he had been since his beating. An inquest the following December stated that he had died of natural causes. To the minority it was one of the most natural causes in the world.' (www.cain.ulst.ac.uk/events/crights/nicra/ nicra).

8. Danny Morrison.

9. *Violence and Civil Disturbances in Northern Ireland in 1969*, p. 121.

10. *Ibid.*

11. *Ardoyne: The Untold Truth*, p. 21.

12. Joe Graham, *Show Me the Man: The Official Biography of Martin Meehan* (Rushlight: Belfast, 2008), p. 39.

13. *Violence and Civil Disturbances in Northern Ireland in 1969*, p. 126.

14. Gregory Campbell MP Interview.

15. *Violence and Civil Disturbances in Northern Ireland in 1969*, p. 131.

16. Tom Holland, 3 January 2014.

17. Marian Walsh, October 2013.

18. *Violence and Civil Disturbances in Northern Ireland in 1969*, p. 133.

19. Interview with Joe Doyle, 15 February 2014.

20. Marian Walsh, October 2013.

21. Eamon McGonigle, 2013.

22. Baroness May Blood interview.

23. *Violence and Civil Disturbances in Northern Ireland in 1969.*

24. *Ibid.*

25. Interview with Patrick Dorrian, 29 October 2013.

26. Joe Doyle interview.

27. *Violence and Civil Disturbances in Northern Ireland in 1969*, p. 162.

28. Paddy Devlin, *Straight Left: An Autobiography*, (Blackstaff Press: Belfast, 1993), p. 106.

29. Sunday Times Insight Team, *Ulster,* (Great Britain: Penguin, 1972), p. 130.

30. Gregory Campbell, 2014.

31. Confidential Letter from RUC Headquarters to Ministry of Home Affairs, 7 July 1969.

32. Brian Hanley and Scott Millar. *The Lost Revolution: The Story of The Official IRA and The Workers Party,* (London: Penguin, 2009), p. 127.

33. Joe Doyle Interview.

34. *Violence and Civil Disturbances in Northern Ireland in 1969,* p. 148.

35. *Ibid.*

36. *Ibid.*

37. *Violence and Civil Disturbances in Northern Ireland in 1969,* p. 162.

38. PRONI BEL/6/1/1/34/58A *Coroner's Inquest Relating to the Death of Patrick Gerard Rooney.*

39. *Ibid.*

40. *Ibid.*

41. *Ibid.*

42. PRONI BEL/6/1/1/34/58A.

43. *Ibid.*

44. PRONI BELF/6/1/1/34/56A '*Inquest into the Death of Hugh McCabe on 15th August 1969.*'

45. *Violence and Civil Disturbances in Northern Ireland in 1969,* p. 172.

46. *Ibid.*

47. PRONI BELF/6/1/1/34/56A.

48. *Ibid.*

49. *Ibid.*

50. Interview with Seamus McCabe, Belfast, 4 January 2014.

51. Seamus McCabe, Belfast, 4 January 2014.

52. Marie Louise McCrory, The Irish News, 13 June 2012.

Chapter Three

1. *Ardoyne: The Untold Truth,* p. 22.

2. *Violence and Civil Disturbances in Northern Ireland in 1969,* p. 176.

3. *Ardoyne: The Untold Truth,* p. 22.

4. *Ibid.,* p. 23.

5. *Violence and Civil Disturbances in Northern Ireland in 1969,* p. 177.

6. *Violence and Civil Disturbances in Northern Ireland in 1969,* p. 178.

7. *Violence and Civil Disturbances in Northern Ireland in 1969,* p. 179.

8. Robert McCargo to the *Scarman Tribunal*: Taken from '*Ardoyne: The Untold Truth*', p. 24.

9. *Ardoyne: The Untold Truth,* p. 23.

10. *Violence and Civil Disturbances in Northern Ireland in 1969,* p. 178.

11. *Ibid.*

11. *Ibid*, p. 183.
12. *Ibid*.
13. *Ibid*, p. 31.
14. *Ibid*.
15. *Ardoyne: The Untold Truth*, p. 32.
16. *Violence and Civil Disturbances in Northern Ireland in 1969*, p. 186.
17. *Ardoyne: The Untold Truth*, p. 31.
18. *Ibid*, p. 34.
19. *Violence and Civil Disturbances in Northern Ireland in 1969*, p. 187.
20. *Ibid*.
21. *Ardoyne: The Untold Truth*, p. 35.
22. *Violence and Civil Disturbances in Northern Ireland in 1969*, p. 189.
23. *Violence and Civil Disturbances in Northern Ireland in 1969*, p. 189.
24. Tom Holland, January 2014.
25. Jean Canavan interview January 2014.
26. *Violence and Civil Disturbances in Northern Ireland in 1969*, p. 197.
27. Steve Bruce, *The Red Hand*.
28. Taken from a CD transcript in Belfast, January 2014.
29. nickgarbutt.wordpress.com/2012/07/17/reading-the-beano-as-belfast-burns (Accessed 9/5/2014).
30. *Violence and Civil Disturbances in Northern Ireland in 1969*, p. 198.
31. Eileen McAuley Interview January 2014.
32. Eileen McAuley Interview January 2014.
33. Eileen McAuley Interview January 2014.
34. *Ibid*.
35. *Violence and Civil Disturbances in Northern Ireland in 1969*, p. 199.
36. Eileen McAuley Interview January 2014.
38. Eileen McAuley Interview January 2014.
39. Robert McClenaghan Interview, January 2014.
40. Danny Morrison, January 2014.
41. Jean Canavan Interview, January 2014.
42. Baroness May Blood Interview, January 2014.
43. Robert McClenaghan.
44. *Ibid*.
45. Jean Canavan interview, January 2014.
46. *Ibid*.

Chapter Four

1. Taken from '*The Men Behind the Wire*' © Paddy McGuigan, 1971.
2. Alban Maginness interview, January 2014.

3. Baroness Blood.
4. According to Scarman, discussions about troop deployment in Northern Ireland '*in aid of the civil power*' occurred in 1966 and in April 1969. Westminster certainly did now want to have a constitutional crisis that would have led to Direct Rule, hence the pressure on Stormont in 1969 to use up all its available security personnel before any request could be made.
5. CAB/4/1458/13 '*Discussion on possible use of troops in aid of the Civil Power arising out of disturbances in Belfast on 2nd-3rd August, 1969*'.
6. CAB/4/1458/13.
7. *Ibid.*
8. Ken Wharton, *A Long, Long War: Voices From The British Army in Northern Ireland 1969-1998* (Solihull: Helion, 2010), p. 55.
9. Ken Wharton, *A Long, Long War*, p. 55.
10. *Violence and Civil Disturbances in Northern Ireland in 1969*, p. 193.
11. *Violence and Civil Disturbances in Northern Ireland in 1969*, p. 210.
12. *Ibid.*, p. 211.
13. *Violence and Civil Disturbances in Northern Ireland in 1969*, p. 212.
14. *Ibid.*, p. 215.
15. *Ibid.*, p. 216.
16. *Ibid.*
17. Wallace Thompson, January 2014.
18. *Violence and Civil Disturbances in Northern Ireland in 1969*.
19. Ibid.
20. Ken Wharton.
21. Ken Wharton.
22. *Violence and Civil Disturbances in Northern Ireland in 1969*, p. 203.
23. *The Sunday Times* Insight Team, *Ulster,* (Great Britain: Penguin, 1972), p. 141.

Chapter Five

1. NAI 2000/6/658 '*Irish Republican Army statement in relation to the situation in Northern Ireland,* by Cathal Goulding, Chief of Staff of the IRA' www.cain.ulst.ac.uk/nai/1969.
2. NAI 2000/6/658.
3. PRONI HA/32/3/2 '*Conclusions of a Meeting of the Joint Security Committee held in Stormont Castle on Tuesday,* 19th August, 1969 at 12 noon'.
4. NAI 2000/6/657 *Statement by the Taoiseach, Jack Lynch, regarding events in Northern Ireland.*
5. Jack Lynch, '*The Situation in the six counties of North-East Ireland: The basis of our thinking and Policy*' (20th September 1969) (http://cain.ulst. ac.uk/othelem/docs/lynch/lynch69.htm).

6. PRONI CAB/9/B/312/1 '*Speech by the Prime Minister, Major the RT. Hon. J.D. Chichester-Clark, D.L., M.P., At a Press Conference in Stormont Castle today, Sunday, 17th August, 1969*'.

7. NAI 2000/6/658 *Seamus Brady, Eye-witness account of events in Belfast, 22 August, 1969*.

8. Danny Morrison.

Chapter Six

1. www.cain.ulst.ac.uk/othelem/organ/corgan.htm.

2. *Ibid*.

3. TSCH-2000-6-658 '*Eye-witness account of events in Belfast, by Seamus Brady. 22 August, 1969*' (www.cain.ulst.ac.uk/nai).

Bibliography

Adams, Gerry. *Before the Dawn*. (Heinmann: Great Britain, 1996)

Ardoyne: The Untold Truth. (Ardoyne Commemoration Project, Belfast: Beyond the Pale, 2002)

Arthur, Max. *Northern Ireland Soldiers Talking*. (London: Sidgwick and Jackson, 1988)

Bell, John. *Voice for all. General Overview Report: Northern Ireland* (Institute for Conflict Research, July 2008)

Bruce, Steve. *The Red Hand: Protestant Paramilitaries in Northern Ireland* (Oxford: Oxford University Press, 1992)

Conroy, John. *Belfast Diary: War as a Way of Life* (Beacon Press: Boston, 1987)

Hall, Michael. *Ulster's Protestant Working Class: A Community Exploration* (Newtownabbey: Island Publications, 1994)

Hanley, Brian and Scott Millar. *The Lost Revolution: The Story of the Official IRA and the Workers Party* (London: Penguin, 2009)

English, Richard. *Armed Struggle: The History of the IRA* (London: Macmillan, 2003)

Graham, Joe. *Show Me the Man: The Official Biography of Martin Meehan* (Rushlight: Belfast, 2008)

Prince, Simon and Geoffrey Warner, *Belfast and Derry in Revolt: A New History of the Start of the Troubles* (Irish Academic Press: Dublin, 2012)

Purdie, Bob. *Politics in the Streets: The Origins of the Civil Rights Movement in Northern Ireland* (Belfast: Blackstaff Press, 1990)

Roche, Patrick J and Brian Barton (eds) *The Northern Ireland Question: Nationalism, Unionism and Partition*. (Aldershot: Ashgate Publishing Ltd, 1999)

Sunday Times Insight Team, *Ulster*. (Great Britain: Penguin, 1972)

Violence and Civil Disturbances in Northern Ireland in 1969. (HM Stationary Office: Belfast, 1972)

The Plain Truth: The Campaign for Social Justice in Northern Ireland (Castlefields, Dungannon, 5th February, 1964)

Walsh, Andrew. *From Hope to Hatred: Voices of the Falls Curfew.* (Stroud: The History Press, 2013)

Wharton, Ken. *A Long, Long War: Voices from the British Army in Northern Ireland 1969-1998.* (Solihull: Helion, 2010)

Marie Louise McCrory. *The Irish News*, June 13th 2012

Archive Documents

PRONI CAB/9/B/205/8 *'Press Release by the Stormont Government'*

PRONI HA/32/3/2 *'Conclusions of a Meeting of the Joint Security Committee held in Stormont Castle on Tuesday, 19th August, 1969 at 12 noon'*

PRONI CAB/129/141

PRONI BELF/6/1/1/34/56A *'Inquest into the death of Hugh McCabe on 15th August 1969.'*

PRONI BEL/6/1/1/34/58A *'Coroner's Inquest Relating to the Death of Patrick Gerard Rooney'*

PRONI HA/32/3/1 *'Conclusions of a Meeting of the Cabinet Security Committee,' 31st July. 1969'*

PRONI HA/32/2/8 *'Confidential Letter from RUC Headquarters to Ministry of Home Affairs, 7th July 1969'*

CAB/9/B/205/8 *'Telegram to the Right Honourable Capt. Terence O'Neill from Paul Rose MP, Stan Orne MP, Hugh Jenkins MP and Patrick Byrne of the 'Campaign for Democracy in Ulster' 2nd January 1969'.*

CAB/4/1458/13 *'Discussion on possible use of troops in aid of the Civil Power arising out of disturbances in Belfast on 2nd-3rd August, 1969'*

NA CAB/129/144 *'Memorandum by the Secretary of State for the Home Department, Northern Ireland, 28th July 1969'*

NA CAB/129/141 *'Memorandum by the Secretary of State on Northern Ireland, 5th May 1969'*

NAI 2000/6/658 Seamus Brady, *'Eye-witness account of events in Belfast, 22 August, 1969'*

NAI 2000/6/657 *'Statement by the Taoiseach, Jack Lynch, regarding events in Northern Ireland.'*

NAI 2000/6/658 *'Irish Republican Army statement in relation to the situation in Northern Ireland, by Cathal Goulding, Chief of Staff of the IRA'*

NAI 2000/6/657, *'Republican Statement on Northern Crisis, 13th August 1969'*

Websites

www.cain.ulst.ac.uk/othelem/docs/boyd69.htm
www.rte.ie/archives/exhibitions
www.cain.ulst.ac.uk/hmso/cameron
www.cain.ulst.ac.uk/hmso
www.cain.ulst.ac.uk/nai/1969
www.cain.ulst.ac.uk/issues/discrimination
www.mary-kenny.com/published_articles/winston-churchill-ireland.
www.libraryireland.com.
www.larkspirit.com/bloodysunday
www.stm.unipi.it
www.rhsroughriders.org
www.mrmichaelstuart.com/uploads
www.malachiodoherty.com
www.scholarship.law.duke.edu
www.cain.ulst.ac.uk/othelem/organ/corgan.htm
www.philipjohnston.com/quotations/ni_union
www.cain.ulst.ac.uk/events/crights/nicra
www.cain.ulst.ac.uk/proni
www.alphahistory.com/northernireland *'King George V opens Northern Irish Parliament June 1921.'*
www.cain.ulst.ac.uk/othelem/docs/lynch/lynch69 Jack Lynch, *'The Situation in the six counties of North-East Ireland: The basis of our thinking and Policy' (20th September 1969)*
www.nickgarbutt.wordpress.com *'Reading the Beano as-Belfast Burns'*
www.belfasttelegraph.co.uk/opinion *Northern Ireland Troubles: Battle of the Bogside*
www.winstonchurchill.org *'Churchill and Ireland'*
www.difp.ie/docs/1922 *'Extract from the Minutes of a Meeting of the Provisional Government'*

Further Reading

Adams, Gerry, *Falls Memories* (Dingle: Brandon, 1993).
Aldous, Richard and Niamh Puirsell, *We Declare: Landmark Documents in Irelands History* (London: Quercus, 2008).
Bell, J. Bower, *The Irish Troubles: A Generation of Violence 1967–1992* (New York: St Martin's Press, 1993).
Bew, Paul, Peter Gibbon and Henry Patterson. *Northern Ireland 1921–2001: Political Forces and Social Classes* (London: Serif, 2002).

Coogan, Tim Pat. *The Troubles: Ireland's Ordeal and the Search for Peace* (New York: Palgrave, 1996).

Cunningham, Michael. *British Government Policy in Northern Ireland* (Manchester: Manchester University Press, 2001).

Dewar, Michael. *The British Army in Northern Ireland* (London: Arms and Armour, 1985).

Falls Think Tank. *Ourselves Alone? Voices from the Nationalist Working Class.* Compiled by Michael Hall (Newtownabbey: Island Publications, 1996).

Falls Think Tank, *'Seeds of Hope': An Exploration by the 'Seeds of Hope' Ex-prisoners* (Newtownabbey: Island Publications, 2000).

Foster, R. F. *Modern Ireland 1600–1972* (London: Penguin, 1989).

Geraghty, Tony. *The Irish War: The Hidden Conflict between the IRA and British Intelligence* (London: HarperCollins, 2000)

Gillespie, Gordon. *Years of Darkness: The Troubles Remembered* (Dublin: Gill and Macmillan, 2008)

Hennessey, Thomas. *The Evolution of the Troubles* (Dublin: Irish Academic Press, 2007).

Hennessey, Thomas. *A History of Northern Ireland 1920–1996* (London: Macmillan, 1997).

Jordan, Hugh. *Milestones in Murder: Defining Moments in Ulster's Terror War* (Edinburgh: Mainstream, 2002).

Kee, Robert. *Ireland: A History* (London: Weidenfeld and Nicolson, 1980).

Lawrence, Michael and Rowan Smith. *Fighting for Ireland? The Military Strategy of the Irish Republican Movement* (London: Routledge, 1997).

Magee, John and Jack Magee. *Northern Ireland: Crisis and Conflict* (London: Routledge, 1974)

Merkl, Peter H. (eds). *Political Violence and Terror: Motifs and Motivations* (London: University of California Press, 1986).

Moloney, Ed. *A Secret History of the IRA* (London: Penguin, 2002).

Moloney, Ed. *Voices From the Grave* (London: Faber and Faber, 2010).

Murphy, Michael A. *Gerry Fitt: A Political Chameleon* (Cork: Mercier Press, 2007).

Neumann, Peter R. *Britain's Long War: British Strategy in the Northern Ireland Conflict, 1969–98* (London: Palgrave Macmillan, 2004).

Northern Ireland Civil Rights Association. *We Shall Overcome: The History of the Struggle for Civil Rights in Northern Ireland 1968–1978* (Belfast: NICRA).

O'Brien, Maire and Conor Cruise. *Ireland: A Concise History* (London: Thames and Hudson, 1999).

Patterson, Henry. *Ireland since 1939: The Persistence of Conflict* (London: Penguin, 2006).

Rafferty, Oliver P. *Catholicism in Ulster 1603–1983: An Interpretive History* (London: Hurst and Company, 1994).

Ripley, Tim and Mike Chappell. *Security Forces in Northern Ireland 1969–92* (London: Osprey Publishing, 1993).

Rose, Paul. *'Backbencher's Dilemma'*, Chapter 12 in: *The Northern Ireland Fiasco* plus *'Appendix'* (A report by the Campaign for Democracy in Ulster on a visit to Northern Ireland in 1967) (London: Muller, 1981).

Taylor, Peter. *Provos* (London: Bloomsbury, 1997).

Tonge, Jonathan. *Northern Ireland: Conflict and Change* (London: Pearson, 2002).

Ulster: Sunday Times Insight Team (Harmondsworth: Penguin Books, 1972)

Van De Bijl, Nick. *Operation Banner: The British Army in Northern Ireland 1969–2007* (Great Britain: Pen and Sword Military, 2009).

Weitzer, Ronald A., *Transforming Settler States: Communal Conflict and Internal Security in Northern Ireland and Zimbabwe* (Berkeley: University of California Press, 1990); www.ark.cdlib.org.

Wichert, Sabine. *Northern Ireland since 1945* (London: Longman, 1991).

Articles and Documents

'A Commentary by the Government of Northern Ireland to Accompany the Cameron Report incorporating an account of progress and a programme of action';

Bishop, Joseph W., 'Law in the Control of Terrorism and Insurrection: The British Laboratory Experience'.

Boserup, Anders, 'Contradictions and Struggles in Northern Ireland'. *The Socialist Register*, Vol. 9, 1972.

Bourke, Richard, '"Imperialism" and "Democracy" in Modern Ireland, 1898–2002', Boundary, Duke University Press, Vol. 2, No. 31 (2004), pp. 101–2.

The Plain Truth, Campaign for Social Justice in Northern Ireland, Castlefields, Dungannon, 15 June 1969; www.cain.ulst.ac.uk/events.

Darby, John. *Conflict in Northern Ireland: A Background Essay*; www.rhsroughriders.org.

Disturbances in Northern Ireland. Report of the Commission appointed by the Governor of Northern Ireland (Belfast: HMSO, 1969); Farrell, Michael, Northern Ireland the Orange State (London: Pluto Press, 1976).

Government of Northern Ireland, Violence and Civil Disturbances in Northern Ireland in 1969 (Report of Tribunal of Inquiry); www.cain.ulst.ac.uk/hmso/scarman.

Harris, Mary, 'Religious Divisions, Discrimination and the Struggle for Dominance in Northern Ireland'

Hepburn, A. C. 'Northern Ireland' Taken from www.mrmichaelstuart.com/uploads/3/2/6/.../noirelandencartainfo.doc Hewitt, Christopher, 'Catholic

Grievances, Catholic Nationalism and Violence in Northern Ireland during the Civil Rights Period: A Reconsideration', British Journal of Sociology, Vol. 32, No. 3 (September 1981), pp. 362–77.

Hull, Eleanor, 'A History of Ireland'; Lynch, Jack, 'A Review of the Situation in the Six Counties' (Dublin: Irish Government).

Jones, Emrys, 'The Distribution and Segregation of Roman Catholics in Belfast'. *The Sociological Review*, Vol. 4, No. 2 (1956), pp. 167–89.

Kenny, Mary, 'Winston Churchill and Ireland'; www.mary-kenny.com/published_ articles/winston-churchill-ireland.

Morgan, Michael, 'How the British Created the Provos', Fortnight, No. 275 (July–August 1989), pp. 12–13.

Munck, Ronnie, 'The Making of the Troubles in Northern Ireland', Journal of Contemporary History, Vol. 27, No. 2 (April 1992), pp. 211–29.

Murray, Sean, article in An Phoblacht, 23 July 2009.

O'Doherty, Malachi. *'The Pogrom Myth'*

O'Neill, Captain Terence, reported in Belfast Telegraph, 10 May 1969; www.cain. ulst.ac.uk/issues/discrimination/quotes.

Interviewees

Gregory Campbell MP
Alban Maginness MLA
Robert McClenaghan
Patrick Dorrian
Seamus McCabe
Eamon McGonigle
Joe Doyle
Eileen McAuley
Jean Canavan
Tom Holland
Marian Walsh
Marian O'Neill Donaghy
Jim Shannon MP
Danny Morrison
Baroness May Blood
Bridgett Cuípéir
Paddy Mooney
Mike Nesbitt MLA
Doreen Gilchrist